Collins

TG 10/13

Introducing English
to Young Children:
Spoken Language

Opal Dunn

Collins

HarperCollins Publishers
77-85 Fulham Palace Road
Hammersmith
London W6 8JB

Based on *Developing English with Young Learners*, Macmillan Publishers Ltd, 1984

Previously published by North Star ELT in 2012

This edition published in 2013 by HarperCollins Publishers Ltd

Reprint 10 9 8 7 6 5 4 3 2 1 0

© HarperCollins Publishers Ltd 2013

Text © 2012 Opal Dunn

The right of Opal Dunn to be identified as the Author of this Work has been asserted by them in accordance with the Copyright, Designs and Patents Act 1988.

ISBN 978-0-00-752255-2

Contents

4 Beginning oral communication 125

5 Oral games 167

6 Verbal play – rhymes, songs, chants, tongue-twisters, riddles and puns 197

About the Author

Award-winning author Opal Dunn has many years of experience in teaching children aged up to 8 years, and has trained teachers all over the world. She has also authored picture books for nursery and young primary children, organised Bunko (mini-libraries) for bilingual and plurilingual children, and has written information books and articles for parents.

About this book

Together with its sequel, *Introducing English to Young Children – Reading and Writing*, this book is an overview of what I have observed and experienced during many years of teaching, training teachers, organising *bunko* (mini-home-libraries) and helping parents of young children. My experience has been in the Far East, Europe, North Africa, South America and also England, where many young children are coming to school with no English. Every English learning situation is different; every child, and his or her home situation, is unique. What I have written aims to help teachers and carers understand better how each child's holistic development is embedded in and entwined with learning language.

Introducing English cannot be thought of only in terms of linguistic attainments. Educationalists including Froebel, Montessori, Isaacs, Steiner, Vygotsky, Bruner, Bruce, Sylva, Malaguzzi (Reggio Emilia) and Whitehead, explain that children acquire and find out about language 'through doing', experimenting and imitating. Children are born natural language acquirers and users; most can acquire English if supportive adults provide them with sufficient language-based 'doing' activities – activities that are right for their developmental level and in which they feel confident to use their personal language-learning strategies. For very young and young children, English is another way of talking about and communicating their needs and interests to sympathetic listeners. It is important for young learners that English should be like learning to talk with their mother – a living and useful skill – rather than being an abstract, taught subject.

More than half the world's young children speak two or more languages outside school and many millions are now learning English in schools.

Some teachers tend to underestimate very young and young children's innate drive and potential to pick up English as another language. Each child is an individual and in order for children to acquire English in school situations and make and enjoy the progress of which they appear capable, adults have to 'tune into' their thinking, language, expectations and society, seeing things 'through their eyes'.

Learning English should be a fun experience for everyone; the child, the teacher and the family all need to 'feel good' about it if the child is to develop the positive lifelong attitudes that are known to be formed before the age of 8 or 9 years. Since many school activities include culture, young children naturally pick up the English language together with the accompanying culture that the adult mediates. The teacher is probably the young child's most important 'window on the English speaking wider-world' – a big responsibility.

These two books are written for teachers and carers working with children of preschool age to 8 years. Oral English needs to be well developed before young beginners are taught to read and write English. *Introducing English to Young Children: Spoken English* discusses holistic development and oral acquisition suggesting useful oral activities, mini-projects, picture books and games. *Introducing English to Young Children: Reading and Writing* introduces reading, handwriting and creative writing skills with suggestions for linked meaningful activities, and more advanced verbal play, games, picture books and projects.

An earlier version of this book was awarded the English Speaking Union Duke of Edinburgh award in 1985 as part of the English Language Teaching Series published by Macmillian Publishers Ltd.

> *The child is truly a miraculous being, and this should be felt by the educator.*
>
> (Montessori 1967)

Terminology used in this book

EFL English as a foreign language

ESL English as a second language (United States)

L1/HL first or home language (sometimes called mother tongue MT)

SL school language (which may be different from L1)

bilingual two languages in the home

plurilingual three or more languages in the home

L2 where English is the second new language

L3 where English is the third new language

L4 where English is the fourth new language

VYL very young learner (nursery school age)

YL young learner (primary school age up to 8 or 9 years)

List of figures

1

Very young and young children and language learning

1.1 Children's and parents' expectations

We become interested in what we are good at, to quote Bruner (Donaldson 1978). This simple truth about attitudes also applies to learning English. How often adults say, 'I like English. I was good at it', or conversely when excusing their poor English add, 'I was never any good at it at school'.

At no other time in life does the human being display such enthusiasm for learning, for living, for finding out (Pluckrose 1979). Very young and young children normally have an inner drive to learn. They are natural language acquirers; they are self-motivated to pick up language without conscious learning, unlike many adolescents and adults. They have their own language learning skills and strategies, which develop as their brain develops and they grow physically (their skull making an effective sound box and their vocal chords and mouth forming the shapes necessary to make sounds). In the womb they hear and are listening to voices. From their first cries, children respond to their mother's soothing words in what is to become their mother tongue.

Young children seem to be 'tuned in' to listen to language, absorb it and then use it through social interaction with supportive others to find out about the world. Their energy to ask, enquire and make sense of their world is remarkable. Parents often feel exhausted by their child's continual drive to find out: *Why? What's this? What for? How?*

Learning is both social and conceptual for a young child. In making sense of every new experience, young children have to make sense of what the other person is saying and doing, confirming the known, whilst stretching and adjusting their own internal categories and theories to take in the new. They become skilled in understanding other people's language and abstracting meaning from it. Young children are quick to decode facial language and can rapidly sense when an adult is not pleased with them.

Language and learning are social and interdependent. Thinking cannot take place without language. Vygotsky (1978) explained that *Language is the tool of thought. External speech is the process of turning thoughts into words.*

We know from observing very young children that even very little language enables participation in a social world and the sharing of meaning: *Gone. Stopit. Myturn.* Through natural, 'tuned-in' supportive dialogue with an adult or more skilled older person, grammar and vocabulary is absorbed and conceptual progress may take place without any planned instruction or conscious teaching by the older person.

Babies learn much through observing carefully and then imitating the role model: the adult or older child. Steiner's work emphasises the great importance of imitation and the quality of the role model. Sometimes young children pick up inappropriate language from other children, which, although it might be annoying, is a measure of their ability to learn through imitation.

From an early age young children have an innate ability to imitate pronunciation and work out the rules of language for themselves. By the age of 6 years, many are capable of adjusting their accent in English to match the local dialect of their playmates, speaking two Englishes, classroom English and playground English, they rarely confuse when to use which type of English, so teachers and parents are often unaware that they also speak playground English. Some young children can speak a little of four or five languages and enjoy opportunities to boast about their language tally. '*I can speak Czech, and I can speak French and I can speak English*' a 5-year-old boasted to other children in the playground. Any idea that learning to talk in English is difficult does not occur to them unless suggested by adults, who themselves may have struggled to learn English 'academically' through grammar-based textbooks at secondary school level. Many adults, who picked up English young, say they cannot remember how, or sometimes, even when, they learned it. 'We just played, said rhymes like "Humpty Dumpty sat on a wall" and sang songs.'

It is now generally accepted that lifelong attitudes are formed in early childhood and usually before the age of 8 or 9 years. If teachers can engage young children and capture and keep their enthusiasm by presenting well-planned language experiences, right for their needs and development level, children usually make progress and feel they are 'good at English'. *The best motivation to learn a language is not an abstract liking of its beauty or utility, but a liking for the person who speaks it* (Taeschner 2005). It is in these early stages of learning English that the foundations for what may be a lifelong interest in English language, literacy and culture are laid down.

1.1.1 Children's expectations

Children come to English sessions or lessons with expectations about what they are going to do and achieve. These expectations are influenced by what their family, friends and society in general expect and what the learners have heard from other children. Today's children may already have heard English spoken on screens and even visited English-speaking countries and seen or spoken to English-speaking children. Technology now brings different languages into the home through TV, DVD, websites, YouTube, Skype, and handheld devices, so children may have many different ideas about English and global English-based cultures. Children like to be entertained and are skilled in picking up audio-visual language and cultural information from the screen. Culture accompanies most English language activities, providing they are not word-for-word direct translations, and young children are especially skilled at picking up information from visual images (see 7.5).

Young children have an inner drive to achieve and when they independently achieve something to what they know to be a high standard it provides an inner, deep self-satisfaction that is important in character development, emotional well-being and in forming lifelong positive attitudes. In today's fast moving lifestyle, many children may not have achieved any one task well enough to feel this inner glow of satisfaction. However, through English oral play and repeated chanting of English oral play, rhymes and tongue-twisters in pleasurable situations, many appear to feel the satisfaction that comes through achievement (see Chapter 6).

1.1.2 Home languages

Monolingual and monocultural children (those who only know one language and culture) appear to find learning English a different challenge from children from binational families, where parents speak their own language to their child at home and their children grow up speaking two languages (bilingual), one of which is usually dominant, as it is the most used. Children who have learned two languages consecutively (L2 introduced after L1) already know how to acquire and communicate in a second language before they go to school. Some of these children may learn English as L4 as they speak two languages at home: school language (SL) is L3 and English L4. Normal young children can cope with acquiring four oral languages if the learning situations are activity-based, right for the child, and within the family's expectations. Amazingly, children who learn English as L3 or L4 generally learn more easily than monolingual children for whom English is L2, as these children have already worked out how to use their own personal language learning skills and strategies to acquire another new language.

It seems that to acquire L2 non-consecutively after L1 (home language or mother tongue) – that is after a gap – is the most difficult way, as a young child has to work out their own language acquisition strategies and skills in order to pick up the new language (although this might also depend on the age at which L2 is learned).

Most children who learn English as L2 at about 7 or 8 years already know to use the main structures of their L1, although they are still using limited language learning skills and strategies to learn vocabulary. Starting to learn a new language, English as L2, means that these children have to work out which of their personal language acquisition skills they can reuse to pick up English successfully. Once they have reused their learning strategies and skills to acquire L2, it seems that L3, and any other subsequent languages, can be learned in the same way, albeit more easily. This is, of course, a generalisation, because learning language depends on the 'feel-good' factor. If the relationship between the adult, who is the mediator of the new language, and the child is not good, learning can be difficult and even frustrating. People who acquire a second language or languages before puberty appear to retain the skill to pick up languages orally throughout their life. In fact some teenagers, who have learned L2 young, complain about using language textbooks at secondary school, saying that they need to hear a language spoken before they can learn grammar rules.

1.1.3 Immediate results

Children are creatures of the moment. They work best and most successfully when the objectives are clear, comprehensible, immediate (Pluckrose 1979). Objectives and language are clearer where activities and the accompanying language are structured to fit them. This enables children to focus more easily on a task without having to sift through all the content in order to find the information and language to be learned. This is an economy in learning energy and time, as young children's concentration span is short.

Young children want to please; they care about what others think about them, especially their loved ones and their teacher with whom they generally have a special, emotional, family-like relationship, sometimes referred to as 'professional love'. *In the Nursery School more than at any other stage of education, a great emphasis is placed on the teacher-child relationship and thereby on good communication – a communicative/emotional relationship between adult and child* (Taeschner 2005).

Children long to 'show off' a new English 'talking' (speaking) skill. From an early age, they work out that a new LI verbal skill is rewarded by some form of praise from adult admirers! They remember how excited their parents were when they recited a complete nursery rhyme by themselves.

Children want immediate results. They expect to go home after the first lesson able to speak some English, even if it is just a rhyme or counting in English, so they can 'show off' and win praise from their extended family and friends. Success motivates; any praise given by parents and other adults, whose approval and love children seek, stimulates, especially in the first stages of learning English, when the child is still gaining confidence.

Rhymes provide good 'show off' pieces and at the same time satisfy children's desire 'to talk a lot of English quickly, just like grown-ups' they may have seen and heard on screen (see 6.2). It is through parents' praise that children find out that they are doing the right thing and understand what is expected of them.

Children are used to communicating in LI and, as soon as possible, they want to do the same in English. They know that it is through talk that they can communicate and exchange ideas with others. However, they expect to use English in real, meaningful experiences. If children are already reading and writing in LI, they expect to be shepherded to do the same in English. Although preschool children are happy with the same all-oral approach they have in LI, to spend months only speaking English is not 'real school work' to young children who can read and write in SL. *Introducing English to Young Children: Reading and Writing* (Dunn forthcoming) explains how reading and writing can be introduced through meaningful, holistic activities from the beginning stages of acquiring oral language.

If children's expectations are not fulfilled and they do not get what they have expected from the English lessons, they can lose interest. Loss of interest sometimes occurs once the novelty of the English lesson fades and the children find they can still say very little in English. With careful planning and working together with the family, this can be avoided. Once a child has lost interest, it takes time, and focused effort and encouragement, to re-stimulate interest.

1.1.4 Parents' expectations

For children to 'feel good' and for learning to be successful, parents' expectations should, as nearly as possible, coincide with those of the teacher. Where parents become disappointed with their child's progress and critical of the teacher's methods, the child becomes confused, which reflects on their learning. It is important that before starting to learn English, parents understand how children learn and how the teacher teaches. Programmes also need to be explained and efforts made to keep families positive by asking for their co-operation in hearing rhymes and singing together and sharing picture books. Later chapters deal more fully with these issues.

Parents who learned English in adolescence sometimes relate their children's learning to the way they learned English. They are frustrated that English grammar is not taught in the way that they were taught in secondary school; this frustration often leads to criticism of the teacher amongst parents, sometimes within their children's hearing, which is damaging to the child's image of their teacher.

When asked, '*What did you do in English today?*' some children reply, '*Played*'. This may cause difficulties as most parents think that the opposite of play is work and associate play with effortless, home recreation, which is different from structured, cognitively complex, school play. Parents need to understand that school play is a tool for learning and acquiring English. Play in the English classroom is purposeful and socially interactive, providing meaningful opportunities for dialogue at young children's level in English. School play or activities are also closely monitored and documented by the teacher, who closely follows each child's progress and needs (see visible learning 2.5.1).

Just as parents' enthusiasm is infectious and can motivate, so their disappointment can reflect on their children, causing them to lose interest and confidence in their teacher. Many parents have not realised that young children learn differently from adolescents, and teachers need to be sure that they understand this from the outset. Teachers may find it helpful to explain to parents that young children pick up English through dialogue-based activities in which a special type of language called *teacherese* is used (see 1.2.3). Many parents, and especially mothers, may have not realised that they successfully taught their child to speak their first language and they did this intuitively by using a simpler form of language called *parentese*. It is accepted that fathers and some older siblings also use this form of speech, but not as well as mothers or female carers to whom, in many societies, it seems to be innate. For this reason it was previously termed *motherese*.

Acquiring any language at a young age cannot be thought of as learning grammar analytically as an isolated subject matter. Acquiring language is a global activity and depends on the whole child's mental, physical, social and emotional maturity and well-being. This global activity is essential if children are to pick up the language they hear (input) and to use language (output). Research shows that language is more meaningful and more easily acquired where the child hears the language whilst being involved physically 'in doing' an activity.

The Reggio Emilia Approach explains that learning is a partnership – teacher–child, parent–child. It seems that learning another language (English) at school needs to be thought of as a triangle: parents, teacher and child, with regular interaction between all three. The parents' role is crucial as the parents, especially the mother, have already been deeply and emotionally involved in teaching their child to speak L1 and know their child's way of learning language intimately.

Recent research records that parents and the home are the strongest influence on a child's life. For this important reason parents, and especially mothers, need to be positively involved as their support and enthusiasm can help in much the same way as it did when their child learned L1.

Some of today's parents, who may only have learned English in secondary school, are much better informed than their parents, as they have been exposed to English experiences through technology and especially on screen. Some may have travelled or even studied abroad and know about learning English as an adult. Knowing more about the use of English world-wide, many parents are really keen for their children to learn English at a young age. Since they were their children's first language teachers, many parents are eager to be involved. They want to monitor and also enjoy their young children's successes in learning English and can, in fact, play an important role in motivating and consolidating learning language – something they innately know how to do. If the teacher/teachers guide parent participation, the child has the advantage of two different groups of supportive adults helping them acquire English.

1.1.5 A young child's learning triangle

The English language learning triangle consists of the child, the parent/ parents, especially the mother if she is the principal home-carer, and the teacher. Each is dependent on the other for success and for making English part of the child's life. Unless the members of the triangle all 'feel good' about each other and the methods used, progress is hampered.

Figure 1 A young child's learning triangle

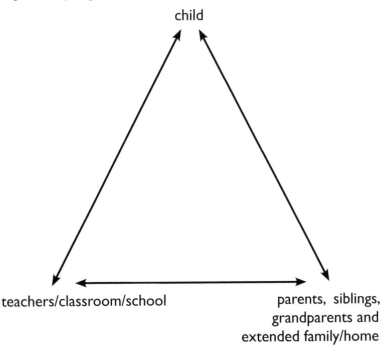

child

teachers/classroom/school

parents, siblings, grandparents and extended family/home

1.2 Starting to learn English as another language

Although every young child is uniquely influenced by the culture, environment and differing opportunities at home, school, and in society, the stages in language acquisition seem to be similar. When a young child learns another language, he approaches it in the same way as when he learns LI, which he is still picking up; *his awareness of what he talks about normally takes precedence over his awareness of what he talks with – the words that he uses* (Donaldson 1978). Thus to achieve the maximum language acquisition in the classroom, young children need to be exposed to rich language dialogues in which there is natural revision of used language and new input of language from an adult/teacher who uses an adapted form of *parentese* language, termed *teacherese*, (see 1.2.3) which fits more closely the holistic maturity of the young child.

1.2.1 Acquisition or learning

The acquisition or learning distinction suggests that adults have two independent but interrelated systems for gaining ability in another language: acquisition and learning. The view of Krashen is that *The good language learner is an acquirer; he may or may not be a conscious learner* (Krashen 1981). Young children are acquirers with remarkable abilities to unconsciously pick up language, or, according to Montessori, 'absorb' language, in situations where speakers communicate naturally using *parentese* language skills with very young children. In these situations, child speakers are more concerned with the use of language to convey meaning than with correct usage. They want to say something and, without thinking, communicate with the language they know rather than analyse it in order to find out the correct way to use it ('rules of usage'). Teaching the rules of usage (grammar) is not necessary for acquirers, as in acquiring LI they work out the rules themselves with the help of adult role models.

The other system, 'learning', takes place consciously. *It is helped greatly by error correction and the presentation of explicit rules* (Krashen and Seliger 1975, quoted in Krashen 1981). In short, it appears that fluency comes unconsciously from what a learner has acquired in interpersonal communication, whilst the formal knowledge of grammar rules has to be learned consciously.

Many young children are still acquiring LI and are therefore still using their personal, well-honed skills to acquire and pick up new language (assuming that they are exposed to language-rich experiences linked to meaningful activities). In young children's desire to communicate, many activities create situations in which language can be acquired. Young children are willing to say something, as their main aim is to communicate, to talk to you, without worrying about mistakes. Some young children find it fun to experiment with sounds, as they did at a younger age in LI. They find rhyming words fascinating and easy to pick up: they enjoy repeating lists of words like *all*, *ball*, *tall*, *small*, *fall*. If they 'feel good' about English and the environment is supportive, fun and friendly, young children rarely show the inhibitions typical of adolescents and some adult English language learners.

Recent research suggests that LI acquisition can be identified on one hand as Gestalt and on the other as analytic or creative. Gestalt psychology stresses the importance of learning by wholes. Gestalt language consists of prefabricated (ready-made lexical chunks) or formulaic routines or patterns (phrases), which are picked up as whole utterances: *Whatsthat? Comehere. Stopit.* (see Figure 2). These meaningful strings of words are memorised as wholes. **Research suggests that these phrases are stored and processed in the brain as individual units** (Zimmer in IHT 2010).

Comment

The child's maturity and the quality of LI and SL experience influence the child's ability to use their own acquisition skills to imitate and memorise.

By contrast, analytic or creative language develops word by word and utterances are consciously constructed by the speaker. In the initial stages of learning, prefabricated chunks of language are more used. However, in time, most children develop use of creative language, which eventually dominates. Research indicates that for many L2 learners, especially children, Gestalt speech (prefabricated language) serves as a short cut to allow social interaction and interpersonal communication with a minimum of linguistic competence. The analytic or creative mode begins to predominate as learners attempt to express specific and also individual ideas.

Figure 2 Types of language in L1 acquisition

Analytic or creative language	Gestalt or prefabricated blocks of language
Creative language	**Prefabricated language**
Includes labeling and identifying objects Word-by-word development eg *a dog, a cat* *a brown dog, a brown cat* *a dog and a cat* *a brown dog and a black cat*	1 Prefabricated routines/chunks Phrases, sentences more complex than a child's linguistic level eg *How are you?* *What are you doing?* *Can you come here?* Rhymes/chants/songs/tongue-twisters (see Chapter 6) Prefabricated patterns 2 Phrases, sentences part memorised, part creative language Prefabricated language constant, creative language changeable: *Can you come here?* *Can you come **into the garden**?* *Can you come **to bed**?*

Language input	
• Regular • Consciously graded • Clear • Easy-to-imitate • Authentic speech	• Very frequent repetition • Quick 'conversational type' • Used socially, in games and classroom management (see Chapter 3) • Simple patterns eg *This is . . .*

Use	
• In beginning lessons, less used and developed than prefabricated • Gradual input and memorisation until balance between creative and prefabricated nearly equal • Later language acquisition situations less predictable, creative language becomes dominant	• From first lesson • Very frequent repetition • As creative language develops less used in activities except for socialising, organising, managing and greetings

Examples of prefabricated chunks of language used by the adult

Survival language	Listen again. Say it again.
	I understand. Please stop now.
Transactional language	Please give me the scissors.
	Pass the paste. Stick it here.
Socialising language	Let's play this game.
	Are you ready?
Management language	How many cards have you got?
	Count them?

All young language learning children understand more than they can express in words. Children need to understand the language they hear if they are going to be able to acquire it. This does not mean that the child has to understand every word; he doesn't when he learns LI. It means that he has to understand what is going on and relate the meaning of the language to it. From a very young age, children have been able to decode the meaning of language not only from spoken words, but also from various clues, which include facial and body language, gesture, realia, situation and timing. This ability to understand without knowing the exact meaning of every word in an adult's utterance is referred to as *gist* understanding (see 1.2.12).

The linguistic environment of an activity based in the classroom is conducive to learning prefabricated patterns and routines whilst not yet understanding how many words and functions are included. When a parent says in LI to a 3-year-old, '*come with me to the toilet*', the 3-year-old may only understand the underlined stressed words but, helped by the outstretched hand and facial gesture, makes sense of the parent's utterance.

Where a lesson regularly follows the same framework, with familiar and new activities slotted into a programme, children have an opportunity to work out the meaning of the language used, since much of it will be familiar prefabricated management language and expanded language based on games, activities and picture books. With regular repetition of the same prefabricated language, children move from making sense of the language to being able to pick it up and then later use it.

There is a natural order through which grammatical structures develop (Slobin 1973). Learning is obviously more rapid where children already have a wide range of concepts and understanding of meanings, some of which they can already express in LI. There seem to be stages, which may be overlapping, through which each child develops at their own pace depending on the frequency and quality of the language input and the mediator. Any upset or lack of confidence generally results in regression, which is usually only temporary as the child regains confidence.

Recognised natural order of steps or stages in language acquisition

1. understanding meaning of simple explanations embedded in activities, but silent except for odd words like *goodbye, no, own name*

2. picking up language – words and some short phrases (blocks of prefabricated language): *green, book, no, stopit, onetwothree*

3. using more and longer blocks of prefabricated language without knowing word content: *getabook, passtheball, myturn*

4. prefabricated language and prefabricated patterns plus <u>creative language</u> = utterance *turnitoverwhatsthat? thats<u>acat</u>/thats<u>pink</u>*

5. combination of four above plus complete creative utterances

1.2.2 Teacher/parent language

How the adult uses language and what quality of language they use in dialogue with children is important for:

- acquiring the sounds of language
- learning how language works
- acquiring vocabulary
- understanding new concepts.

When they are very young, children learn language through one-to-one dialogue with a caring adult, who uses *parentese* language skills to match the child and the activity. Most very young and young L1 learners are still using some modified personal language learning skills and strategies to pick up new vocabulary and structures. It is thought that many monolingual English L1 children have learned most of the structures of English by the age of 6 years depending on the frequency of L1 input and the quality of the mediation by caring adults.

1.2.3 Motherese to teacherese language

Motherese or *parentese* language skills for talking to babies and toddlers are innate in many world languages. **Motherese deploys prosody, melodic overtones of speech that transcend culture and that are much the same whether the mother speaks Mandarin Chinese, Urdu or English. Motherese always sounds friendly and playful** (Goleman 2007).

It is said that young children can successfully learn English without the help of a modified form of *motherese* or *parentese*, often termed *teacherese*. However, teachers who can intuitively use *teacherese* in the beginning stages provide very young children especially (and young learners generally) with a richer, more emotional and sociable holistic learning environment. This environment is one in which children can be shepherded more easily by a supportive adult to use their acquisition skills and strategies. This shared attention creates a 'feel-good' factor that is vital if learning and enthusiasm is to be sustained at an early age.

Women appear to be innate users of *parentese*, whilst many men find it more difficult to adjust their voice, gesture and speech to fit activities with very young children. *There is a fundamental, biological difference in the way in which women tackle verbal communication. If this inherent skill is combined with another of women's inborn qualities – a more caring, nurturing temperament – it is obvious that certain major areas of social life should be dominated not by men but by women* (Morris 2010). Although men may find it more difficult to talk to very young children and get down to their language level, it should be remembered that children, and especially boys, need male role models, as men use language differently from women and can enthuse on different subjects, too. There is genuine worry about the 'over-feminisation' of education in the early years.

A lot can be learned about how to develop language by listening to a mother skilled in using the adult complement to baby talk, *motherese*, with her young toddler and watching how she develops her voice and language and affectionately encourages her toddler to use language by eye contact, body language, use of realia and even mouthing or whispering replies as role-models for her child. The mutual empathy and emotional connection creates a special glow. *At Nursery age emotional relationships are central to a child's growth.* (Italian National Educational Nursery School Programmes (Orientamenti) in Taeschner 2005.)

Women intuitively 'tune into' and adjust to a young child's language, interacting with the child and shepherding the child to their next level of language whilst scaffolding conceptual competence. This is much more effective when conducted one-to-one and face-to-face. For a young child to get more than a surface understanding of quickly changing screen images, an adult sitting next to the child has to add a running commentary, which helps mediate feeling and make a connection with the child's feelings.

Language scaffolded by a teacher in a dialogue with a child

Child	car (*taking a red car out of his coat pocket*)
Teacher	Oh you've got a car. It's a red car.
Child	red car
Teacher	There's the wheel, the steering wheel. (*showing how to turn the wheel*) Be careful! The car's coming.
Child	Vroom, vroom – car coming (*child taking the car on a journey in the air*)
Teacher	The car's coming fast.
Child	Vroom, vroom, car's coming fast
Teacher	(*holding up a hand to stop the car like a policeman*) Stop! The policeman says STOP!
Child	Stop! Car's stop stop
Teacher	Put the car in the garage. Here's the garage. (*holding open the child's coat pocket*)
Child	Car garage (*closing pocket*) car garage

Teacherese is a modified form of *motherese* adapted to fit the level of understanding and output of a child in L1 and the child's all-round maturity and emotional needs. Young children need to forge their own link with the teacher, and through the emotions conveyed in *teacherese*, they can feel a close connection.

After initial lessons, *teacherese* tends to be used when introducing new material (activities, games, picture books) and scaffolding children's thought from their present level to a higher conceptual and language level. Even if some adults feel shy to use *teacherese*, the young child does not feel it is boring or patronising; for them the over-dramatisation adds fun and makes understanding and acquiring language easier.

Top tip: Make learning language fun — funny voices, rhymes, noises and singing all help children to learn language. Be silly — often the daftest things gain their attention.

(I can 2010)

Teacherese styles for interactive interacting and learning

Voice	soft, possibly higher pitched than normal, caring and friendly
Pitch	range of pitch for dramatisation and to add fun/ suspense and aid management by conveying mood (eg to hold attention, keep order, show disappointment, sadness)
Volume	vary between quiet and loud
Stress	important words stressed, exaggerated intonation (melody of the language)
Articulation	precise, providing mouth movement model within view of child
Speech content	language simple, structured to child's need and level of understanding, initially single words and phrases, delivery slower (fewer words per minute) than normal speech, embedded in here-and-now activity, more profuse than usual, to increase input for the child, adjusted unconsciously to shepherd child's understanding of concepts and language.
Facial expression and gesture	exaggerated to aid understanding and imitation of sounds.
Eye contact	to reassure and encourage speaking (output).
Listening	obvious sole attention
Reply	allow longer time for child's reply, support a reply to increase child's output, which may include taking child to a higher conceptual level and thus language level (scaffolding)

Adult/teacher language input can take the form of:

- a running commentary (talking aloud) about what is happening
- repetition of new language and useful management language, enlarging phrases (rephrasing) as understanding increases (repetition helps the child to confirm the language to pick up and helps them to correct mistakes)
- reflecting back the child's language and enlarging it

> **Child**   Yellow.
>
> **Mother**   You like the yellow one. Here it is. Here's the yellow one. Let's see. Yellow, red and here's the brown one. I like the brown one, do you?

- scaffolding concepts (see above)
- questions
- commands
- paraphrasing and recasting language introducing new structures and vocabulary.

Non-native speaker, qualified teacher of 7- to 8-year-old children divided class of 24 into three groups and invited two English native speaker mothers to come once a week to play games like the *Memory Game* (see 5.1.9) with the same group each week for several weeks. By the end of the term, children in the two groups who played with the native speakers using *teacherese* were more fluent and confident than children in the third group, who had always played with the class teacher, whose spoken English was not sufficiently fluent to use *teacherese*.

The voice belongs to both the body and the mind and is unique to each of us. It is fundamental for the use of *teacherese*, and the teacher of VYLs and YLs depends greatly on their voice to 'shepherd' learning, modulating pause, pace, pitch and power to make their delivery colourful and memorable as well as to convey emotions.

Young children need to be talked *to*, not talked *at*. The way a teacher uses her voice will affect everything from the way she manages classes, reads picture books, says rhymes and dramatises jokes. *The voice both reflects and mediates our relationship with the outside world, and can be used to express attitudes and feelings that would be derided or dangerous if articulated through words* (Karpf 2006). Developing the full potential of the voice can take time, but with regular practice (including self-recordings before introducing new picture books, rhymes etc.) teachers often discover how many different voices they have and improve their vocal delivery skills.

Teachers need to check that they are providing sufficient language input of the right quality for children to be able to pick up language. The quality of the dialogue used makes a substantial difference to the rate children acquire and use language. Too much silence whilst children are playing games or colouring pictures is a waste of language learning time as each 'doing' activity provides time and opportunities for short, natural one-to-one dialogues. *You start. Are you ready? it's your turn. Put your card down. What is it?*

Once young children begin to create language, adults intuitively feel less need to use *teacherese* language except when introducing new language or activities. As young children mature and their English skills increase, they can pick up language when spoken to as a member of a small group, so the need for one-to-one dialogue for learning diminishes. However, children who are slow to pick up and use language or who make mistakes or seem to be disturbed still need some focused one-to-one dialogue each lesson, with the empathy that goes with it, if they are to feel more confident and make progress.

1.2.4 Scaffolding

Scaffolding is a term first introduced by Bruner, although both Piaget and later Vygotsky use it. Scaffolding represents the strategy used by an adult that enables the child to understand something beyond his present language level. The scaffolded language experience is embedded in an activity and to the outsider might look like a casual conversation, but is in fact a powerful, unconscious teaching/learning interaction. Once the child feels secure with the new learning, the scaffolding is gradually removed so that eventually the child can take control of the activity. The fewer the child's scaffolding experiences with a supportive older person, the fewer their opportunities to connect emotionally and acquire new language and thought. *What a child is able to do in collaboration today, he will be able to do independently tomorrow* (Vygotsky 1978).

This instructional scaffolding, like scaffolding on a building, provides a helpful temporary support framework to access new meaning and also new language. As language and learning are interdependent, speech is a critical teaching tool in scaffolding for both thinking and responding. In L1 it is through scaffolding that both new language and new concepts are introduced, often unconsciously. However, in learning English, scaffolding may be used just to introduce new vocabulary and language structures within known concepts, when an opportunity arises.

Adults who are 'tuned in' to young children intuitively know when children are ready to take part in a scaffold and know how to introduce language in small, absorbable chunks to make a scaffold. It is through scaffolded dialogues that children focus on language and discover how English works; these intimate, caring dialogues are the most important contribution to very young and young children's acquisition of English. In order to learn language, children need a considerable amount of dialogue experience even if, to begin with, their replies are limited and the adult has to compensate for the child's limitations by using *teacherese* techniques to make it easier for the child to listen and learn.

Scaffolding is a sociable interaction linking meaning, language and emotions naturally to a child and their activity or interest. Many adults, and even older children, when explaining something to younger children use this powerful, innate teaching skill. As the older speaker discusses the activity, she builds on the young child's language to develop the concept and introduce new words. A scaffold can extend naturally and playfully over several exchanges, depending on the child's receptive ability and understanding. A scaffold is not pre-planned and includes no overt, formal instruction. As the child loses interest, which can often be seen by the eye contact waning, and the eyes begin to wander, the adult speaker understands intuitively the child has reached their potential developmental level and interest for that encounter (ie the top of the scaffold) and together they move on to another activity.

1.2.5 Interaction

> *Language is acquired in the course of human development*
> *as a means of interacting with those 'significant others' who*
> *are most involved in the life of children.*

(Wells 1981)

Children learn language through a social dialogue with an older role model. In the first stages some teachers find it can be useful to use a doll or soft animal or even a glove puppet that only speaks English to create added dialogue with the teacher. This interaction enables the children to hear a role-model dialogue in English between two people as, initially, children have to find out how dialogue in English works and what language they have to use to reply. It also provides another English-speaking 'person' to ask questions and engage in dialogue with the children, which increases, in a natural way, the amount of repetition. For this to work, however, the teacher has to keep alive the mystique, as well as the fun, of the English-speaking toy, as some younger primary-aged children may begin to feel too sophisticated for this type of fantasy.

As English ability increases, interaction between a child and the older role model/models provides a child with added experience in:

- spoken language (output)
- new language acquisition (input)
- language repetition
- confirmation and development of concepts
- introduction of concepts.

Where children have little opportunity for quality language interaction, progress in English is unlikely to be rapid or good. Some children are, of course, better language acquirers and users than others; it is now generally accepted that boys differ from girls in acquiring and using language (see 1.3.2).

1.2.6 Extending concepts

T. S. Eliot, the famous poet once commented *TV permits millions of people to listen to the same joke at the same time and yet remain lonesome* (T. S. Eliot 1888–1965).

The role of the teacher is that of mediator (see 2.2), interpreting to the child the realia, the activity, the game or the picture book. In fact the mediator controls and extends the child's world, and the way they see the world (culture), through these selected, new experiences.

Mediating and gradually extending a concept requires patience. Young children need to return again and again to the same activity if they are to absorb both the concept and language. Young children's threshold of boredom is not as low as that of adolescents and adults. The child is content to return again and again to the same type of activity or game. Watch how, day after day, children play the same game in the playground, working at improving their game skills. Revisiting a game in English helps them to confirm what they know about the language and game concept and contributes to their 'I can' factor. To feel that 'I can' is very important for young children; it increases their confidence and self-esteem and subconsciously aids their progress in English.

1.2.7 Hearing and listening

Children need to feel that an adult is listening to them and concentrating on what they say. For this reason it is important that adults do not confuse hearing and listening.

Hearing involves receiving and understanding sounds and is easily done at the same time as something else, like talking on a mobile phone. In these cases a reply involves mere recognition (indicated by *Hmm* or *Yes*) that the speaker has said something.

Listening is more concerned with paying attention and deducing meaning from what can be heard. It requires some degree of concentration, as the listener has to record accurately what the child is trying to say and deduce meaning from it. In a dialogue where the adult only hears but does not listen, their response may not provide the child with a quality learning opportunity. A confirmation only with *Hmm* or a single word reply *Yes* or *No* does not provide any meaningful reason for the interaction to develop further.

1.2.8 Interference between languages

Although many parents are keen for their children to learn languages early, some worry that learning another language might interfere with children's ability to speak and write in LI or their SL. *Spending time learning one language does not slow down the development of language proficiency in another language at least not that aspect of proficiency which is related to success in school* (Swain 1981).

Mixing languages or getting confused as to which language to address to which person rarely happens once young children have worked out unconsciously, in their own time and without being continually told about their mistakes, which language to use to each adult. Young children have a remarkable ability to classify and compartmentalise their users and languages from an early age. They even seem to have worked out which gestures go with each language, too. On the occasions where languages get mixed, it is best to make no comment and continue as normal, letting children self-correct in their own time.

As children's English ability develops, some, often unconsciously, begin to compare similarities and differences between languages. Teachers report that in some cases, adolescents with a knowledge of several languages appear to use a richer vocabulary in LI or their SL, especially in written work. *He who knows no foreign language does not truly know his own* (Goethe 1749–1832).

1.2.9 Code-switching

As young children become more competent speakers a type of mixing occurs, referred to as *code-switching*; that is, they may include an LI word within a created English phrase. They may say 'He's eating a (LI word)', because they have not yet heard or acquired the word in English. If the adult repeats the missing word in English and then reflects back the phrase in English, including the missing word, depending on the developmental level of the child's language skills, the child may pick up the English word. Although the child may have picked up the word, a child rarely uses it straight away. Adults need to return to the same phrase later, by which time the child may be ready to use it. Some children need to hear new words several times in consecutive lessons in order to acquire them and then use them. Few children can use a new word immediately after they have heard it. Absorbing takes time and it takes longer for some children than for others.

Code-switching may occur when a very young child has had a new experience and wants to talk about it in English, but does not know a word (often a noun) to describe it. Again, the adult, without making any comment, reflects back to the child what he has said in English, so the child hears the new word in English. The child knows how to pick up the new word and although he may not use it immediately, he probably will in his own time.

Code-switching is not an error. It shows that children have understood meaning and also how language works, as the foreign word is usually inserted in the correct word order for English. If given more experience a child will correct himself when he is ready.

Children know how to listen and self-correct their speech and gradually match it to the role model's. However, this takes time. It may take several days or even weeks, depending how often they hear the correct model. Learning English cannot be forced; children need to be able to work at their own speed. They also need to be motivated and encouraged if they are to speak uninhibited by a fear of not knowing all the vocabulary, and if they are to say what they think and to reach their potential. Parents sometimes put pressure on children and cause them stress, as they expect them to absorb language more quickly than the child's natural speed. Teenagers and adult learners can repeat language from a textbook with little or no delay; young children learn differently.

1.2.10 Mistakes

> *Correction has little value as children need to 'learn by experience' and work out their own system. What a child works out for himself has quite a different status in his mind from what he is told by an authoritative adult.*

(Donaldson 1978)

Correction of speech by an adult has little value to a child and even may be off-putting. What a child works out for himself, in his own time, is remembered, providing he hears the adult repeat the correct version several times. Young children have an innate ability to self-correct by trial and error. Unlike young adults and teenagers, who are usually embarrassed to make mistakes in front of others, young children willingly try and continue to correct their speech over a period of time until they reach close proximity to the adult speaker's version.

Young children assume that adults will understand what they say. Their parents understood them when they began to speak in L1. Parents were used to understanding their intended meaning, especially when what they actually said was not correct or was a word and not a full phrase. Listen to parents; they rarely point out a mistake saying 'You've made a mistake' or 'That's wrong'. They know intuitively not to stop the flow of conversation and that, if they did, they might inhibit the child. They do not scold them or correct them either, but just edit what they said and demonstrate a correct spoken version. The next time the child uses the language, he may have self-corrected. If not, the child may need to hear the correct utterance several times more before he self-corrects; parents are patient. Teachers of young children need to adopt the same strategies. To be criticised or told that you have made a mistake by a teacher, when you have been trying your best, can be hurtful to a young child and can even affect the mutual emotional bond, which is so important for learning language. Young children are upset if they feel the teacher does not like something they are doing.

Some young children make the same mistakes over several months. Teachers need to be patient and increase the opportunities of one-to-one dialogue that include the correct speech. Imposed corrections by adults have little value for the child, even if they might satisfy the adult. What children work out for themselves, they remember. What adults tell or impose is generally forgotten. Where a mistake persists there is still nothing to gain by correcting or tutoring; children's language learning strategies are not tuned to picking up imposed corrections. A child will refine and adjust to the adult model in his own time, if he is motivated and feels supported.

1.2.11 Transferring language

In learning L1, very young children develop skills to transfer (recycle) the little language they can use to make meaning in other related situations. Many adults use these same skills when they try to make themselves understood in foreign situations, reusing the few phrases they know in that language.

A young child used *allgone* (a prefabricated phrase) in different situations:
Allgone (referring to juice)
(then pointing to the window) *Car allgone*
Dada allgone (implying the car had gone and Daddy was in the car).

If children are to begin to use their transfer skills in English, the adult needs to show them how, by providing role models of language. Planned transfer of management language is useful as it also exposes a child to repetition of meaningful language.

> ### Transfer (same language, different context)
> *Come here, children.* (getting ready for Rhyme Time)
>   Then later in the day:
> *Come here, children.* (getting ready for a game)
>
> ### Transfer (same management language, same context)
> *Put the book on the table.*
> *Put the crayons on the table.*

1.2.12 Translation/Understanding

Using only English in the classroom (*total immersion*) takes a lot of effort on the part of the teacher, but after a slow beginning children seem suddenly to break through to understanding. It is worth a slow, somewhat exhausting start in English when all the input comes from the teacher, as eventually children understand how to use some of their innate skills to make meaning and feel 'I can'.

> ### Balance in talk and understanding
> Stage 1: Initial language input: Teacher dominates/child listens.
>
> Stage 2: Language input changes: Teacher talks/child replies.
>
> Stage 3: Language input changes in specific familiar activities (eg games): Teacher-talk is less dominant/child-talk more dominant; child replying and instigating language.

Young children's ability to focus, analyse and understand, if they are engaged, develops fast and should not be underestimated. As in L1, young children understand much more than they can say.

In L1 very young children are used to understanding only some key words and guessing the rest – getting meaning from the speaker's body language and context clues around them. This is termed *gist understanding*. As adults we also use gist understanding to make sense of what a new speaker says until we 'tune in' to their voice and pronunciation. Developing sufficient confidence to use gist understanding skills is important if progress is to be made in language learning. Many language learners are held back by their own expectations that they should understand every word.

> In this example the English is structured and accompanied by body language to help understanding.
>
> *Put* the *book* there. (pointing at the table)
>
> Child picks up the book
>
> *Put* the *book* on the ·*table*. *Put* the *book* in the *English* Corner on the *table*. (pointing at the English Corner)
>
> The child understood the underlined words and filled in the rest.

As young children get used to transferring the gist understanding skills they use in L1 to make meaning in English, their understanding develops rapidly, along with their confidence.

When both a new concept and new language are introduced at the same time, it may be necessary to give a quick translation once, using a whisper, followed directly by the English. However, if a translation is given more than once and again in following lessons, a child may get used to waiting for the translation instead of using his own clues to decode the English to get meaning.

Adults can intuitively sense when what they have said is beyond the child's ability to understand. In such situations they can often see bewilderment on the child's face. However, some children may not be adventurous and may not try to understand. This is a challenge for a teacher, who needs to build up the child's confidence by repeating the language with added gestures, hoping that the child has understood and is motivated by the teacher's encouragement – *See you can. Well done!* – and their own feeling of achievement.

1.2.13 Beginning to think in English

By using simple English with plenty of repetition in familiar activities, adults help children to begin unconsciously thinking in English in specific, familiar activities like often-played games. Where children are secure, can predict what is going to happen, have begun to initiate dialogue and create their own English, it is possible that during a very familiar activity, like a game or picture book, they (as they would in a total immersion situation) begin to think in English. For this reason it is important to revisit favourite picture books and games, as these might be important for consolidating learning (see browsing 7.8). Adults need to remember that children have a higher boredom threshold than adults and are generally happy to revisit enjoyable experiences if given the opportunity.

At the end of three months at an English school, teachers related that from one day to the next, Japanese children began to talk. In fact the Japanese children were so pleased with their newly acquired skill, teachers found it difficult to stop them chattering. It was as if something had happened overnight that made it possible for breakthrough the next day. Suddenly these children found that they could create their own language to say what they wanted and to talk about things within their own experience. Unconsciously they were building new language, combining it with bits of language they already knew. To their delight they found they could initiate a discussion and sustain it. Although they continued to speak using prefabricated language, the amount of created language they used increased daily to become the most important part of their speech.

This 'overnight breakthrough' is not unique to children learning English as an additional language in British schools in the UK. Teachers in elementary schools in America report similar experiences with immigrants after about four or five months learning English. French teachers report in French elementary schools that non-French children take about the same length of time to achieve breakthrough.

The length of the pre-breakthrough period depends on:

- the amount and varied types of exposure
- the degree of home support
- the position of English within the family, society and the environment.

Where there is no home support, learning takes longer. Where parents understand very little English, but are still supportive and willing to co-operate with home tasks, children are motivated by their positive attitudes. Parents who have only followed two- or three-year English courses at secondary school need encouragement as their English is insufficient to support their children. Some schools run successful short courses for parents who have forgotten their school English – classes geared at how to help their children with English.

1.2.14 Encouragement and praise

Young children look for adults' praise. It helps them to 'feel good', and through praise they know they are making progress in English and they can confirm that they are doing what their parents expect of them. Young children have an ability to sum up adults they know well; they are quick to sense their approval and soon find out how and when to please them. By finding out what adults think about them and what they do, children work out what is expected of them and what is right or wrong. Young children feel more secure when they know what is expected of them – when they know 'the rules'.

Young children also work out how to attract praise. However, to be able to do this in English, teachers need to provide them with some 'show-off' pieces, such as easy English rhymes or songs that attract praise. For the 'show' to be successful, parents and family need to understand what to expect and not to be critical or compare the show with what they did in English at school. Parents need to understand that young children learn language in a different way from adults and that English is another way of talking about things that interest them and about the experiences they have had.

Praise is not the same as encouragement, but both serve to motivate and are needed by children if they are to learn. Praise is generally given for a completed activity. *Well done. That's cool. You did try hard. That's very good.* Encouragement, on the other hand, is given whilst the child is doing something. Encouragement is intended to assist successful achievement and effort. *Just a little more. It's nearly finished. Try once again, you can do it. You have worked hard. Well done.* Praise should not be given just for ability – *Clever boy, you are clever* – as this can make children complacent and thus lose the drive to try new activities.

Encouragement can be used more liberally than praise. Praise should not become routine although children may be craving for it. Children know when something merits praise and when a teacher gives praise unjustly; children have clear-cut views on what is right and what is wrong and expect justice from a teacher. If children have a feeling that they are clever, they might give up trying, so it is important to give encouragement and praise where it is merited, including when a child has worked hard.

If the relationship between the teacher and each child is good and the activities right, young children will happily do their best as they want to please the teacher and gain their praise. The teacher's praise and understanding, even when a child has an 'off day' satisfies emotionally, motivates and makes children 'feel good'. Young children trust their teacher and develop a special bond with them. A reward system of giving stars is unnecessary and over-competitive for very young children, who are doing their best. Stars are an adult marking system that can result in children feeling cheated and let down by the teacher if they are not awarded a star when they feel their work merits one. There are other more child-friendly ways of recording work and progress (see 3.6) including exhibiting all the work in the classroom, boys' work in one corner and girls' in another, for everyone to see and learn from.

1.2.15 Imitation

An enormous amount of learning from infancy and childhood goes on through modelling – observing how others act and bringing that into the brain as part of the potential repertoire for behaviour and then using it in the right situations.

(Goleman 2007)

Young children have a natural biological predisposition to imitate and unconsciously look for their role models in adults and older children both in real life and on the screen. They enjoy copying and mimicking. How often do Bob the Builder and other screen personalities become copied heroes? Unconsciously young children imitate adults' behaviour and also speech, facial and body language without any direction or instruction, learning in a stress-free environment and at their own pace. It is through watching the adult's mouth movements, linking them to the sounds they hear, that children learn how to make sounds and words in English. For this reason children need to be able to see the adult's face clearly. Learning how to make sounds by watching adults on the screen may be more difficult as the child has to imitate the sound without confirming the accompanying mouth movements, as there are fewer close-ups of the face than in real life.

> (South London suburb)
> *You speak like a local kid. Where did you learn your English?* Japanese professor
> *Playing. All summer I went out into the park and played.* Japanese child, age 7

Opportunities need to be carefully planned so that imitation is easier. For example, in leading Circle Time, Rhyme Time or picture book reading, it is better for the adult to sit on a seat at a higher level than the children so they can see and imitate the mouth movements of speech. If children cannot see the mouth movements, it is possible to imitate the sounds, but it takes longer and more effort to work out how to make them.

1.2.16 Transferring concepts

Concepts learned in one language are not only applicable to that language. Teachers will have noticed, when teaching children to count in English, that children who already know how to use numbers in LI learn number names quickly in English. In fact, they are transferring their concepts of numbers from LI and merely learning a new linguistic label or name for each number in English. The same applies to literacy skills. Children who can already read in LI learn to read in English quite quickly once they have been introduced to decoding text. This is partly due to the fact that they are more mature, but also because they have LI reading skills and knowledge of how to decode text to get meaning, both of which they transfer to English.

Some teachers trying to teach new concepts in English to children who have not yet learned them in LI are left in doubt as to whether the children have fully understood. Swain points out that *instruction in the first language can benefit second language and spending time learning in one language benefits both languages equally with respect to developing those language-related skills essential to academic success* (Swain 1981). Where children have insufficient oral ability in English, it may be better to wait to teach a new concept in English until it has been taught in LI. Once the concept has been taught in LI, children generally transfer it easily to English as it only involves learning the new language, and not both a new concept and language at the same time.

1.2.17 Child and adolescent/adult language learning differences

It is thought that an important relationship may exist between physical, mental and emotional maturation and the development of puberty, which has an effect on language learning. It seems that monolingual children who have reached puberty before learning English have lost their innate ability to pick up language and to learn by trial and error, taking risks using it in front of others. Monolingual teenagers at secondary school are ready to learn English as a separate grammar-based course whilst for VYLs and YLs, acquiring English is part of their natural holistic development and something they do innately and unconsciously by taking part in activities. Linguistic considerations alone are not a sufficient measure for evaluating how young children learn English.

Teachers and parents remark how quick young children are at successfully acquiring another language and how error-free their speech (and in particular their pronunciation) is, in spite of being given little or no formal grammar instruction. They marvel at young children's ability to imitate English and rapidly become indistinguishable from native speakers.

Adults who learned English at secondary level generally retain some accent long after they have reached fluency, whereas children who acquire a second language by imitation before puberty usually manage to speak several Englishes with no accent. This is summed up by a frequent situation where the recently arrived adult immigrant speaks English with a marked accent, whilst his young son speaks a neighbourhood dialect indistinguishable from his local friends.

1.3   The developing child

> *Unfortunately, human evolution has been working against the genderless ideal for more than a million years and has ensured that significant differences in male and female thinking exist deep inside our brains. We know, for example, females are much more fluent verbally than males*
>
> (Morris 2010)

Boys' brains develop differently from girls and this affects how boys pick up language and use it. Too often co-ed classes make little provision for boys, who may be overshadowed by girls' natural ability to use language. If young boys are to reach their potential, they need some different language experiences from girls and their achievements should not be compared to those of girls. Parents also need to understand this as it can be very demotivating for boys to be compared with girls.

Although YL classrooms are expected to give the same learning opportunities to both girls and boys, most teachers and parents recognise that each child is unique. However, few adults make accommodation for the differences between how boys and girls learn. Most teachers appreciate that girls love to chatter and use language, whilst boys tend to be more economical in their utterances, but few organise different English learning activities according to gender.

Since the 1990s it has been acknowledged that in the UK boys are underachieving in reading and writing and seem to have more difficulty in communicating and learning language than girls. It is now accepted that there are fundamental differences between the learning skills and interests of the two sexes. These differences show up from the very first months in the way babies develop (nature) and may be accentuated by the way that adults mould babies to fit the cultural stereotypes that individual societies expect of male and female behaviour (nurture). In most Western societies boys are spoken to differently from girls from birth and are treated to more vigorous 'rough and tumble' play, especially by fathers.

Development disparity is greater in the early years of development and it is generally accepted that most young girls reach the accepted 'developmental milestones' before boys. However, where some boys may have difficulty in reading at the age of 6 years and write slowly and laboriously, by the age of 8 years most boys have caught up with expected levels.

1.3.1 Brain development

Through recent research, which incorporates the latest technology, the differences between the male and female brain and their ways of working are becoming more widely appreciated. Newberger (1999) explains that although the adult male brain is 15 per cent larger than the female brain, this is not as important as the male and female brains' different methods of functioning.

The two lobes of the female brain are more abundantly connected in more complex ways. This feature appears to create marked functional differences and may explain girls' tendency to use both sides of the brain, giving rise to females' ability to multitask. *In more than 50 per cent of women, processing the sounds of speech seems to involve both hemispheres* (Field 2004). This suggests that women are better at integrating information, which may be why they are often more successful at language learning.

An outcome of research in 1981 was the notion that brain functions could be divided into left or right brain functions. Today neuroscientists consider this to be an over-simplification and it is thus viewed as inaccurate to typecast people as *left-brained* or *right-brained*. It now appears more important and appropriate to think in terms of *whole-brain* learning and holistic education where each child can gain the experiences they need for learning.

Evidence also suggests that reading appears to use both sides of the brain simultaneously and that this may account for the fact that most girls have better literacy skills than boys. Research data in the UK shows that many more young boys than girls have reading difficulties in their home language, are dyslexic or stammer. This could also have an effect on young male learners of English (L2).

Recent research is resulting in scientists rethinking how deeply culture – language and values – shapes the brain. The new field known as *cultural neuroscience* is discovering unexpected differences in the function of the brain. For instance in 2006 a study showed that to do simple sums, native Chinese speakers use a different region of the brain from native English speakers, even though both use Arabic numbers. The Chinese-speaker brain uses areas that process visual and spatial information and plan movements, whilst English speakers use language circuits. *It seems as if the West conceives numbers just as words, but the East imbues them with symbolic, spatial freight. One would think that the neural processes involving basic mathematical computations are universal, but they seem to be culture-specific.* Professor Nalini Ambady *attests to the strength of the overlap between self and people close to you (in collectivistic cultures) and the separation in individualistic cultures* (in Begley 2010).

This has implications for adults working with young children who are beginning English, as concepts and consequent behaviour cannot be thought of as universal. Apart from explicit differences in teaching handwriting in English (eg compared with Chinese and Japanese ideographs, which are classified by the number of strokes, and Arabic handwriting, which is from right to left across the page), there are also hidden differences, including mother–child relationships that should not be overlooked. In playing games in groups, different ideas on how to play are likely to exist between children of different linguistic and cultural backgrounds; home culture will be dominant and 'universal notions' of how to win or lose should not be expected, unless they have been carefully explained.

1.3.2 Gender differences

Hearing

Newberger points out that girls' senses of hearing, touch and smell are better developed and this advantage remains throughout life. Boys appear to have less sensitive hearing at all ages, which may reflect on their ability to imitate and pick up language and songs. Girls tend to be better listeners than boys and this could be linked with their hearing as well as their ability to concentrate for longer periods than boys. In Western societies boys are frequently talked to differently from girls, so some of the language they hear and use as a model on which they base their learning varies, too. This may result in boys using language differently and possibly not as fluently in some situations as girls.

Voice

Boys tend to speak more loudly than most girls and many appear to have less control of their voice than girls. Boys also have problems as their voice prepares 'to break', which sometimes make them reluctant to perform in front of others. Young girls' voices tend to be softer and girls appear to find it easier to modulate their voice, which makes dramatic reading easier for them.

Muscular control and eye co-ordination

Unlike girls who can sit still and work at activities like colouring for a longish period for their age, boys need to move and wriggle a lot especially around the age of 6 and 7 years. This may be connected with their muscular development and, according to some experienced teachers, the effect of growth of new molar teeth around the age of 6 or 7 years.

Boys especially can benefit from the recent research in the US, which finds that short physical activity breaks of as little as five minutes can improve classroom attention, behaviour and achievement, and can also boost academic performance.

Boys generally read later than girls and reach fluency later. Some boys show little interest in stories, preferring to read information books. Many boys have difficulty with handwriting and take longer to reach the same standard of co-ordination as girls. Producing a beautiful piece of handwriting may be difficult for many boys. This could be due to later muscular development.

Frustration

Boys tend to be more aggressive and competitive; they are risk-takers. Girls are more inclined to be people-pleasers. Boys flourish in situations where they need short, sharp spans of concentration and where their abilities are not compared with those of girls. Young boys find it difficult to accept comparison by teachers of their school skills with that of girls'. Many boys feel that girls are always more successful at schoolwork (often confirmed in their eyes by marks); this can lead to a loss of self-esteem and confidence in using language. Girls, on the other hand, soon feel they are cleverer and harder workers than boys. Most young children, and especially girls, have opinions about the abilities of other children and their behaviour, too.

Young boys also tend to be more restless in class than girls and if they are not involved actively in things that interest them, they can become disruptive and inattentive. Girls are usually more attentive, more tolerant of – and capable of – learning in non-enjoyable situations and thus, from the teacher's point of view, easier to manage.

In the pre-puberty years (aged 8–9 years old) boys become naturally boisterous and their high-spiritedness needs to be directed into topics that match, in some way, their growing masculinity.

Concentration and perseverance

Young boys' concentration spans seem to be shorter than girls' as they manifest a need to move around. Young girls seem to have an ability to persevere and finish off an activity from an early age. They generally complete a piece of work neatly and rarely give up even if they find something is a bit difficult.

Girls aged between 1 to 3 years generally learn to talk before boys, giving them a 'head start' in using language and learning through dialogue. It is suggested that girls' constant desire to chatter may give them more practice and opportunities to acquire different levels of language and vocabulary. This factor may be especially relevant in the period just before they become fluent readers.

The length of time a child can concentrate on doing one activity also varies from child to child. Some young children can only manage to concentrate for about five minutes, others for very much longer periods of up to 14 or 15 minutes. Once children have lost interest in an activity and their attention and eyes have wandered, little or no more learning takes place. It is best to change an activity before children lose interest so that they are left wanting more and looking forward to the next opportunity to do the same activity. Over-exposure to an activity leads to boredom. As children develop, so their span of concentration lengthens. It is important not to confuse a child's span of concentration with his need to move physically.

1.3.3 Intelligence

Previously it was thought that the intelligence quotient (IQ) was innate, could not be changed and could be measured in one type of test. Most classroom teachers who do different activities with the same group of children know that boys and girls show evidence of different types of intelligence and have preferred ways of learning. However, too few methods of assessment, including tests and school exams, value these different abilities and skills.

The psychologist Howard Gardner challenged traditional IQ tests, suggesting that they only measured logical/mathematical and linguistic/language thinking abilities. In his theory of multiple intelligences (MI), Gardner now identifies a possible 8.5 types of intelligence (Gardner 1983).

Gardner suggests the following:

Linguistic	good listeners and users of language
Logical–mathematical	good calculators and reasoners
Musical	appreciative of rhythm, sounds, and love music
Spatial	learn through drawings, charts, graphs
Bodily	kinesthetic learners with a sense of body awareness
Interpersonal	interested in others and learn through interaction
Intra-personal	introverted, in tune with own personal feelings and desires
Naturalistic	in tune with the environment
Existential	(half) (has yet to be fully listed)

According to Gardner, each child has a different and unique profile of strengths and weaknesses, which, if learning is to be successful, adults need to recognise and nurture in a way that ensures that the child can achieve and can build up confidence.

While some neuroscientists do not fully accept Gardner's theories, there is no doubt that Gardner's MI theory has broadened the way in which many educators look at children and caused some to consider altering the types of learning experiences they provide. *His theory has made teachers ask the inclusive question, 'How is this child intelligent?' rather than the exclusive, 'Is this child intelligent?'* (Barnes 2005).

The theory of multiple intelligences is not intended to label children, but to support teachers who, by following Gardner's list of intelligences, may find they can better identify individual children's strengths and weaknesses and so organise activities that match their learning styles more closely. Where the classroom provides holistic experiences, including physical and creative activities as well as reading picture books, which cater for many learning styles, children can select what is best for them and for their individual ways of making meaning and acquiring language.

However, there is a danger in labeling a child, for example, a spatial learner, as this can be an inadequate description for the rapidly developing young child. Such descriptions need to be used with care as they are only, as Gardner terms, 'entry points' to learning and finding out about children, and are not proven. Labels are quick ways for talking about children's abilities and can stick (especially within families) and become a self-fulfilling way of coping with and explaining limitations and failures. *Males have better spatial and mathematical abilities than females. We see this every year when GCSE results are published. Men have larger brains than women and a larger brain gives more brainpower, just as a larger computer gives more computing power* (Lynn 2010).

1.4 How a child learns oral English

1.4.1 Holistic development

Without an understanding of a child's various stages of cognitive, emotional, physical, social and language development, and an ability to recognise the changes as a child develops, it is difficult for an adult to plan an effective learning programme. Piaget's view that *all children pass through the same stages of cognitive development, but at different rates* still provides a comprehensive outline for the study of intellectual development. The importance of both emotional and social intelligence and development is now recognised as fundamental in early years' learning, where relations with a supportive teacher are central to holistic development.

Experienced teachers of young beginners are aware of these different stages and know how to recognise developmental changes as they take place. Changes can take place within a week or even within a lesson, which means that teachers need to be flexible, adjusting lesson plans where necessary to cope with new developments. In some cases there seem to be periods of concentrated, and sometimes rapid, development (which Montessori refers to as sensitive periods), followed by periods of self-satisfaction with little further advancement when it seems the child is on a plateau, but a higher plateau than before. The inset below gives an actual illustration of this.

> One morning during a short school holiday, this little girl brought a pencil and paper to her mother and asked her to show her how to write. Previously she had not been interested in writing. For the next three days she continuously asked for more information and practised writing. On the fourth day she discovered that she could copy the print from her picture books. After copying from some of her books at random, she suddenly stopped writing and changed her activities completely. When she went back to school, she showed her new skill to the teacher and was moved into the special 'writing group' for the few children in the class who could write.

The rate of development may not necessarily indicate a young child's ability. An intelligent child may be a slow developer or even a late developer. Children who make little progress may have some physical difficulty, which may not have been recognised, or a temporary health problem like a bad cold, which impairs hearing.

In addition, teachers may face the challenges of managing varying concentration spans, and differing maturational stages of voice, hearing and sight co-ordination. These characteristics may be gender-specific, depending on the cultural and home context of the learners. The following section will address the question of how to meet this range of complex developmental differences within the YL English classroom. In particular, it will consider ways in which authentic picture books might meet such challenges effectively.

The rest of this section considers key areas of development in the child that the teacher needs to be aware of, pointing to some of the important themes to consider.

1.4.2 Early language acquisition

Children instinctively know how to learn language through communicative interaction with adults or older children. It is as if they have an innately guided programme that is pre-set to go through the same processes irrespective of the language being learned. They also appear to have an inner drive to succeed if they 'feel good' about what they are doing.

A child's ability to use LI or the dominant language (most developed language but not necessarily LI), which he uses for thinking and storing concepts, is a crucial factor in learning English. The degree to which he can use LI to communicate and think will reflect on his ability to acquire English. Teachers find that where they plan activities already known in LI or SL children know about the activity and can concentrate on picking up the English used in the activity. Teachers can also advise parents on suitable language experiences, which may help improve the child's use of LI (see 3.9).

Children learning language all pass through the same three stages. In learning LI the stages stretch over approximately three years. In learning English the initial silent period (the period in which the learner is not expected to actively produce any language) is shorter depending on the age that the child begins to learn English and how well they know LI and other languages. If the child is monolingual and English is the L2, the silent period may be longer in comparison with children of the same chronological age who know more than one language, because the latter already know how to use their learning strategies to acquire another language and can reuse them to acquire English.

Acquisition occurs through language used in meaningful situations and generally in dialogue with an older, more experienced, language user.

> Activities, which impose what the teacher would wish to take place, but which are beyond the child's level of development ... are difficult and even in some cases impossible for the child to understand.

(Donaldson 1978)

New language not connected to an activity, and thus without context clues, may not be understood by the child listening and so will not be acquired. When children find they cannot understand, they begin to lose confidence and concentration. This often results in a restless classroom, or in discipline problems in large classes.

1.4.3 Silent period (non-verbal phase)

All children go through a silent period in learning a new language. During this period communication takes place only through the eyes, facial and body language; a smile has a wealth of meaning. This period lasts for the longest time and is most evident when babies are learning L1. During this time children are building up their own bank of knowledge of the sounds and structures of English and working out their own strategies of how to acquire the language. The quality of the input is crucial at all times. Children are continually updating and refining the language they acquire. The adjustment continues throughout a child's life as they match their output to that of the model speaker. Children cannot be rushed; they need time and each child works at his own speed. As much as adults long for children to speak, there is no short cut or magic way to make them speak before they are ready. However, use of carefully selected useful rhymes, chants and songs – forms of prefabricated language – from the first lessons help, as they involve children in focused, limited listening and in repeating language in fun ways. They provide short cuts in which the speaking part is prefabricated without any need for a created dialogue.

Apart from exposing children to many of the sounds of English and giving them experience in making them (especially important if sounds are made very differently in L1), rhymes give children a feeling that they are speaking some English from the first lessons, which is what they expect to do (see Chapter 6).

1.4.4 Intermediate period

Children are ready and have confidence from the first lessons to begin to use some individual English words or short prefabricated blocks of language, which they say by repeating the sound (intonation pattern) without knowing how many words the prefabricated language comprises. If they are encouraged by adults to use the little English they can speak in dialogue, they soon begin to use more English, not only to speak to the teacher, but also amongst themselves. Prefabricated language is central to the development of English at this stage.

Children usually begin by using blocks of management language to organise games and activities and some social survival language – *sitdown*, *gotothetoilet*, *mybag*, *tidyup*, *timeforsnack*, *notme*, *myturn*, *stopit*, *whatsthat* – accompanied by facial and body language to make their point clearer.

Playing the same games reinforces the use of commands like *sit down/ stand up*, *turn round*, *your turn*, *that's yours*, *count/how many*.

Most children seem to get great satisfaction from being allowed to repeat language to themselves. It's form of practising or browsing, which they know about because as babies they babbled, repeating the same sound over and over. This form of practising enables them, step by step, to gain control over their mouth and lips so that they can move them in the way needed to imitate sounds and say English words. Children sometimes repeat words aloud in their normal voice and sometimes in a whisper, as if they were only saying sounds. Parents often report that they say the same words and phrases over and over again, when they are playing and even when the word has no relevance to what is going on: *stopit*, *megoal*, *noyou–me*.

Children need time to play with language, as they need time to browse with books; it is a way in which they consolidate learning. Children know how to learn if we give them time and the right experiences. Lesson by lesson children become capable of taking a more active part. As ability increases so does the confidence to use language and to create prefabricated patterns (see Figure 2). In fact they create their own English, which they are confident to use and put it together with prefabricated blocks of classroom management language.

That'smybook. Where'sthe ball? Where'sthe red? Timetogohome.
Putitaway.Tidyupthere. Not yet. Go away. It's mine.

Young children learn language through language – listening and talking with 'tuned-in' others..

1.4.5 Breakthrough

Breakthrough often comes overnight or from one lesson to the next. Children find they use blocks of language and create sufficient prefabricated patterns to organise games and activities, which are a regular part of a lesson. This overnight breakthrough is reminiscent of what happens when a young L1 toddler breaks through to using whole sentences and becomes a non-stop, chattering talker, who revels in his new skills.

The length of the pre-breakthrough period depends on the amount and type of exposure to the foreign language. Naturally in classrooms where the lesson is managed only in English (total immersion), the breakthrough is quicker.

The quality of home support also contributes to the speed of the breakthrough (see 1.5.2). Where there is no home support, learning takes longer. Where parents do not understand English, but are still supportive, learning is quicker as the support motivates and creates positive attitudes.

However, this breakthrough is still limited to known experiences in English, such as those that go on in the classroom. It does not mean that, for example, children can cope with total immersion screen experiences (DVD, Internet etc.) experiences in English. However, children's newfound breakthrough gives them confidence to broaden their experiences and, guided by suggestions from the teacher, they keep their confidence and feel they can understand something and so develop their range of language abilities.

After about five months in total immersion schooling, parents often report that their 7- and 8-year-old children begin to criticise their way of speaking English. Their children compare their parents' pronunciaton with that of their role model – a remarkable analytical achievement for young children. Apart from giving us an insight as to what is going on in their minds, this is an indication of the depth of understanding they have acquired of the sound structures of English and of their own language or languages. *You don't say it properly. It isn't 'led', it's 'red'* (showing how to make the r sound).

It is interesting that criticism is only about their parents' pronunciation and not word order, which is often different as it is influenced by the L1. This is probably due to the fact that children at this stage are still using prefabricated language blocks and are not yet readers (thus not conscious of the individual words of which the blocks are comprised).

As children became more fluent, after about seven months in a form of total immersion, parents reported that their 7- and 8-year-old children had begun to act as their interpreters. In situations like shopping, in restaurants or even in discussing their work with the teacher, they interpreted meaning from English into L1 or L1 into English, sometimes adding cultural information to make understanding easier. Switching from one language to another and interpreting seemed to come quite naturally to them. Some teachers make use of these interpreting skills in the classroom when introducing new materials, as it helps young children to consolidate their learning and develop their innate skills of interpreting.

1.4.6 Cognitive development

A child's language learning skills are not isolated from the rest of his mental growth. It appears that concepts that he has learned in L1 can be transferred to English as well as other languages.

Children find it easier if learning a new concept takes place in L1 rather than in English. It is also easier for the person explaining the concept, as the child's use of L1 is more developed and thus explaining is easier. Teachers who have no other way but to explain in English will find it helpful to consult books that deal with introducing concepts to young children in a structured way. They also need to plan a longer active learning exposure as children will take longer to work out and learn about the new concept.

> *Until a child is ready to take a particular step forward it is*
> *a waste of time to try and teach him to take it.*

(HMSO 1967)

Teachers of young children are conscious that children reach a certain point when they are ready to learn something new. This 'readiness' stage is very clear in activities like numbers, reading and writing. If a child is asked to learn a certain skill before he is ready, he cannot do it. This failure results in disappointment and sometimes loss of interest. It is, therefore, very important for a teacher to be able to recognise children's 'readiness' to learn a certain concept and make use of the enthusiasm that often accompanies it. This is particularly the case in an oral 'reading readiness' programme where children need to be very familiar with spoken language before they decode letters to make words and get meaning from them (see 4.5).

Teachers also need to know what concepts children in their class already know and what concepts they are likely to learn during the school year. Some textbooks for learning English include concepts that are too difficult for young children. Where teachers are faced with this type of problem they can substitute different activities that are right for the developmental age of the child and at the same time provide the same language experience (see 3.4).

Since the individual differences and especially cognitive differences between young children of the same age are great, to teach a class as one unit does not give each child the individual attention they need.

Where classes are very large, teachers can divide the children into small groups and within each group give individual attention.

However, young children until about the age of 8 years are still dependent on adult emotional and social support for much of what they do. This is especially so in the English classroom and although they may work in groups, their relationship still has to be strong with the teacher. Only when they are older are they ready to have less contact with the teacher and relate more with the group leader.

It is essential to be able to judge how much new material children can absorb at one time. The amount that they are capable of taking in depends on their developmental level, enthusiasm, interest and on the teacher's skill in presenting and mediating the material.

It also depends on a factor that is often overlooked: the class's mood. Children are excitable; snow or heavy rain, a birthday to be celebrated or an approaching festival can excite them. If they are excited they cannot concentrate for as long as usual. Mood is infectious; if one or two children are excited, this can spread to the rest of the class. When a class is in such a mood, they generally do not want to settle down to quiet or new activities. In this case it is better not to force the children, but to leave these activities until the next lesson, when things have usually gone back to normal.

Some teachers worry that they may be making young children work too hard. If a child is learning by taking part in activities, it seems to be impossible to push him further than he wants to go. Once he has reached saturation point, he 'switches off' his interest; he no longer concentrates on what he is doing and lets his mind, and in some cases even his body, wander to other activities. However hard a teacher tries to attract his attention back to the original activity, once he has 'switched off', the attempt is generally not successful.

It is impossible for children to learn everything perfectly in each lesson. For this reason part of every lesson should consist of going over previous work (revising) to help children to consolidate the language and the concepts they have been exposed to. Failure to consolidate new language at any one stage of learning affects the next stage of learning. If new activities are presented before sufficient consolidation of previous activities has taken place, a gradual accumulation of things not properly understood begins to grow. This often leads to a feeling of 'not being good' at English.

On the other hand, activities that are right for the stage of development and are properly consolidated give a feeling of satisfaction and of being successful, which in turn motivates. If children can go from one successful activity to another, motivation takes place naturally.

1.4.7 Emotional development

It is difficult to examine all aspects of a child's emotional development. However, teachers should be aware that young children differ in temperament. Some children are aggressive, others shy, some are over-anxious to please and in some cases frightened of making a mistake, others are moody, especially if they do not get what they want. Temperament affects their ability to take part in language learning activities. If teachers are aware of differences in temperament they are in a position to help children make the best of an activity. By watching children in the classroom, in the playground or with their parents, and by talking to parents about their children, teachers can gradually find out about the children's temperaments. Once a teacher knows what sort of temperament a child has, she can allocate particular activities to him, which give him an opportunity to develop his character. She also knows better when to give praise and encouragement.

Children need to 'feel good' if they are to learn easily. Serotonin is the neurotransmitter that generates feelings of well-being in the brain. If the 'feel-good' factor is absent, children are likely to be less co-operative listeners and their frustration may even lead to disruptive behaviour. This type of behaviour is generally more usual amongst boys, who are known to find new (English) language learning more difficult than girls.

Learning how to recognise and manage personal emotions is an important part of growing up. This is especially so in the pre-puberty years, when children become more self-conscious. In some cultures, children may be exposed to many forms of stress and SL education may give little help in emotional management. SL education may be formal and standardised, involving testing and providing little opportunity or support for emotional and social development.

1.4.8 Physical development

Cognitive and physical development play important roles in determining what activities are right for the young child. *Patterns of physical growth tend to be broadly similar for all children. As coarse muscle control becomes finer, a child can make more complex and differentiated movements* (Tucker 1977).

Muscular development affects a child's ability to focus his eyes on a page, line or word – a prerequisite for reading. It also affects his ability to hold a pencil, a pair of scissors or a paintbrush. Before a child has developed a certain degree of muscular control, some activities are too difficult for him.

Teachers often complain that young children have difficulty in sitting still. They want to move, to wriggle and touch everything. To quote Millar, *The fact that children find it less easy than adults to sit still for long periods, not to bang their heels against a chair, not to jump up, or move their arms, or touch objects, to execute fine movements with their fingers and modulate their voices, is not a question of having more energy to spill, but of comparative lack of integration and control of movement systems* (in Tucker 1977). Activities need to give children an opportunity to move around within the classroom. Rhymes, for example, can include activities like jumping or dancing, and games can include physical activity games. In many cases the need to wriggle and move might look like a loss of interest, but if the learning level is right for the child, the child will still be involved and listening even if he is wriggling.

Early childhood illnesses, such as middle ear infections, can leave some damage, which may go undetected in LI because hearing has been partially replaced by lip-reading. Hearing disabilities may only show up when learning another language. Colds can cause temporary loss of hearing. Children who have hearing problems often find out about these when learning English in a classroom situation where the teacher cannot be so close to the child as the mother, and where learning includes hearing English spoken to a group or at a distance.

Children aged 6 years sometimes have some pain and general malaise caused by the cutting of their 6-year molar teeth. This may make them slightly moody and less able to settle down and concentrate. Around 6, 7 or 8 years old, children lose their top and bottom front teeth, which is embarrassing for many and makes pronunciation difficult. During this period it is better not to make children work orally by themselves; if they work with a partner or in small groups, their temporary sub-standard pronunciation is less noticeable. Similar considerations apply to children fitted with an orthodontic apparatus to straighten teeth.

1.5 Adults' and parents' roles in learning English

Personal relations appear to form the matrix within which a child's learning takes place.

(Donaldson 1978)

1.5.1 The teacher's role

A young beginner is entirely dependent on his teacher for all English language learning in the initial stages. The responsibility for his success is, to a large extent, in the hands of his teacher and how well she manages to build up a personal relationship with the child and his family (see no 3.9). Through this personal relationship, adults mediate attitudes to learning English and English culture.

The role of the teacher is supportive not tutorial. In some societies children, often by mistake, address the early years' teacher as the equivalent of 'Aunty', which is an indication of the emotional trust, special bond and social relationship with their teacher. The teacher, like the mother, is the mediator, interpreting the English to the child through the realia, the activity, the game or the picture book. In fact the mediator extends the child's world and the way the child sees the world (culture), through the selected, new experiences in the security of the classroom.

Early years' English teaching differs from upper primary teaching as the child up to the age of 7 years (or beyond depending on the child and society) is still emotionally and socially involved with the mother who continues, informally through dialogues, mediating the world and extending and consolidating L1. When the child begins English, the early years' teacher, especially if this is a woman, unconsciously assumes and adjusts to the mother's language-teaching role, mediating using *teacherese*. The child responds to the social and emotional contact and is shepherded to apply his language skills to learning English.

At this stage of English language learning the young child is not ready for a more formal teacher–child relationship with taught instruction. The transition to a different, less dependent social and emotional relationship with the teacher develops gradually as the child matures to become a fluent reader and begins to initiate his own interest activities. Each child matures holistically at his own pace; this cannot be speeded up externally.

Mediating and gradually extending a concept requires great patience by the adult and frequent planned repetition. Young children need to return again and again to the same activity if they are going to absorb both the concept and language and sufficiently reconfirm what they have acquired to be able to use it in dialogue. Without adequate consolidation children sense that they are not making progress and gradually begin to feel 'I can't' instead of 'I can'.

Young children already know unconsciously what they need to learn and, remarkably, they know how they learn. They also need to feel that the teacher is happy with them, too. The emotional 'feel-good' factor should never be underestimated, especially in early years' language learning, as progress and success is socially and emotionally linked to mutual empathy with the supportive person – the teacher.

Adults, in the role of mediator, need to be flexible, adapting to each encounter as, like adults, young children have their 'good days' and 'off days', when sometimes for unpredictable reasons (like a rainy day) they are not ready to settle down and concentrate. Children cannot switch on readiness to learn without an adult's mediation to help them switch their focus and mood. Lack of focus can often be successfully changed by abandoning any prepared plans and returning to a favourite, familiar activity, game or picture book. The activity should be easy to use, playful and require little effort on the part of the children.

A teacher's enthusiasm and interest is generally contagious. Young children are eager to build up a relationship with their teacher especially if she is a happy person. If they feel her interest in them and her support of them they are unlikely to be inhibited or shy. To build up a personal relationship, children have to feel the teacher respects them and understands their needs; they, on the other hand, have to feel a respect for their teacher.

Young children are dependent on the teacher for input of language and for planning language acquisition activities. In the classroom where only English is used, children depend on the teacher in the initial stages for all interpersonal communication; she is usually the only English speaker. It is up to her to sustain this communication and develop and extend it. Through careful planning and emotional support, she can ensure most children's individual progress and give the right level of encouragement and praise necessary for motivation.

1.5.2 The parents' role

Societies differ, even within Northern Europe, as to the role of the parent vis-à-vis the school. In some societies there is no tradition for a parent to work in close co-operation with the teacher. In fact any interest could be considered as interference on the part of the family and even show a lack of respect for the teacher, who may even be addressed as 'Teacher'; that is, by profession, rather than by personal name. Teaching English to very young and young learners is relatively new and many people have not yet understood that learning language in nursery school or lower primary school is different for young children than learning in the top years of primary school when children have begun to study the structures of language and expect to do the same in learning English.

Continual positive support, encouragement and praise from both mother and father, as well as the extended family, help to build up self-confidence and motivation. In the early stages of learning, encouragement is especially important and praise for any small success or hard work motivates. You are doing well. Go on, it's good. That's really nice. Great work.

Once young children can say rhymes and have memorised some short picture book stories, the support need no longer be so intensive. By this stage, some English phrases, rhymes and stories are likely to have been playfully transferred into family life. In-family English can be bonding and is often the beginning of positive lifelong attitudes to English.

What 'home' says or even thinks about how a child is achieving in English is important to the child's self-esteem and consequently his self-motivation. Many children spend most one-to-one time at home with their parents, carers, siblings and members of the extended family and like to please them and look for their praise.

'Sasha's in the school play and he has to say something in English. He's getting very good in English,' Mother told Grandpa over the phone within Sasha's hearing. Imagine how proud Sasha felt and what effect this has on his attitude to English at school.

Conversely, if parents are not pleased with the way English is being taught at school, their criticism may be felt by the child, even if it is not actually verbalised in front of them.

Good liaison between the school and home is very important if participation is to be successful and beneficial for the young child.

Many parents show more interest in English and the way it is taught than in other subjects like History or Science. This could be because many parents, especially mothers, are innate language teachers who have already successfully taught their children to speak their 'home' language. Parents who began English in secondary school, and learned through grammatical analysis methods, sometimes expect their young children to learn in the same way and so can be initially sceptical about primary school language acquisition methods. Young children's expectations can be influenced by their parents' attitudes. *I only play at school. When am I going to learn?*

Research shows that parents and the home are the strongest influences on a child's life. If parents are interested in their children's achievements in English and show appreciation of their successes, their children will be motivated. What parents think and say about what a child is doing and achieving is important to the child. A child wants to please his parents and is happy when they become involved in what he is doing.

> *As teachers of primary-aged children, we have found out that learning is most successful when home and school are working together. ... This is particularly true in the teaching of a foreign language.*

(Farren and Smith 2004)

2

Fitting the syllabus to the child

2.1 The syllabus

In children's minds learning a foreign language is not a subject, even if it appears on the timetable as such, and parents talk about it as a subject when they ask, '*What did you do in English at school today?*' If the school gives each child a textbook for English, this can help adults confirm their idea that English is taught as a subject using an English textbook in a way familiar to them from their experience of secondary school. In young children's minds, learning English is another way of communicating about activities using differently pronounced words and phrases. For them English is embedded in and entwined with learning about everyday life and surroundings. If there is some logical reason to use English and they are motivated, they accept it as part of their holistic development and intuitively use their skills to pick it up. Young children are natural language learners and enjoy learning language.

In most countries, teachers are given a structured syllabus to be followed for every year of learning English. A syllabus provides a useful guide as to what is expected by the school and parents at the end of a year's work. In some nursery schools there is no set syllabus; it is then up to the teacher to devise their own syllabus. In these cases it is advisable for teachers to work with a hidden syllabus in order to assess what children are actually learning. Without some guidance from a syllabus, regular documentation and informal assessment, teachers can drift and may not plan sufficiently challenging learning activities to match young children's potential and desire to communicate in English.

Set syllabuses are a useful guide to what language should be introduced during an academic year. However, they generally need to be supplemented linguistically to follow young learners' needs and to enable children to talk about (narrate) their life and interests. Some set syllabuses introduce only the present forms of verbs in the first year, which holds young children back. Although children live in the here and now, their natural way of talking is to narrate what has already happened in their life and thus they need ways of expressing the past: *Yesterday I went, I saw, I ate* etc. and, at a later stage, simple language to project: *On Sunday I am going to see my grandma.* Children are excited about learning English and want to use it from the first lessons. If they find they cannot speak any English, bonding with a monolingual teacher is more difficult and children become disappointed and sometimes frustrated.

2.1.1 Textbooks

Textbooks (or coursebooks) are written to follow international, country or set examination syllabuses, and in some schools teachers are expected to follow them closely. Although over the last 30 years textbooks have developed to meet syllabus requirements and also to include what adults feel young children need to learn, they rarely provide sufficiently rich language programmes or include items relevant to local conditions. Children see the world holistically and pick up language by taking part in activities, so teachers need to dip in and out of textbooks, mixing and matching their own class activities with structures introduced in their set textbook. Some teachers work on mini-projects for most of a term or year, only using the textbook and supporting CDs, DVDs etc. towards the end of a term or year, when, to most children's delight, they find they already know most of the content. In fact most children can use much more language than can be found in the textbook's content.

Textbook illustrations often appear dull to young children in comparison with the quality artwork in picture books. Colouring picture outlines drawn by adults, which are not necessarily drawn the way children see objects, occupy children but rarely motivate them, and give few real opportunities for children to listen to and use English.

Information about how to learn English is no longer controlled by educational publishers' textbooks with accompanying CDs or DVDs. Today's parents and children have the means of getting information on screen when the child is as young as two years old, even in remote places where books cannot survive the humid climate or the hunger of termites. Today's new technology and social networking is changing the way information is created and distributed. Young children are born into the world of new technology and they expect to use it. Very young and young children can listen on screen, join in with rhymes, hear picture books read, and see or even talk to other children around the world in English. Many young children have their own form of computer, have Wi-Fi games, or have access to the Internet and are skilful in using it – sometimes they are even better than their teachers.

Technology makes many different experiences available in English, but for children to learn from them these experiences need to be well selected by the teacher and, initially, be mediated by the teacher or parents, who expand the commentary to facilitate understanding at a deeper level for the child. Selected screen experiences can be introduced in the classroom and then suggested to parents as supportive programmes to be shared at home. Young children soon *learn how to learn* from these programmes, provided they have been initially well mediated. Children can be disappointed and demotivated by listening to programmes that are far too difficult for their level of competence, unless they are well mediated and played back many times. A single exposure is not sufficient for acquisition, as the child is busy making meaning of first the concepts and then the language. In subsequent playback sessions the child already understands the content and can concentrate on the English.

2.2 The teacher's role as mediator

Mediation means 'interposing' – within a child-led or teacher-led activity the teacher interposes some language or object that helps the child to react and the teacher to guide or shepherd further understanding. The teacher, as the elder and more experienced person in the dialogue, acts as the mediator for the child, helping them to make meaning of most English experiences. Through a natural, encouraging, targeted mediation the child can:

- decode and make some meaning of new language in an activity or picture book
- take understanding to a deeper level
- be helped to discover eg information on a topic
- link ideas to similar or related topics.

As the teacher is the more experienced speaker in the one-to-one, or one-to-group dialogue, the teacher has a hidden aim in the mediation to introduce new language (teacher-led). However, stimulated by a child's enthusiasm to show-and-tell, or to comment, the teacher has to be prepared to alter her aim in order to mediate the child's interest to the other children. Experienced child-led teachers know that to ignore child-led enthusiasm is to waste an additional learning opportunity.

In all cases it is important that the role of a mediator (teacher, parent or older child in family grouping situations) is:

- to give time for the child to make his own reply in a dialogue. Children need more time than adults to formulate a reply. (In the initial stages of learning English this may be only eye contact or a grunt to show some understanding.)
- to be ready to listen attentively and encourage a reply and then adapt the mediation to take account of the content of the reply
- to judge when the mediation has gone as far as the child can go for this session. A signal is often when the child's eyes are no longer engaged with the mediator. Eyes are said to portray the soul.

The mediator's language

- *teacherese* and scaffolding when introducing new experiences or language
- exaggerated facial language and gesture to get across meaning
- realia to support meaning
- easy-to-copy demonstration of 'how to make something'

The teacher is the principal mediator between the syllabus and the child. When preparing a syllabus for very young and young beginners, the teacher needs to have a clear idea of what the programme aims to achieve. In the words of Hawkes, *age, cultural context and general educational priorities influence content more than purely linguistic considerations* (Hawkes 1981).

The teacher also has to mediate activities, setting the scene so that everything is prepared for children's immediate participation and raises their curiosity. Success depends on how well the teacher has planned and structured an activity and how flexible her mediation is in the first lessons. First impressions are lasting; bad impressions are difficult to eradicate.

Learning is more successful when there is an emotional 'feel-good' factor. This can only develop where the children and teacher feel confident and calm about what is expected of each of them. To achieve this, the teacher needs to plan aims and class language content. This includes thinking about:

- daily programmes/monthly programmes/term attainments
- routine management phrases that can be expanded gradually
- flexibility – having alternative activities ready for immediate implementation, when necessary, to bring out about change and re-motivate
- basic classroom rules (procedures) known and understood by everyone including respecting others' work, sharing and putting away equipment etc. (these expectations are to be explained in the first lesson in L1 or SL).

2.3 Supplementing the syllabus

Many experienced teachers of young children have long been aware that purely linguistically based programmes are not successful with young beginners. Many teachers therefore supplement these with their own materials and activities, which they feel cater more closely to their children's developmental level, needs and interests.

However, where programmes are based entirely on the needs and interests of the child, without an underlying syllabus design, they tend to be too haphazard and less effective than those that have the guidance, often hidden, of a linguistic programme designed for young beginners.

Very young children want to be able to talk (narrate) in English about:

- themselves *My hair/My birthday*
- what they like. *I like/I don't like… yuk*
- their family *My Grandpa/My little sister*
- their home and immediate environment *My dog/The swimming pool*
- what they have done *I went to …/I saw…/I ate…*
- how they and others feel *I am sad/She's cross ….*

Young children are interested in many of these same topics, but at a more profound level, which includes a wider exploration of their environment and how it works.

If young children are to learn language from syllabus-related activities, they need their own space and time:

- to use language
- to be listened to
- to interact one-to-one
- to reflect (browse) in order to consolidate language.

2.4 A beginners' syllabus

In the 1960s and 1970s when teaching English to non-native-speaking children was a relatively new subject, administrators felt it was easier if classes world-wide were categorised into three main linguistic groups based on the type and length of the exposure and language content:

- English as a foreign language (EFL)
- English as a second language (ESL)
- Total immersion or Bilingual.

As the age for beginning to learn English is getting younger and many millions of young children and very young children between 3 and 8 years old are now learning English in schools globally, these linguistic classifications have become inadequate terms for reference. This is especially the case for very young and young children beginners, who are:

- **still** acquirers of LI and/ or SL
- already speaking two or three languages
- non-readers in nursery school
- emergent readers in LI or SL and non-readers in English in lower primary school
- fluent readers in LI or SL and emergent readers in English in lower primary school.

Children in nursery schools need a programme based on meaningful and playful activities that match closely the activities they are already familiar with in SL classroom experiences. In order to match such activities, teachers need to know not only the names and ages of the children, but also:

- the level of children's linguistic skills in LI and SL
- the degree of exposure to other languages; L2, L3 or LI dialects (eg Chinese national language and regional dialect spoken at home).

as these different language abilities can reflect on their ability to acquire English and English pronunciation, especially in the very beginning stages of learning.

It is also important to know the amount of exposure young children have to the screen watching of English programmes and playing of computer games etc. Although such exposure is non-social, passive and rarely interactive, via these media children are often already conscious of many of the different sounds of English and may be familiar with some of the mouth movements that make English sounds. Some may be able to imitate the different mouth movements, like the letter o sound when you say the word *open* in English, which may differ from any sound in their L1 or SL. Others may have learned to imitate words or phrases in English – *Hiya, Thank you, Goal* or *No* – or numbers in English.

Some of today's parents may have lived or travelled abroad before having a family and are eager for their very young children to learn English without understanding how children pick up language. In their eagerness, they watch carefully to see what English their children learn in each lesson and may be critical about their child's progress. Some may have their own ideas about 'how to learn' based on their own secondary school English programme. Teachers need to gain parental approval and support, as parents or carers can help by sharing activities at home, providing added opportunities for consolidation and motivation. Research shows that children's progress is markedly better where parents support and encourage in the home.

School regulations may restrict teachers questioning families about languages spoken at home and in children's home life and holiday experiences. However, through informal conversations with parents, it is often possible to find out about children's home language exposure and also judge the level of English support parents will be able to give at home. The following checklist may be helpful as a guide when talking to parents.

Whatever their background, all young children want immediate results. They expect to talk, to say something in English straight away and add more in each subsequent lesson. They need to acquire sufficient English for interpersonal communication to take place as soon as possible, otherwise they are disappointed and motivation gradually diminishes. Some children, by the end of the first term, say they no longer like English; this demotivation can occur for many reasons, but is often because they have

Figure 3 A young child's language background

Child's name	❏ male ❏ female	Date of birth

Parents' language background	Mother	Father
Home language		
English level		
	❏ Lived overseas as student ❏ Worked overseas in English-speaking country ❏ Overseas holidays	❏ Lived overseas as student ❏ Worked overseas in English-speaking country ❏ Overseas holidays

Child's language background

❏ Monolingual L1   ❏ Learning L1   ❏ Bilingual/Bicultural   ❏ Plurilingual/Multicultural

Child's position in family

❏ Eldest child   ❏ Child #2   ❏ Child #3   ❏ Other _____

Other children in family learning English?   ❏ yes ❏ no   Comments _____

Previous exposure to English

❏ Nursery school   ❏ Lower primary   ❏ Upper primary
  (age 3–5 or 6 years)   (age 5 or 6–8 or 9 years)   (age 8 or 9–11 or 12 years)
❏ Out-of-school English/clubs   ❏ Home tutoring sessions   ❏ Sports clubs in English

Type of language exposure

❏ Monolingual   ❏ Bilingual   ❏ Plurilingual
❏ Total immersion eg International   ❏ Short fixed lesson x times   ❏ Short session x times embedded
  schools/English-medium schools   per week with English specialist   in the timetable with class
                         teacher

Teacher information

❏ Class teacher   ❏ Specialist native-speaker   ❏ Specialist native-speaker English
  bilingual/monolingual English   teacher (not Young Learner   English teacher (Young Learner
             trained)   trained)
❏ Native speaker informant   ❏ Club organiser

Technology availability

❏ School (computer, IWB, Internet access etc.)   ❏ Home (mobile, computer, Internet access etc.)

Notes _____

_____

no visible record to show that they can speak some English (see 3.6).

Once children begin to communicate, acquisition takes place quickly and naturally. The initial stages of acquiring sufficient English to begin communicating is common to all beginners, whatever their learning situation. This initial oral first stage should include fast-changing, rich acquisition experiences that give children sufficient opportunities to begin to work out the sounds of English and find out how the language works. For convenience it can be termed Part One of a child's language learning syllabus. Part Two is introduced when children have greater oral ability, and are more conceptually mature and physically skilled.

2.4.1 Part One of a syllabus

Part One aims

1. To equip children with the means to communicate at a basic level in simple spoken English in predictable situations by:

    a) exposing them to prefabricated language (including survival language and management language) and prefabricated patterns (creative language) in the initial stages (see Figure 2)

    b) leaving any unsuitable language, including conceptually too advanced or structurally too complex language, until Part Two of the syllabus

    c) exposing them to constant, natural recycling and repetition of the same language.

2. To enable children to talk and, if already writing in L1, learn the names and sounds of the 26 alphabet letters and read basic language embedded in projects, simple picture book texts and rhymes, riddles and tongue-twisters.

The length of time it takes to complete Part One depends on the:

- length and frequency of the exposure to English
- age of the children
- type of teaching in SL

- quality of materials
- number of pupils in the class or group
- teacher's ability to plan and mediate
- children's ability to write or read in L1 using a Roman alphabet or different scripts.

Once Part One has been completed successfully children have sufficient grounding and self-confidence to move onto a more formal syllabus (Part Two). At the same time, they are ready to recycle Part One at a linguistically and cognitively more advanced level, including simple reading and writing embedded in projects, games, picture books and creative activities.

2.4.2 Part Two of a syllabus

Once children have an oral foundation and are conceptually and physically sufficiently mature they can be introduced to reading, handwriting and creative writing in English. Some children, who have been able to enjoy browsing familiar picture books, may have already begun to teach themselves to read. These children will be ready to make quick progress in Part Two of a syllabus and enjoy the more formal introduction to English (Dunn forthcoming).

Due to children's increased oral ability, Part Two of the syllabus includes more local cultural content to teach children about customs and daily life in English-speaking countries, and may even involve screen contact with English-speaking children. Young children begin school with few fixed ideas and prejudices and *a second language programme which teaches cultural information along with language can produce a more tolerant, less prejudiced child* (Donoghue and Kunkle 1979).

2.4.3 Adapting a syllabus

Existing syllabuses can be adapted to ensure Part One builds up oral listening and confidence in readiness for the more formal Part Two syllabus. The following are suggested adaptations.

1. Controlling the introduction of material

a) introducing prefabricated language in the first lessons: young beginners quickly and easily acquire prefabricated language in simple rhymes. To help children acquire and use English, include more prefabricated language and accompanying explanations in simple language in the first lessons and through the early stage of Part One than in the average L1 classroom for children of the same age.

b) reducing the amount of vocabulary: a young beginner needs only a basic minimum of words to begin to communicate. For this reason, many items of vocabulary can be left until later in Part One, when children are more 'tuned in' and have increased their listening and oral ability and so can acquire new language more easily and quickly.

c) adding prefabricated language to make communication only in English possible:

- survival language
- organisational language
- management language.

Without these categories of prefabricated language it is difficult to organise an all-English-speaking classroom that is a similar to a form of total immersion.

2. Introducing additional activities

The syllabus and textbook often do not provide sufficient opportunities for young children's acquisition needs and attention span, which is shorter than in SL, as listening to a new language is tiring. For this reason, activities within lessons need to be fast-paced, which means that there needs to be careful planning to keep up speed and motivation. Too often children are left doing activities like colouring pictures where there is little or no acquisition or browsing opportunity, resulting in language learning time being wasted. At times like these, discipline problems often start, especially amongst 7-year-old boys. If the teacher supplements activities that are right for the children's interests and developmental level, the children's interest will be engaged and stimulated and, providing they have the linguistic tools, they begin to communicate. In some cases young children may be so stimulated that, if they have not got the linguistic tools in English, they communicate half in English and half in SL (code-switching). This was so in the case of a little French boy aged 6 years who shouted, *'Twenty. J'ai twenty!' (I have twenty)* in a game.

Ways of supplementing a syllabus:

- projects
- picture books
- games
- cultural activities (celebrating festivals)
- rhymes, songs, jokes, tongue-twisters, chants
- themed show-and-tell sessions.

3. Increasing the opportunities to talk about children's immediate interests

Children want to talk in English about the same things they talk about in SL. Although they may not have sufficient English to talk about things at the same level or in such detail, activities can be selected that are more or less parallel to those in the SL classroom.

A good syllabus follows children's interests; where a set syllabus introduces items that are beyond children's present interests, these items can be left until the end of Part One or until Part Two, when children have greater oral ability and are more conceptually mature. At this stage local cultural content can be extended to learning about customs, daily life and festivals in English-speaking countries (see 9.4).

2.4.4 The syllabus and the textbook

Many teachers may not be involved in syllabus design and may not have any choice in the textbook with which they are provided. However, they need to understand the underlying principles of the syllabus if they are to use the textbook effectively and adapt it to their own situations. Teacher's books, which accompany textbooks, generally include helpful advice. Few textbooks are ideal for VYL and YL or beginners, as many are written for international use, yet each country and each individual classroom is different in its needs. However, with adaptations and the addition of activities and materials, teachers can manage to make them fit the needs of the children they teach and can get surprisingly good results.

2.4.5 Adapting a textbook

Each child is an individual and every classroom and school is unique, as is their surrounding society. No textbook, however well written, can hope to satisfy the learning needs of all children. For success and ongoing motivation, teachers need to be prepared to supplement textbooks.

Teachers need to think carefully about:

- where their textbook material needs supplementing
- how to supplement their textbook material
- how best to present their textbook material.

Teacher's books may include some useful suggestions and additional activities.

When adapting a textbook, the teacher may find the following suggestions useful:

1. Oral introduction

VYLs and YLs generally find it easier to learn from real objects than from pictures in books. Where the oral introduction in the textbook illustrates objects common to any classroom (pens, pencils etc.) children find a lesson easier to understand if real pens and pencils are substituted. This also allows the teacher to be more flexible and playful in the presentation of new vocabulary.

2. Speed of introduction of material

Children find it easier to learn one concept at a time. Where a page in a book presents children with a confusing amount of new material, it is better to take one item from the page and deal with it, if possible, by relating it to children's personal experience. For example, a page in one textbook introduces *my father*, *my mother*, *my sister* and *my brother* and then *Mr* and *Mrs*, all referring to the child in the textbook. This is best divided into two steps, which are initially taught by relating the language to the children's own families (see 8.2).

3. Simplifying too complex material

Methodological techniques need introduction, as adult methods of coding language (eg substitution tables) are too abstract for young beginners. For example, where textbooks use substitution tables or brainstorming diagrams, teachers can introduce the language orally in activities. Once the more mature children are familiar with the language and they can use it in games etc. the teacher can mediate the tables to them. Some more mature children find them to be a challenge, and some boys have said 'it's like cracking a code!' It is also common to find books that introduce too much vocabulary on one page for young beginners to absorb at once, something which young children expect to do. Teachers can find ways of introducing the vocabulary orally in steps and later consolidate it in games before young children are asked to read the page, eg playing *What's This?*, *Memory Game*, *Snap* and *Bingo* using the items of vocabulary (see Chapter 6).

4. Supplementing the text

A text may be culturally too far removed from children's experience for them to be able to interpret the photographs or pictures meaningfully. This is particularly so in the case of texts prepared for European primary schools; children with a completely different life-style, for example in the Middle East, often have difficulty in relating to them. In such a case a teacher may find it helpful to transpose the activities in the book to the children's own society, thus making them more meaningful.

5. Introducing and consolidating reading

Children sometimes find it difficult to remember prepositions such as: *in front of, beside, near, behind* etc. Before reading them in the textbook, the teacher can introduce them orally in simple hide-and-seek games or *Picture Lotto*.

2.5 Working without a textbook

Many teachers, especially teachers qualified to work with Young Learners or those with many years' experience with young beginners, prefer to work without a textbook. This is often the ideal method of working providing it is backed by a 'hidden syllabus' (see Figure 8). In these cases VYLs and YLs are taught through structured:

- projects
- picture books
- games
- cultural activities (celebrating festivals)
- rhymes, songs, riddles, tongue-twisters, chants
- themed show-and-tell sessions.

As long as each encounter includes rich opportunities to listen to English and interact in meaningful ways with an adult role model individually or in groups, children pick up a wider range of English than is included in a textbook. Children are in fact exposed to a type of total immersion that not only benefits their holistic development, but enables them to acquire an all-round base in understanding and using English. This gives them confidence to use it beyond the classroom. It is important that the teacher as mediator is positive about all she introduces as it will influence the child's first impressions of, and attitudes too, learning English.

2.5.1 Assessment

When a teacher works without a textbook, it is important that regular documentation and records of each child's progress and learning needs are kept. Apart from adults monitoring children's progress, children also like to monitor their own progress. Making learning visible is important for children and parents; visible records can include photographs, DVDs and picture book sharing, reciting rhymes and other oral language games. When children begin to formally read and write, the range of visible learning and visual documentation increases and children become capable of keeping some of their own records.

Assessment and documentation take time, but are invaluable for getting to know the real needs of each child and for checking that each lesson includes the right type of activities with appropriate language content. It is easy to forget how children responded in a lesson, so quick recording is best done immediately after the lesson. Some teachers record something quickly in a pocket notebook to act as a reminder when writing fuller notes later. Methods of documentation are suggested in Chapter 3.

2.6   An examination syllabus

Most hidden syllabuses will have introduced the main points covered in an exam syllabus for young children. Knowing how to participate in a test is important, and if children are to remain confident and thus able to show the English they know to the examiner, they need role-play practice before the exam. This can be done in a fun way, sometimes by inviting other native speakers into the classroom so that young children get used to other voices speaking English. If they are well prepared and confident in their use of English, children with a wide experience usually gain top marks as the test is to see how much a child knows, not to find out how little they know. Parents also need to be told that the teacher will be preparing them by using some fun role-play, otherwise some parents become too anxious and their stress reflects on their child's self-confidence.

The grammar of some language is simply not logical enough to express complex ideas.

Guy Deutscher

3

Planning lessons

3.1 Class framework

Children see the world holistically. English for young children is another tool for communicating things about themselves, what they are doing, did and will do and the concepts and new interests they are finding out about in the classroom.

To teach very young and young children English successfully, teachers need to understand child development and respond to individual children's ever-changing needs, as they grow rapidly physically and as they develop mentally, emotionally, socially and linguistically. Many of today's children are stressed. They want and need adults to listen to them. They need support to understand and manage their emotions and without it they are often not sufficiently relaxed to learn successfully. Learning English can be an additional frustration for children, more especially boys, as it takes time and effort before they can use sufficient English to talk about themselves and their needs and interests as easily as in SL. This is especially the case if their teacher is monolingual English. In some situations the frustration may be compounded as the relationship with the English teacher may be more friendly and relaxed than with some of the other teachers at school and the activities more fun, too. Young children may long to share their joys and problems with the English teacher, but if she is monolingual and they have not yet acquired sufficient language in English, they can be frustrated as they cannot link socially and emotionally sufficiently to get the type of support they need. Frustration may be present in many YL beginners' classrooms and often goes unrecognised.

Young children appear to learn more easily when they know what to expect in a lesson and what the teacher expects of them. Apart from making them feel more secure, this gives them confidence. It also enables them to predict situations and the language likely to be used in them.

For this reason, teachers often find it helpful to use the same class framework for each lesson. This framework becomes the basis of a routine that is followed in each lesson, the activities being slotted into the framework. After a few lessons children get to know the routine and often feel so 'at home' that they move on to the next stage of a lesson, making the preparations themselves even before the teacher has given any instructions.

The security of knowing what comes next enables young children to concentrate on the activity in which they are involved, free from the worry that they will not understand what to do next. The calmness of a class that is used to a routine is quite noticeable, especially when compared with a lesson that has been haphazardly planned with little or no regular routine.

3.1.1 Optimum learning times

Each child is unique; their approach to learning is different. Recent research in male and female brain development shows that boys learn and use language differently from girls (see 1.3).

Most young children have an inner, innate drive to explore and find out. Very young children have periods when they seem to be more eager to learn than others. During these intense learning periods they concentrate and stretch themselves to capacity; such phases can last for hours, overnight or for several days depending on the child. Maria Montessori referred to these learning spurts as 'sensitive periods'. Once over, the child returns to a less frenetic mode of work, but at a more developed level. Although tired by their efforts, the child appears satisfied, realising that they have achieved something that other children can do. It seems that there is a period of calm work, like a plateau, until the next 'sensitive period'. 'Sensitive periods' can occur at any time and when they occur it is important to support the child's uncontrollable desire to learn, answering their questions and giving them the means to keep on repeating and researching to achieve their aims. Frustration can occur if teachers block a child's drive to learn during a 'sensitive period' by making them join in class activities. It is better to let the child continue with their own 'work' without disturbing the others. Once they have achieved their aim, they are generally ready to join in.

3.1.2 A class framework

The class framework that follows (Figure 4) is very basic and can be modified to fit different teaching situations by altering the duration of the three phases. The time spent on each phase can also be altered from lesson to lesson to fit in with the aims of the lesson, the children's development and attention span, as well as their particular needs. It is important for teachers to be flexible, judge moods and respond to them.

Introduction

The social function of greeting people and saying goodbye (interpersonal relations), although limited linguistically, allows the teacher to have personal contact with each individual child at the beginning and end of each lesson. An experienced teacher uses this to sum up a child's mood at the beginning of the lesson, and to add a few caring words of encouragement in an effort to build up emotional trust. This is important in the first lessons as many children may be feeling insecure about a new teacher and a language they cannot understand. Where there are two teachers to a class, one teacher can greet the children, whilst the other is already sitting on the mat ready for Circle Time.

Phase One

As soon as all the children have been to their places, organised their things and seen any new realia in the classroom, children are ready for Circle Time. Children sit informally on the floor on a mat round the teacher, who sits on a chair, slightly elevated so that the children can see her face and especially her mouth. Sitting close to the teacher enables children to see the teacher's mouth movements and hear clearly, which is essential for imitation and self-correction.

This type of Circle Time begins by a revision of rhymes, songs, tongue-twisters etc. as a 'warming-up' activity, which helps children 'tune into' listening to and using English. This initial revision period is followed by other oral activities: some introduce new language items and some revise familiar ones, which can involve the whole class, groups or pairs of children.

Figure 4 A Class framework

Phase	Aim	Activities	Place
Introduction	Cultivate 'feel-good' factor	Welcome individuals	Classroom door
Phase One Class activities	Warm up Introduce personal things (teacher and child)	Revision of oral play including rhymes Show and tell Introduce new oral play	On mat, sitting round teacher's chair
Phase Two Individual or small group activities	Completing new activities/consolidating at own level	Practical activity	Sitting at own place or moving around the classroom
Phase Three Class or small group games, drama or other activities	Further consolidating experiences	Acting, puppets, language games, projects etc.	In an open space or sitting in groups
Ending	Cultivate 'feel-good' factor	Class tidies up then sits on the mat Discussion about and show of day's work Repeat rhymes, sing 'goodbye' song Teacher says goodbye and adds a personal comment to each child	Mat Classroom door

As the children get used to the teacher's way of working, they can take over some of the organising themselves. This session ends by preparing for the activity in Phase Two. This lesson may be extended on occasion for special projects and can include a show-and-tell, introducing objects brought from home (see Chapter 8).

Phase Two

Children sit at their own tables or desks in small groups, pairs or as individuals doing the activities introduced at the end of Phase One. This is a calm period during which the teacher goes round the class, talking to individual children in turn about the activities they are doing. The children get on at their own speed, working by themselves and talking to other children, with occasional words of encouragement from the teacher to sustain their interest. As the teacher goes round she keeps up a running commentary on what is going on and what is being achieved. *Pierre has drawn a great plane and I can see the window where he is sitting. The plane is up in the blue sky.*

Children who finish more quickly than others can sit quietly looking at picture books or take plain paper and crayons and draw until the class is ready for Phase Three.

Phase Three

By the end of the lesson some children are getting tired and may become restless, wanting to move around. Phase Three is planned to give children the opportunity to take part in games, activities or projects, which can include creative activities.

The lesson ends with a quiet group activity on the mat, the teacher reading a picture book, revising the new rhyme, and talking about what children can do at home and some plans for the next lesson, so children have something to look forward to.

If the teacher needs parents' support, she will have prepared a note in simple English for the children to take home.

Ending

At the end of a lesson the teacher makes sure she sends each child home with a few words of praise and a comment on his participation. *You did work hard today. Well done. See you tomorrow. We are going to play the same game tomorrow.* Young children look forward to this special, bonding time with their teacher and her personal words contribute to creating a motivating 'feel-good' factor as well helping them look forward to the next lesson.

3.2 Class organisation

3.2.1 Length of lessons

The frequency and length of lessons is generally fixed by school timetables or local circumstances. Where teachers have some choice in arranging lessons, the length and frequency of lessons should neither be too short (for example 20 minutes for 7-year-old immigrant children in a British infant school) or too long (a pre-school class with an unplanned three-hour programme in Italy). Lessons that are too short do not give children enough time to get 'warmed up' or for sufficient experiences to take place for adequate acquisition and consolidation. Longer lessons are best broken up by a snack time between Phases Two and Three, which give a natural opportunity for the children to use polite language. (*Would you like a …? Yes, please. No, thank you.*). Ideally, lessons for 7-year-old children should last 45 minutes and should be more frequent than once a week.

3.2.2 Class numbers

Young children need to be treated as individuals by the teacher if optimum learning is to take place. For this reason classes should not be too big. The ideal number seems to be somewhere between 12 and 20. Classes that are too small are also not ideal for learning as too few children make it difficult to play some games and there is less interpersonal communication.

Some teachers, however, are faced with classes of more than 40 young beginners. It is possible to manage large classes the way suggested in Figure 4, but children have to work in pairs or groups instead of individually. This takes careful preparation, organisation and management. It may also entail training children to work in groups, unless they already work in this way in other lessons.

3.2.3 Equipment and layout

Atmosphere is important for children, and if teachers expect them to use only English in the lesson children need as much help as possible to make the transition from SL. It is possible to create an English atmosphere in a classroom with pictures, posters, notices and books in English or by playing English songs on an iPod.

The 'warming-up' period at the beginning of Phase One also helps to create an atmosphere to get children into the mood for using English. Where the classroom is used for other subjects and it is not possible to keep English pictures and notices on the wall from lesson to lesson, or where children use the same room with the SL teacher, teachers find it a good idea to have a portable teacher's kit of English things. The experience for children of unpacking the kit at the beginning of the lesson with the teacher and putting it away at the end of the lesson is an added opportunity for interpersonal communication.

If children are going to take part in real-life activities in the classroom, furniture has to be arranged to allow this to take place. Furniture has also to be set up to allow for maximum communication between children. Desks in straight rows have to be grouped together so that a child can talk to the child next to him or across the table to other children. A great number of teachers are faced with far from ideal classrooms, such as small rooms equipped for adults with lecture chairs, a desk and writing board. But with a little enterprise and furniture moving, the worst situation can generally be improved sufficiently for some activities to take place. This can begin by pushing the teacher's desk into a corner and using it to store equipment.

Basic needs for a young beginners' classroom are listed here. See Figure 5 for a sample classroom layout.

✓ An area, possibly a corner, where children can sit on a mat or carpet round the teacher's chair for Circle Times in Phase One and picture book reading in Phase Three.

✓ Desks or tables to provide a flat top, for painting or creative work. These can be pushed together for group work to provide a bigger surface. Some children find sloping surfaces difficult to work on.

✓ An area in which to play games, act, etc. Desks and tables can be pushed aside to make this bigger area. Card games can be played on tables or on the mats on the floor.

✓ A blackboard, whiteboard or equivalent, low enough for children to read from and write on. Sometimes boards and display areas are too high for young children to see the work clearly.

✓ An exhibition area for pictures, homework etc. Where there is no wallboard, it is possible to prop up work on window ledges at the end of a lesson. Portable kits can include display boards or cloths on which to pin pictures.

✓ Equipment for creative work including crayons, round-ended scissors, paste, staplers etc. These can be stored in easily accessible labelled containers. (Labels give natural reading practice.)

✓ Where possible, classrooms should have technology (a computer) for additional experiences and especially listening to different Englishes.

✓ Ideally a classroom should have an English Corner. If not possible there should be a Picture Book Corner or bookshelf with chairs or rug and cushions to make individual browsing possible.

Figure 5 A basic Young Beginners' classroom: sample layout

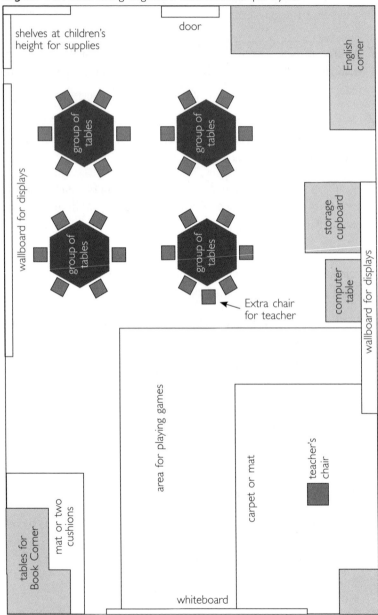

3.3 Planning activities

3.3.1 Organising activities

At this stage teachers should not expect language acquisition activities initiated by children to take place spontaneously in the classroom. Activities have to be planned before the lesson to fit with children's developmental needs and interests. The teacher needs to 'set the scene' for the activity to take place and 'stage manage' the activity whilst children are participating. It is important that activities should lead on from previous activities, and should give ample opportunity for repetition and transfer (recycling) of old and new language items as in the following example.

Colour Pairs – an activity game that develops over several lessons

Step 1

- Children are given a pair of hand-sized cards and asked to colour the circles on one side red. As they finish they show them to the teacher who asks *What colour is this?* They are then given another pair of cards and asked to colour the circles blue. They are then given two more cards and asked to colour the circles green.

- The teacher revises the colours by calling out the colour names and asking the children to point to the colour.

Step 2

- In pairs children place their cards, mixed-up and colour down, on a flat surface.

- If the first child, picking up one card, says *red* and picking up a second card says *red*, then he can hold them both up and say *red and red (good)* and keep them. If the child picked up two different cards, *red* then *blue – (no good) –* the child replaces them where they were and the other child has a turn.

- The game continues until all the cards have been picked up.
- Children then arrange their cards in colour pairs and count how many pairs they each have.
- The winner is the child who has the most pairs.

Step 3

- Children return to Step 1 and make three more colour pairs – brown, yellow, purple.
- The teacher then revises all the colours.
- Children play the game as in Step 2 but with 12 pairs of colour cards per game. (NB It takes longer to play the game this way.)

Often young children like to make their own set of cards to take home so that they can play with their family.

3.3.2 Frequency of activities

For maximum acquisition the same activity needs to take place at least twice on two different occasions. It seems that the first time an activity takes place children rarely acquire the maximum input, even if they are familiar with a similar type of activity in SL, as they are partially occupied in working out what is going on. The second time the same activity takes place they are already familiar with it and can concentrate more on the language and even on using some of it. This is very noticeable in creative work activities. Some activities may stretch over several lessons. In these cases language input needs to be carefully structured and planned to make sure the children gain the maximum benefit from the activity.

3.3.3 Variety of activities

Within a lesson there should be a variety of activities, some of which are familiar to the children, others new.

- Familiar activities give opportunities to revise, consolidate and expand language items.

• New activities should offer a challenge and require some effort.

Without making any effort, children have no feeling of satisfaction in achievement; but where an activity is too difficult, they quickly lose interest and feel they have failed. No lesson should consist of more new experiences than familiar ones as this would be too confusing for children, who seem to thrive on the security of knowing what to expect next.

3.3.4 Integrating activities

Some activities begin in Phase One of the lesson and are continued in Phase Two. Other activities such as projects may be continued through the three stages of the lesson with an initial Circle Time at the beginning of the lesson and another at the end. The time planned to be spent on different activities often has to be modified on the actual day to fit in with the children's mood and span of concentration. If an activity involves all the class, and about one third of the children lose interest, it is time to change to some other activity.

Throughout a lesson with 6-year-old children, activities were planned using language connected with time:

Practicing language connected with time

Phase One   Revision of a rhyme and using it as a game:

Tick tock tick tock
Listen to the clock.
Tick tock tick tock
Listen to the clock.
One two three four five

instead of saying the numbers the child says '*ding*' the relevant number of times; the child saying the rhyme then asks another child *What time is it?*

the reply is   *Five o'clock.*

Phase Two   Creative work – making clocks. Either cutting out clocks and hands from cardboard, or drawing different types of clocks and watches showing different times and displaying them.

Phase Three   Playing the game *What's the time, Mr Wolf?* (see Chapter 5).

3.4   Managing and mediating

The role of the teacher is that of:

* organiser of the classroom
* manager of activities, games, picture book reading
* mediator, aiding understanding (see 2.2).

Mediating and gradually extending a concept requires patience. Adults, in the role of mediator need to be flexible, continually adapting to meet children's moods and needs.

Young children need to return again and again to the same activity if they are going to absorb both the concept and language. Young children's threshold of boredom is not as low as that of adolescents and adults; they are content to return again and again to the same type of activity or game. Playing the same game many times helps them confirm what they know about the language and concept and 'feel good' about it. To feel 'I can' is important to children; it increases their self-esteem and gives them confidence to tackle new challenges.

Children's attention can often be held by asking different children, in turn, to take part in an activity (for example, reading, singing or playing a game). The suspense of waiting for a turn excites children and holds their attention. Whilst waiting for a turn and listening to others, some language acquisition seems to take place. When a class is very excited, it is better to shorten the time spent on quiet activities in Phase Two and spend more time on physical activities in Phase Three of the lesson.

If children are to be involved for the maximum length of time in language acquisition activity, it is essential to keep up a momentum by changing activities throughout the lesson. To help do this and switch smoothly from one activity to another while still holding children's interest, some teachers slip a card into their pocket on which they write the order of activities. In this way they do not lose time, or control, in having to refer to their lesson notes to check what is planned next.

3.4.1 Managing disruptive children

Teachers may face the challenges of managing varying concentration spans and differing maturational stages of voice, hearing and sight co-ordination as well as the change of physical ability due to teething. These characteristics may be gender-specific, and may depend on the cultural and home context of the learners. Some female teachers of YLs report that they have trouble in holding the attention of boys (aged 6, 7 or 8 years) who seem to need to move around and disrupt activities. In these cases teachers have not managed to engage the boys sufficiently and make them feel they can be successful. Teachers need to look at this problem from two angles: their own lesson plan and why boys become disruptive (see 1.3). The following suggestions may help teachers to look at the problem.

Organisational considerations

- Avoid judging the length of activity by girls' attention span – boys' concentration span is often shorter.
- Avoid feminisation of the classroom (boys feel unwelcome). Include visual aids and activities that stimulate boys like football information and superheroes.
- Boys admire risk taking – include games, realia and picture books that reflect this and show them you know about their world.

- Girls always tend to 'get it right'. Avoid this by dividing boys and girls into groups, giving each different tasks and displaying both groups' achievements.
- Ensure the selection of activities is balanced for both boys' and girls' interests.
- Girls generally acquire oral skills before boys, which affects classroom situations such as answering questions – make sure boys have sufficient time to listen to adults and partake in one-to-ones with them.

Boys learn differently from girls and learning language tends to take longer for them. Many teachers may not have had experience in educating boys of this age and may find this checklist useful when considering their potential. Boys are quickly bored if they do not find things in which they are interested. Women teachers have to include relevant interests that makes English special for them.

In the bush in Tanzania 5-year-old boys could read the names of all the English football teams, even some of the players and also knew the colours of each team.

Boys' learning needs

- Physical development – 6–7 years – sitting still is difficult, they need to move more often than girls.
- Competition – boys need opportunities to compete with other boys in separate groups, eg in games.
- Challenge – offer a choice of shorter oral challenges, eg tongue-twisters, as learning may take more effort and time.
- Picture books for boys' interests – make sure picture book selections include information books, sports books etc.

- Fun – jokes: boys like to laugh and make others laugh.
- Opportunities to work at their own interests in a group together. Boys are often annoyed by girls' 'goody-goody' and 'people-pleasing' attitudes and may react against them.

3.4.2 Managing activities

According to the size of the class, activities can be for:

- all the class
- boys/girls
- groups/pairs/individuals/younger and older pairs
- readers/non-readers
- writers/non-writers

Children should be encouraged to help each other. They appear to consolidate their own knowledge through teaching someone else, which is a good exercise in communication. Older children can help younger children, quicker children can help slower ones, readers can help non-readers and so on. Other children from higher classes can be invited to take part in activities like plays. English-speaking visitors can also be invited and recruited to contribute to activities or play games.

In some activities planned for the whole class the situation can arise where the quick children always answer first or win, giving the slower children little or no opportunity to practise language. In these cases the quick children can be asked to organise the game or take some managing responsibility, thus removing them from actually playing the game and so giving the slower children a chance.

Other activities can be organised for groups or pairs (for example, reading, creative work and playing games). However, unless children are used to working with other children, they may be unable to benefit from a group situation. Some young children are not ready to work with other children and, although they are placed in groups or pairs, they continue to get on with their own individual task. In these cases they should be allowed to continue as individuals. In time, they will probably gradually join in.

If possible, all work achieved in a lesson should be shown to the rest of the class and discussed with them. This can be done by a quick exhibition at the end of a lesson, Phase Three, when work is displayed in some corner of the classroom or even on the window ledge. It can also be done at the beginning of the next lesson during Phase One, when the children are gathered round the teacher. The teacher can hold up each piece of work in turn and make some comment, remembering that there is no right or wrong, but rather personal best. A permanent exhibition of work can be displayed on the classroom wall, though for this to be of any value it should be changed quite frequently.

3.4.3 Managing a class

Managing a class, keeping everyone occupied and learning is not easy and is tiring, too. Apart from being caring and supporting, teachers have to show they are leading and in control. Children respond to leadership and like to know what is accepted and what is not. At the beginning of each school term some teachers explain simple classroom rules such as sharing and not interrupting when someone is talking.

To help each child achieve their potential, teachers need to be active in the classroom, multitasking as they move from group to group using their voice to control and manage.

Using voice as a personal teaching tool

All teachers of young children need to develop the qualities of their voice as it is vital for managing a class (as any teacher who has lost her voice well knows).

Through the voice teachers can:

- control – altering the volume: a softer voice generally gets everyone to listen

- mediate
- scaffold for learning
- dramatise picture books
- develop choral speaking
- sing songs
- translate using a whisper.

Children are natural language learners and they take it in their stride if they are learning meaningful English in a playful way. VYLs and YLs know intuitively when they have had enough of an activity and switch off. This can be detected by their eyes, which are the first part of the body to show a loss of concentration. Experienced teachers recognise the signs and know that it is advisable to change an activity as concentration begins to wane. Ideally it is best to stop as soon as interest begins to wane but whilst most children are still keen to continue.

3.4.4 Managing stress

School performances and class shows can cause stress. Stress can affect the teacher, the children and the parents, for whom it is not only an opportunity to see their own child's attainments, but also for other parents to judge them. To avoid too much stress teachers need to explain their aims to parents, pointing out that such shows/performances should be an enjoyable experience for all involved. In selecting the type of performance teachers would be well advised to repeat work children already know well, such as story rhymes and songs that are easily dramatised, tongue-twisters etc. Teachers should remember that the learning process is always more important than the final product.

Stress may also occur if parents or schools want children to take external English exams. If possible, it is better to delay the taking of these exams until children are older and have a better command of English and are thus likely to enjoy the actual dialogue with the examiner, without realising it is an examination. A lot of examination pressure and stress come from parents and is passed on to the children. A note of explanation to parents explaining that their children are ready for the examination and that at school you are acting out (role-playing) the examination to give children added confidence, helps to limit stress all round.

3.4.5 Young children's expectations of their teacher

Very young and young children need to like and develop a special emotional bond with their teacher if they are to pick up language easily in dialogue. When they have developed a bond, they really look forward to meeting the teacher each day and are even disappointed on days when the school is shut. *Can I show this to Ms Jackie? Ms Jackie says 'Don't push.'*

Children need to recognise in the teacher many of the same qualities they know in their mother/parents:

• trust
• warm care – emotional understanding
• friendship – social relationship
• leadership
• fairness – following rules/knowing what is negotiable and what is not
• enthusiasm
• fun – playfulness.

3.5 Making a lesson plan

Many teachers find it useful to break a syllabus into smaller units or schemes of work, so that they have a clearer idea of what they should have achieved at the end of a week, month and term. It also helps in planning individual lessons. An example of a scheme of work designed to last a month is given in Figure 6 on page 110.

It is essential to plan lessons carefully if children are to make progress from lesson to lesson. It is also necessary to plan more activities than may be needed in any one lesson, just in case children are not in the mood to work individually at some quieter activity or to do one of the planned activities. Teachers will find it useful to record any new ideas for activities or games in a book to which they can refer when looking for new ideas. This plan is written out in full; most teachers develop their own way of recording.

3.6 Documentation

3.6.1 Monitoring children's work

Assessment and documenting is time-consuming, but is invaluable for getting to know the real needs of each child and checking to see that each lesson includes the right activities to interest each child with appropriate language content.

Recording after each lesson is important, but it should not take away time from lesson preparation time. For this reason it is important to devise quick-to-complete record templates, to provide:

• Visual documentation for children and parents
• oral records (of ability to read picture books, recite rhymes, say tongue-twisters etc.)
• Visual long-term records (portfolios)
• teacher's records after each lesson (on individual child participation/ activity follow-up).

A list of children in the class should record absences, but also note which children did not have an adequate opportunity to speak or read during the lesson and who had an 'off day'. This list helps the teacher to see at the beginning of the next lesson which children need added contact opportunities. Unless the teacher records this type of observation, it is quite possible for a shy or quiet child to go from lesson to lesson using little English.

In some part of a lesson plan file, teachers should keep more detailed

Figure 6 A scheme of work

Ages 5–7+

Step	Identifying	Oral	Reading	Consolidation
1	Numbers 1–10		Arabic number mini-cards	Game *How Many?*
2	10 animals eg a dog/a cat	picture	picture cards	Game *What's This?* Game *Bingo*
3	10 classroom objects, eg a book/a pencil	picture	mini-cards	Game *What's This?* Game *Bingo*
4	10 objects or animals with an, eg *an* elephant/ *an* ant/an orange/an apple	picture	mini-cards	Game *What's This?* Game *Bingo*
5	joining 2 different objects already introduced **with** *and*, eg a dog and a cat	2 pictures	word cards joined with *and*	*Memory game 'a dog and a cat'*
6	plurals: 2 objects already introduced ending in /s/, eg two cats	2 pictures Poem: 1 cat, 2 cats	new word cards	*Memory game 'two cats'*
7	plurals: 2 objects already introduced ending in /z/, eg two boys	2 pictures Poem: 1 boy, 2 boys song	word cards	*Memory game 'Snap' using /s/ and /z/ plurals*
8	plurals: 2 objects already introduced ending in /iz/, eg two matches	2 pictures Poem: 1 match, 2 matches	flash cards	*Memory game 'Snap' using /s/ /z/ and /iz/*

Notes

a) The steps are graded and can overlap, for example in consolidation work.
b) Steps can last for several lessons. Length of time to complete a step depends on the progress in a lesson. This scheme of work is planned to last a month.
c) Mini-cards should be hand-sized.
d) Instructions for the games are given in Chapter 5. After the end of the work scheme game materials are placed in the English Corner for free play or taken home to play with the family.

notes on individual children, their home background, their parents' knowledge of English, their general school progress in L1 or SL and their progress or difficulties in English. This information should be regularly updated (Figure 3).

Follow-up notes are best completed directly after the lesson, as details of what exactly happened during the lesson soon fade. The right-hand side of the lesson plan can be left for follow-up notes (see Figure 7). Follow-up notes form the basis from which the next lesson's plan is made. Follow-up notes should include:

- points to be consolidated in the next lesson
- language to be used in the next lesson, listing children needing more one-to-one time
- activities to be repeated or extended
- new ideas to be included.

3.6.2 Types of assessment

Modern technology is changing the types of assessment and evaluation now available to teachers and parents as well as changing children's self-assessment. In contrast to the traditional assessment of one piece of work by a teacher comment, a child's weekly or monthly progress is now visible to the child as well as parents. New forms of assessment – audio and visual – stimulate wider awareness at a younger age of present achievements and participation as well as allowing the teacher to reflect on and plan future ways to maximise class and individual potential. Even very young children are aware of other children's achievements and learn from them and sometimes use them as a role model to be copied. From an early age children are competitive and can be critical of others – this is most visible in playing simple games (Dunn forthcoming).

Teacher assessment
- after every lesson – quick assessment of children's spoken participation and problems (note summary at side of lesson plan and suggestions for next time)

111

Figure 7 A Lesson Plan

Time 1 hr	Class 66 Age 5+	Lesson No 4	
Equipment	LESSON	INPUT	FOLLOW-UP
Introduction 5 mins	Hello + name. How are you? Put your coat here.	Fine, thank you	Pairs
Phase 1 10 mins	<u>Circle Time</u> <u>Revise</u> Rhymes 1, 2, 3, clap with me Open them, Shut them <u>New</u> Tommy Thumb → Little finger <u>Revise</u> Red Yellow Green <u>New</u> Red for stop, Yellow get ready, Green for go (Rhyme) <u>New</u> Blue Brown Violet Explain making own colour cards	Stand up, Sit down. Again, Let's do it again. Boys stand up. Girls only say it. Well done, Good Colour game. This is red. This is yellow, etc Give me yellow.	Boys in pairs Girls solo Make finger faces to show
Phase 2 10 mins	Give out hand sized cards with circles. Children colour in circles red, yellow green. Show how to play Colour card game	Sit down. Colour like this (Showing red card) Well done. Now colour yellow and now green.	Make blue, brown violet cards Extend play
Phase 3 10 mins	In small groups play with 3 colours What colour is this? Keep own cards (rubber bands) Where's the monkey? (Game) on mat	Put your cards like this. Yes, that's red. No, that's not red. Where's the monkey. Here's the monkey.	Play with 6 colours
Ending 5 mins	On mat sum up & talk about next lesson. Goodbye everyone (Song) Goodbye individuals.	Shut your eyes. Count to 10 with me.	
Notes	<u>Absent</u> Alberto. Maria, Anna Additional 9 cards. Check boys saying colours		

- summary at end of week
- end of month – long-term planning
- monthly checking of work covered in relation to syllabus.

Self-assessment by child

- reporting self-appraisal of achievement and making suggestions for improvement
- commenting on oral ability, participation, socialising through:
    - photographs and short videos of child-led discussion
    - audio-visual recordings
    - audio voice recordings with playback opportunites for self-correction.
- Making own portfolio over a term, semester or year.

Parents' evaluation

Parents need guidance on evaluation as they may be influenced by how they learned at school. Parents tend to compare their child's achievements with other children's achievements.

- participation in weekly schoolwork rhymes, songs, sharing picture books
- attending class shows.

Portfolio assessment

A portfolio stores the child's personal collection of work from the first week of the school year often to the final week of the year. Work completed at school should be taken home before being stored in a child's portfolio as children want to 'show off' work to get immediate praise.

Young children like to browse through their portfolios and those of other children; they like to see their progress and often laugh at how little they knew when they were younger! First self-portraits reveal no personal traits and even no eyebrows and sometimes no ears either. In order for the child to recognise the changes over time, it is better if portfolios are not stored by children and are brought out by the teacher on occasions when several items of material need to be added.

A VYL's portfolio may consist of self-portraits drawn in pencil at various intervals, creative work, copies of rhymes known by heart illustrated by the child and photos of participation in games, class events etc. Portfolios are considered to be holistic in their representation of a child's work and progress.

3.6.3 Analysing mistakes

Teachers have to decide what type of mistake a child is making and then analyse why these are being made. Mistakes can be thought of in these general categories:

Misunderstanding

A young child has misheard or misunderstood the information or the instruction given. Repeat the instruction: *Look again. Cut it here.* Add more supporting gesture than before and wait to see if the child has understood.

Grammatical

A young child applies a generalisation to an exception in working out the system that governs English. These errors are natural in the process of learning how English works and should be welcomed as they show the stage the child has reached. Repeat the correct language, eg *I goed to the seaside*. Reply: *Oh, you went to the seaside*.

Pronunciation

A mispronunciation of a sound or word. The child says 'zee' rather than '*the*'. Repeat the word or phrase again checking that:

- the child is listening or hearing properly. Hearing can be temporarily difficult if a child has a bad cold.
- the child can see the mouth movements of the adult speaker clearly
- the type of control the child has of mouth movements. Losing and gaining front teeth and wearing braces all interfere with pronunciation and can embarrass some children.

Intonation (tune)

If the tune of a phrase is wrong, repeat the phrase with the right tune and then move on.

Word order

The degree of interference of L1 or SL in acquiring English continues to be a matter of debate. Very young children seem to have little interference as they learn language initially in blocks with fixed word order. As they begin to create language patterns and there is a mistake in word order they soon self-correct if there is sufficient role-model and adult input.

When children make a mistake in a lesson, it is important not to stop the flow of dialogue, but to continue reflecting back the corrected language. A few children can correct themselves immediately, but most need to hear the correct utterance several times more before they have assimilated it sufficiently to use it.

Some young children make the same mistakes over several months. Teachers need to be patient and increase the opportunities of one-to-one dialogue that includes the correct speech. Where a mistake persists there is still nothing to gain by correcting: children's language learning strategies are not tuned to picking up imposed corrections. A normal child will refine and adjust to the teacher's model in his own time, if he is motivated and supported.

3.7 Classroom language

What language does a teacher need?

For teachers working only through child-led activities, it is useful to have a Hidden Syllabus to check that children are being exposed to the range of language needed for communication (see Figure 8). This may include:

- Questions: closed questions that give *Yes* or *No* answers; open questions like *How did you do it? What do you do next? And then?*
- Suggestions: *Do you want …?*
- Discussions and negotiations: *What do you think? Have you got an idea?*

116

INTRODUCING ENGLISH TO YOUNG CHILDREN: SPOKEN LANGUAGE

Figure 8 A suggested Hidden Syllabus

Item	Examples	Accompanying questions
Numbers		*How many? How much?*
Alphabet		
Colours	*brown, blue, green, orange, etc.*	*What colour is this/that?*
Nouns	•classifications (some things are uncountable like water •with indefinite articles (*a* or *an*) •with definite article (*the*) •plural nouns	*What's this?* *Where's the …?* *How many are there?*
Conjunctions	*and, or*	*Is this a … or a …?*
Verbs	*to be (I am …), to have got (I've got …)* simple present	affirmative and negative question forms *Are you? Aren't you?*
Prepositions of place	*in, on, under, neart*	*Where is it?* *Where are they?*
Imperative for instructions	*Stop, Go, up, turn right/left* (affirmative) *Don't stop. Don't turn right* (negatives)	
Adjectives	*big, little, sad, happy, etc*	
Pronouns Subject pronouns Possessive pro-nouns	*I, you, he, she, we, you, they* *my, yours, his, hers, its, ours, theirs*	*Who* *Whose?*
Verbs	*want* + noun *want an apple, don't want an apple* *want* + infinitive *want to go, don't want to go*	*Does he want a bat?* *Does he want to go?*
Verbs	*can* + infinitive *can run, can jump, can't run*	*Can he dance?*
Verbs	*like* + noun *like bananas, like ice-cream, don't like bananas* *like* + verb *like playing the piano, don't like playing the piano*	*Do you like bananas?* *Does she like playing the piano?*

116

Item	Examples	Accompanying questions
Time	days of the week parts of the day (*morning, afternoon, evening, night*) meal time hours and minutes months and years seasons	*When?* *What time is it?*
Nouns for the family	*mother, father, sister, brother, etc*	*Who is …?*
Nouns for parts of body	*leg, arm, head, etc*	
Nouns for clothes	*T-shirt, dress*	*Whose is ….?*
Nouns for home	rooms (*kitchen*, etc.), furniture (*sofa, bed*, etc.)	
Prepositions for transport	*by bus, on foot*	*How did you go?*
Classifiers	*a piece of, a bottle of, a glass of, a box of, etc*	
Veb forms Present continuous Simple past Future	**affirmative** *I am eating* *I went* *He will buy* *I am going to sneeze*	**negative** *I am going* *He didn't come* *I won't go* *He isn't going to get a book*	*Are you listening?* *Did you win?* *Will you ask?* *Are you going to come with me?*
Professions	*a doctor*	*What is he/she* *What are they?*
Places	*station, supermarket, hospital*	*Where is ….?* *Where does he work?*
Adverbs	*slowly, quickly, now, soon, sometimes, here, there*	*How?* *When?* *Where?*
Adjectives Comparative Superlative	*smaller* *smallest*	*Which is smaller?* *Which is the smallest?*
Irregular adjectives	*good, better, best*	*Is this better?*

- Explanations and justifications: *This is red. The line's here, so cut here.*
- Discipline and instructions: *Please, don't do that now. Tidy up, please.*
- Encouragement and praise: *That's nearly right, try again. Well done.*

3.8 Linking home and school

3.8.1 Pre-participation

Before children start learning English it is useful for parents to have some brief explanation, either in the form of an English newsletter or through an informal meeting, about the following:

1) How young children pick up English

Parents often think that their young children will learn English like they learned it at secondary school. They may be confused that there is no textbook or similar activity that confirms grammar. Once they understand that they taught their child to speak L1 and children are still capable of picking up English in the same way through activities, they are likely to be more supportive.

Explain that teaching via formal lessons is not how young children pick up language. Young children pick up English using many of the same skills they used when their parents were teaching them how to speak L1.

Explain that much of what children say in English initially will be single words or blocks of language. Girls may be quicker than boys to use English and it is not helpful to make comparisons between the sexes. At this stage parents should not expect children to know anything about the grammatical rules of their utterances or even how many words they comprise (eg *Whatareyoudoing?*).

Parents also need to be understanding about mistakes and only give praise when it is genuinely merited. Children have usually worked out when praise is merited and are disappointed when they do not get what they think is just.

2) Parents' support

Support at home in English should be similar to that which parents gave when they were helping their children to begin to speak their home language. Support can take place at a regular time in the day (eg an English Time or English Book Time) or at any time when the child shows he wants to speak English (eg the child starts a rhyme and mother and child go on together). Support is different from tutoring. Sharing English should always be fun and not be associated with formal homework tasks.

3) Links to activities

There has to be some logical reason for the child to use English instead of LI at home. English-language-based activities can provide a reason for communication. Using the English language to communicate is only part of the learning that takes place whilst participating in activities. Activities can also broaden the child socially, cognitively, emotionally, creatively and even in some cases physically. In any English-based activity there is usually some cultural content that naturally leads to comparisons of differences and similarities.

3.8.2 Parent participation

The degree of participation allowed by education authorities or individual schools varies from country to country. In some countries the system of Parent Teacher Associations (PTA) is not allowed.

Even if formal parent participation is restricted, some form of sharing between the child's two worlds of home and school is natural for the child and, if positive, can also be beneficial. Parents often encourage sharing by asking, '*What did you learn in English today?*' The parent should not be disappointed if the child replies '*played a game*' in their home language, as it difficult for the child to repeat odd new phrases in English that are not linked to an activity or to some action that is going on.

- Participation is easier for a parent when it is based on some activity that is familiar to them and the child, like sharing a picture book. A parent needs to be confident about how to participate in the English activity that the child brings home. If a parent is unsure of what is expected, this can give the child negative feedback about his parent's English ability and the place of English in the home. Where activities are new, parents need a note of explanation from the teacher and suggestions of what English phrases to use.

- Activities to be shared should not be sent home until they have been well prepared in class and children feel confident enough to take the lead in sharing, so being able to 'show off' their English ability. Success starts off a chain of praise, *well done, you have worked hard*, which motivates and stimulates the child to go on. Any criticism can demotivate and regaining confidence is rarely immediate.

- Discussion about the activity can be in either English, LI or in bilingual speech where the child speaks in LI and code-switches to use English words he knows well or words he does not know in the home language. *Tu as vu (Look at) Dirty Bertie. Tu as vu his hands. Dirty, yuk!* As children become more fluent, the use of LI diminishes.

- Parents should be encouraged and feel comfortable using some of the same innate, updated *parentese* skills they used when they taught their children how to speak, like repeating back, stressing important words, speaking more slowly and giving praise more generously.

Rhymes and other 'show-off' pieces

Rhymes and other oral language plays (see Chapter 6) are ways that parents can assess that children are learning English and that there is continual progress. The experience of reciting a rhyme is satisfying for both the child and the parent.

- Children like to say rhymes aloud to adults and they expect their praise.
- Once children know a rhyme well, they can take a rhyme card home so that parents can follow the rhyme as they recite.
- Rhymes and other forms of language play will be built up over the term. Children will want to share them with their family. Explain to parents that

listening to the same joke or tongue-twister over and over again is tiring and needs patience, but it is a valuable learning activity.

Sharing picture books

Picture books provide parents with a ready-made activity in English that is easy to share. Sharing a picture book creates a bond. Phrases in a text often become in-family English phrases whose relevance is only understood by family members as they are related to some shared experience ... *Not now, Dirty Bertie.* When sharing, children can read the text in English and discuss the pictures in LI, broadening their visual literacy skills.

- Selected picture books with short texts, that have been read and re-read many times at school, can be borrowed and taken home. By this time the text has generally been picked up by heart and a child is ready to 'read-recite' it aloud to others.
- Young children also find satisfaction in 'reading-reciting' (pretending to read) to themselves semi-silently.
- Each reading increases a young child's skills and confidence.
- Children enjoy having their own time to browse with a book at home, looking again and again at the pictures and possibly copying and 'reading-reciting' the text, matching it to the pictures (see Chapter 7).

3.8.3 English Times at home

Many parents are eager to know what their child is doing in the English lesson and others ask how to help by watching DVDs, TV etc. at home. It is important to sustain this interest and enthusiasm as, apart from being motivating, it helps to consolidate children's holistic experience. It also gives an added opportunity for interpersonal communication in both LI and English.

Home activities

The following suggestions may be helpful to parents:

- Create an English Time when everyone tries to speak simple English. *Please.*

Thank you. Sit down. An English Time may last a few minutes or 10 and can take place once or twice a day or week depending on circumstances. The more frequently English is used, the quicker it is absorbed.

- During English Times focus on your child without any outside interruptions. Young children come to love English Times as they associate it with a special time with their parents' undivided attention.

- Young children are logical thinkers; they need to have a reason for speaking English, since both they and their parents can speak L1. Picture books, rhymes, birthdays or a game in English can be good reasons.

- Young children may find it difficult to switch from L1 into English, so it is important to 'set the scene'. *In three minutes we are going to have our English Time.* Setting the scene for English Time might involve moving to a special place in the room *Let's sit on the sofa. Now, let's talk in English.* Warm up in English by counting or saying a familiar rhyme as this helps to switch into English before introducing some new activity. When English is taught by a monolingual teacher who gives no translation, activities need to be shorter as children's attention span is generally not as long as in L1. Listening only to English can be tiring.

Home and school are closely linked in the young child's mind and some activities in the classroom should reflect what children do or talk about at home, for example new additions to the family, pets or bicycles.

Most parents of young children are interested in knowing exactly what goes on in English lessons, especially if they can speak some English or have lived in an English-speaking country. Teachers generally find that parents appreciate being informed or invited to informal class functions. Parents can be kept in touch with in the following ways:

- a parent's notebook in which the teacher writes information in the parent's L1 and the parent replies by writing in the notebook. This is a good way of keeping parents who do not understand English informed.

- notes in English written jointly by the teacher and children asking parents to come to a play or read a rhyme together with children

- a special time, once a month, when parents come into the classroom to fetch their children and see a small exhibition of work
- an end-of-term concert. This can be a simple Rhyme Concert or a dramatisation of a picture book.
- Parents who speak English can be asked to help in turns by the teacher or be asked to come on special days like birthdays to help with the snack. There is no reason why parents who do not speak English cannot help their children.
- Some teachers prefer to keep parents in touch via email, class blog, etc. This all takes up precious time and is generally written after lessons, so children are not directly involved.

There is a noticeable difference between the achievements of children who have parental support and children whose parents cannot speak English or do not make any effort to help them in any language. Parents who cannot speak English can show interest, praise their children's efforts and ask their young children to 'teach' them what they did in class. Young children without some kind of parental support are undoubtedly at a disadvantage.

> *Perhaps we need to consider the way that we support parnets and families through positivity and the building of self-esteem, just as we would for the children in our care.*

Helen Bromley

4

Beginning oral communication

4.1 Using English from the start

Primary level teaching materials are likely to be communicative in general character rather than building up a communicative competence by systematic steps (Hawkes 1981). Children acquire language by taking part in activities, and to take part in activities, they must want and need to communicate. The desire to communicate using English is immediate as that's what learning English means to a young child, so from the first lesson activities should and can take place in English.

When discussing how a 4-year-old Chinese boy learned English, Krashen explained that *Gestalt speech (prefabricated language) served as a short cut, a prefabricated tool to allow social interaction with a minimum of linguistic competence. Analytic (creative language) eventually predominated* (Krashen 1981).

In order for activities to take place in English, even from the first lesson, the teacher needs to rely heavily on prefabricated language for class organ-isation and activity management. Many activities and games (especially if the same or similar ones have taken place in the SL classroom) have predictable language, which can be picked up quickly. This language consists mainly of prefabricated blocks or chunks of language (phrases, short sentences).

Spoken language comes naturally before reading and writing or, as Montessori believed, writing and then reading, but this depends on the way reading is taught and the types of experiences individual children are exposed to.

As when a baby learns their home language, there is a similar, but shorter 'silent period' when a child looks and listens and, although is not yet ready to speak any English, may communicate through eyes, facial expression or gestures. During this time teachers should not force children to take part in spoken dialogue by making them repeat words. Spoken dialogues should be one-sided; the teacher's talk providing useful opportunities for the child to pick up language. Where the teacher uses *teacherese* – modified *parentese* – to facilitate learning, the child can use many of the same strategies used in learning home language.

4.2 Instructional words and phrases

In the first English lessons plan to use words and simple phrases in English accompanied by gestures in order to:

- organise the classroom
- manage activities
- play games
- make social contact with children (this needs to include basic survival language: *Toilet, please. Can I go to …? My bag is lost. I feel sick/bad.*).

This instructional language consists of words and prefabricated phrases introduced as whole blocks of language. Without this language it is not easy to organise a class using only English (total immersion), which is what helps children to pick up language and eventually, in some very familiar activities, begin to think in English. *It is mainly the knowledge of these chunks of language that allows non-native speakers to advance towards fluency* (Zimmer 2010).

As children get used to hearing these phrases repeated over again in lesson after lesson, they pick them up and then begin to adapt them to form prefabricated patterns (see Figure 2). *Sit down. Sit down everyone. Sit down everyone, here* (pointing to a mat on the floor). Initiative and confidence to build on to language unconsciously is fundamental to children's progress in beginning to learn English.

Teachers, especially many non-native-speaker teachers, are often amazed that lessons can be run using only English. They are equally surprised by the ease and speed with which young beginners can pick up and use quite long and complex phrases and sentences. To be able to run an all-English lesson, teachers need to structure, organise and mediate activities more carefully than they would in a SL classroom, so that all children have opportunities to listen to and get meaning from the repeated prefabricated language. With constant repetition of the same routines, children soon acquire the language involved and can begin to use it themselves to organise activities or games.

Starting an activity

To start an activity the teacher can 'set the scene' by:

* reviewing related activities done previously
* showing examples of work done by the children on previous occasions
* capturing the children's interest by explaining the new activity and showing and explaining the materials.

Checklist of language for starting an activity

Listen/Listen everyone/Are you ready? Then let's start.

Listen carefully.

This is yours and this is his/hers.

Do this like me/Watch me/Now copy me.

Follow me.

Have you got a pencil? Have you got some glue?

Has everyone got some paper? Have you got some scissors?

Have you got everything?

Draw a …

Colour this red/Colour this picture.

Cut here/Cut along the line like this/Fold it here.

Checklist of language for sustaining an activity

Listen again/That's right/Put it here.

Say it again/John and Mary say it/Boys say it/Girls say it.

Now everyone say it again.

What's this? Yes. It's …

Try it again, you can do it.

Now copy this/Now colour this.

What's this? What colour is this?

What's he doing? What's Sonia doing?

Where's the …?

Well done/You are working hard/You've nearly finished/I like it.

During an activity the teacher has to watch each child carefully, participating and helping and, where necessary, adding a comment to guide children or sustain their interest. Young children need to feel that the teacher knows what they are doing and that she is available, so that they can show their work to her or discuss it with her. This close contact can only be achieved if the teacher moves round the classroom or sits in some place easily accessible to the children – for example, on a chair at one of their tables. To sit formally behind a desk creates a barrier for communication. Some teachers take the opportunity, whilst their class is doing creative work, to move around to talk to individual children in a loud enough voice for all the others to hear and benefit from hearing an English dialogue. Some teachers often re-cap after the dialogue, explaining how the child has done it as this gives children a chance to hear the same English phrases over again. Others put on an iPod or recording of rhymes, so that children can listen to something whilst they paint. This is a good opportunity for the teacher to work in a corner of the classroom with a small group or with individual children who need some further consolidation.

Ending an activity

Before putting things away at the end of an activity, it is a good idea for teachers to show the work to the class and talk about what different children have achieved. As children gain oral fluency, they can show their work themselves and explain what they have done in simple English to the rest of the class. All creative work should be displayed so children have time to browse over the styles of work, which inspires and helps to consolidate an activity.

Checklist of language for ending an activity

Have you finished? Has everyone finished?
Stop working/Stop writing.
It's time to stop/Show me your book.

Put away your things.

Please put away the pencils/Put everything away.

Please tidy up/Tidy the classroom.

It's time to go home/It's time for play.

Give your books to me/Give your pencils to Rebecca.

Please collect the pencils/Please collect the crayons.

Put the crayons on the table.

Take your aprons off and hang them on your peg.

That is nice and tidy. Thank you everyone.

Put your books in your bags/Put everything in your desk/locker.

The following list gives additional examples of prefabricated language useful in the classroom.

Language for socialising

Greetings

Hello/Hello Toru/Hello everyone.

Hi, I am pleased to see you Aisha. How are you?

I'm very well, thank you/I'm fine, thank you.

Can I sit here, please?

Let Mia sit next to you, please.

Good morning/Good afternoon/Goodbye.

Apologising

Excuse me/Excuse me, please.

Sorry/I'm sorry/Say sorry to Tom/Sorry Tom.

That's all right.

Language for agreement/disagreement

Yes/Yes, that's right.

No/No, try again, please.

I don't like that. Please don't do it again.

Language for praise

You have worked hard.

Good/Good, well done/Good work/Very good.

That is very good writing/That's beautiful.

That is kind of you. Thank you.

4.3 Modifying language levels for young beginners

Perhaps we acquire by understanding language that is 'a little beyond' our current level of competence. Optimal input includes structures that are 'just beyond' the acquirers' current level of competence.

(Krashen 1981)

If the concepts in an activity have already been understood in SL, when the activity takes place in English, young beginners can predict much of the meaning of the English used. To help in this, the language items used in the first lesson should be as simple as possible. Once children have understood these first language items and in some cases are capable of using them, the teacher can gradually expand them and introduce more complex language so that the language used is always 'just beyond' the children's level of understanding. This requires careful overall planning and schemes of work as well as careful planning from lesson to lesson. *Put it there. Put it on the table. Put it on the table by the crayons.*

When young children are learning L1 their understanding is always greater than their ability to speak. Young children are used to not understanding every word that is said, even by their parents. To cope with this they have developed skills, which they use much of the time to get the gist. Gist understanding works by understanding a few important words in an utterance and filling in the rest of what has been said. In this way children make meaning by using different context clues and accompanying gestures and facial and body language. Children are shrewd observers and are quick to decode meaning from a tone of voice and facial gestures. Most young children rapidly work out that they can transfer their gist understanding skills to get meaning in English.

To help in the initial stages of learning, language items can include words that identify colours, numbers, classroom objects, self and personal items. In this way children have enough information to work out the gist of utterances referring to these things. In addition, facial gestures and gestures made with the hands, similar to the type of movements that accompany speech to toddlers, can be exaggerated, especially in the first lessons, to help understanding. Children are motivated once they find out that they can actually understand something in English. This breakthrough often takes place with number names (one, two, three), as children already know the concepts.

In an acquisition-rich classroom children are continually understanding by gist at their own level of comprehension. However, it is wise to plan one or two additional, new activities in each lesson, which include gist understanding. In this way, from lesson to lesson, gist experiences are made progressively more complex, so providing children with added input and at the same time increasing their skills and confidence in understanding by gist. Rhymes, reading picture books, news discussion, classroom and games management language all provide opportunities for this type of new language.

4.3.1 Loss of concentration

If the level of the teacher's language content is too advanced and children cannot understand, they lose concentration, their eye contact switches off and they become bored. Just one bored child in the classroom can easily infect others, causing trouble.

Once this happens the teacher needs to reword what she has said in an attempt to try to retrieve interest. If this is not successful, it is best to conclude the activity and change to something familiar, possibly asking one or two of the bored children to take some responsibility – through this they often become re-engaged.

Next time the same activity is reintroduced, the teacher needs to use simpler, more structured language, and insert more fun. In doing this it is wise to involve those who did not understand in a mini-scaffolding, which is focused on the more difficult parts. In this way children understand more of the language and have fun. Any negative behaviour should be a signal that the disruptive child is having difficulty in understanding and therefore learning. In this case it is best to change the child's mood by introducing a well-known game or rhyme game (see Chapter 6), before the child loses face and becomes demotivated. It is important to record and analyse a child's difficulty in lesson documentation and make sure that he understands the next time. A problem like this may be temporary; it could be difficulty in hearing because of a cold, teething problems or an 'off day'. However, it is important to make an effort to check and erase any problems in their initial stages, before they grow and have a demotivating effect.

4.3.2 Translation

If young children understand that in the English lesson they are going to use only English, they are quite at ease and appear to enjoy the challenge of understanding and using English. For this reason, it is a good idea to explain to children at the beginning of the very first lesson in SL and then in English that *We are going to learn English by talking. This is an English classroom and in this classroom we try to speak only English.*

At the same time it is a good idea to explain simple classroom rules in both languages. Young children like to know boundaries – that is, what is or is not allowed. It makes them feel more secure than total freedom. For some the informality of an English classroom can confuse them if the other lessons in their school are very formal with little opportunity to interact with the teacher spontaneously.

Only speak in English.
Only one person speaks at once.
Do not shout.
Move about the classroom quietly.
Help others.

To use only English (total immersion) with no translation or explanation in SL needs careful structuring and planning of activities and adequate support of new material with visual aids, stories, rhymes and so on. If teachers find that children have not understood the first time, they can repeat a second time or even a third time, adding more gestures or miming an action to help. Teachers have to be prepared to dramatise and add fun to the initial stages of learning. Generally some children understand the first time and they often act as leaders for the other children, even translating for them into SL. If this is the case, let them make the translation once, in a big whisper, as being able to translate is a skill that needs to be encouraged. In some classes, teachers let children make the translations when they can. However, teachers have to be careful in case children who are slower get used to this and do not bother to translate them-selves – knowing that if they wait the translation will be done for them by other children.

In the very beginning stages some teachers may, when introducing a new concept, rhyme or picture book, feel that it is better to give a rough translation once quickly, if they can. In this case it is a good idea to use a different tone of voice or even a whisper so that children realise that it is not something that regularly happens in an English lesson. Once children understand more English, teachers often find that it is no longer necessary to give a rough translation, providing they plan and structure the new language items of their lesson carefully.

However, children need to understand that the teacher translates something only once in an English lesson, otherwise some children may get into the habit of not 'tuning into' the English and waiting for the translation. Once a translation has been given and a child asks a question in L1, the adult should repeat the question and reply in English, stressing the important words, so giving children an opportunity to pick up the new language needed to continue the discussion. Sometimes it is effective to let the quicker children help the child by giving the translation in L1, which helps to develop children's natural ability to translate.

In the classroom children should be in an atmosphere where they are ready to communicate in English. Care should be taken to avoid breaking this atmosphere by translation or allowing the children to lapse into SL. If there is a short break or playtime halfway through the lesson and children go out into the playground, they usually immediately switch into the language of the playground. When they return to the classroom after playtime, it is necessary to get them back into the mood to use English. This takes time and effort. In such cases it is worth trying to organise games in English in the playground during playtime. Teacher-led games on one or two occasions act as a role model copied by children, who afterwards happily include English games in their own play.

Where lessons are full of activities, a break, if required, can be taken in the form of a snack within the classroom. Where groups are small, children can take it in turn to bring a snack for every child. Snack time provides a good opportunity for children to use suitable social language, as if in a real-life situation.

A Can I have a blueberry muffin, please?
B What would you like?
A This one, please.
B I liked the chocolate cake. It was delicious!
A I Liked the muffin.

These phrases are learned as prefabricated blocks or chunks of language that can be transferred to other situations and even used when parents or English-speaking visitors are invited into the classroom.

The habit of some children of translating aloud every new item the teacher says into SL should be broken. It is possible to do this by playing fun games in which, for example, any child using SL has to stand up and turn round twice. If, at the same time as introducing the game, the teacher takes care to use simpler language than usual and introduces no new language items for two or three lessons, the habit is often broken naturally. Once children get out of the habit of translating, they are excited by their new ability to use only English. They also seem to make quicker progress than before, especially if they are given some one-to-one support through interacting with the teacher.

It seems that if children are to make rapid progress they need to 'edit out' one language when using the other. Continual translating aloud back into SL or L1 gives confidence, but appears to waste energy and learning time. Instead of learning to 'tune in' to English, the child is getting mixed messages and does not learn to stay in one language at a time. With constant repetition most young children get beyond the need to translate routine activities and become better skilled and more confident at understanding new activities by using gist understanding. However, it takes time and patience to reach this position. Adults, parents and teachers tend to be impatient but should remind themselves of the slow start when very young children were working out the sounds of language and how language made meaning when they were learning their L1. A repetitive beginning supported by rhymes, language games and simple activities generally builds a strong foundation for later, faster progress.

4.3.3 Simplification

> *Teachers need to use deliberate strategies that parents generally use quite intuitively.*
>
> (Tough in Brumfit et al. 1991)

The type of simplified speech, referred to as *teacherese*, is, in the case of many young beginners, the only model of English they will hear. In the first lessons the teacher is in sole charge of the content of the lessons and any language interaction that might take place. Young children pass through a similar form of *silent period* as they did when they were a baby learning L1, but truncated to match their stage of development. At this stage, VYL and YL beginners are silent observers except for the repetition of rhymes or language items directed by the teacher. Carefully selected songs, chants and rhymes as well as games that consist of repetition of blocks of language help teachers shorten the silent period as they are quick ways for young children to acquire blocks of useful language.

The teacher's concern in the beginners' classroom is to ensure that activities can be organised and within these activities some communication can take place, even if this is only a facial response on the part of the young child. In order for communication to take place from the very first lesson, teachers need to modify their speech to *teacherese* with

Lesson plan (see Chapter 3)
Phase One

The teacher held up a bag containing a toy monkey, car and boat and said, *Look! A bag.* She then opened the bag so that the children (aged four to five years) could see inside and said, *Look. What's in the bag?* A child replied, *A car.* The teacher then said, *Yes. A car's in the bag. Look again. What's in the bag?* A child replied, *A boat.* The teacher said, *Yes. A boat's in the bag. Look. What's in the bag?* A child saw the monkey and replied, *A monkey.* The teacher pulled the monkey out of the bag and said, *Yes. A monkey. A monkey,* and as she said it, she added fun by making the monkey jump on each child in turn.

Phase Three

The teacher plays the game *Where's the monkey?* (see Chapter 6) in which she hides a soft toy monkey in the room.

exaggerated body language and eye contact. Teachers often complain that they are 'performing', acting and exaggerating the use of their voice to aid interaction, but children enjoy it. Simple 'free conversation' is likely to fail, as it will often not be understood and so no dialogue can begin.

Some teachers find it difficult in the initial stages to alter their 'free conversation' to simple language and are often surprised that children cannot understand their complex instructions. If communication is not taking place, it is difficult to manage an activity-based lesson. To work out the right sort of language to use, teachers may find it useful to bear the following points in mind:

- Children acquire structures in a relatively predictable order, which is similar to the order in which they learn L1.
- Situations in the classroom are controlled and give opportunities for the exaggerated use of prefabricated language, repetition, transfer and the recycling of language.
- Techniques for suitable language can be copied from the way in which parents communicate with their children.

Once certain language items have been introduced and understood the teacher can build on them from lesson to lesson, keeping language 'just beyond' acquisition level. New items can be introduced by:

- using new language supported by realia or pictures
- later consolidating the new language in an activity or game.

4.3.4 Scaffolding

Scaffolding is usually recommended when introducing new material or when a child has some learning difficulty (see 1.2.3).

Some non-native teachers worry that they may not have the fluency to manage scaffolding in English. Scaffolding becomes much easier if an activity and the accompanying language are worked out at the same time. In spite of this preparation, the actual scaffold language needs to be flexible in order to follow children's interests and moods.

Scaffolding is always easier when a child already knows the concept from work in SL, as then the scaffolding is only concerned with introducing the new language, English.

Scaffolding is only successful when the adult starts from the child's level and builds the scaffold from that point. Teachers intuitively know at what level to begin with a child and rarely get this wrong. They know that a mistake in the level at the start of a scaffold means that the child will not be sufficiently engaged to build the scaffold. Vygotsky referred to the Zone of Proximal Development (ZPD) as being **the distance between the actual development level and the level of potential development with adult guidance, or in collaboration with a more competent speaker** (Vygotsky 1978).

In interacting, listening to other people and responding, a child has to stretch to understand other people's intentions, thoughts and replies.

Teacher's role in scaffolding English

- content – generally built on a child's initiated interest
- listens carefully with empathy, encourages
- supports and gives guidance
- praises – *Yes, that's right. Good.*
- language – short phrases providing a climb: *a cat/a black cat/look at his eyes/green eyes*
- extends and sustains until interest is lost
- has hidden goal (teaching not instructing) revising known language and including a new language structure and/or vocabulary
- stresses key words
- uses exaggerated intonation and playful gestures
- repeats
- rephrases
- if child uses L1 to reply, reflects back same language in English and then continues the scaffold.

A good scaffold may last less than a minute, but if both speakers are concentrating it is likely to be a good learning experience. It is important for the teacher not to take the scaffold too far, as the child's interest may then be lost. Children need to look forward to these precious 'feel-good' times when there is sharing and mutual empathy. Very young children and young children want adult attention and seek it from teachers!

Scaffolding contributes to development in that as a result of scaffolding the child:

- builds up evidence of how language works
- is aware from adult praise and support that he is making progress
- gains confidence and understands more clearly what is expected.

In a later session, the adult can go back to the point just before they left off, to scaffold further. Montessori records sensitive periods when children's desire to learn is almost unstoppable. Teachers and parents are familiar with these periods, which may last hours or several days, after which follows a period of calm and satisfaction. When these enthusiastic spurts of learning are recognised, teachers need to be flexible to accommodate them.

As children become more mature, types of scaffolding can work in small groups or in pairs with older children or more competent English-speaking children teaching younger children in the class. Family group classrooms are ideal for scaffolding as younger children learn from their elders and grow to respect them. The older child also benefits from teaching, as, in working out how to structure information to scaffold, they internalise it. English-native-speaker children or bilingual English-speaking children within a beginners' classroom can be encouraged to lead small groups of peers and often scaffold naturally, especially in playing games.

Scaffolding is useful when a child has some learning difficulty. It can also be used to oral scaffold before writing creative language. Once children begin to use English, scaffolding can be used at a more advanced level to include predicting and recalling past experiences (Dunn forthcoming). Some young children skilled at using computers have worked out how to self-scaffold to obtain information.

4.3.5 Repetition

Meaningful repetition helps to consolidate language. For many children, meeting a language item once or twice is not sufficient for them to use it in dialogue. They need further planned opportunities to consolidate new language before they can use it. Consolidation may be in many forms – for example, games, repetition of a rhyme or repeating an activity. Some teachers are hesitant about repeating the same game or rhyme many times in case it may bore children. This seems to be an adult way of thinking; young children enjoy repetition as it gives them another chance to improve their performance.

Repetition appears to give very young children a feeling of satisfaction and achievement, which helps to motivate them. They appear to enjoy doing the same thing again and again as can be seen in the playground, where, child-led, the same game is selected and played over and over, day after day. Too often teachers and parents do not create sufficient opportunities for VYLs and YLs to repeat familiar activities or picture book experiences necessary for consolidation. Where children move on to new language before they have had the time to absorb the language of previous activities, they may have accumulated language that is understood but not sufficiently acquired to be reproduced and used. Where teachers find young children are incapable of joining in dialogues about things they have done many times in the classroom, teachers need to introduce more similar activities at the same level, giving the child time to consolidate their knowledge and opportunities to use the language.

4.3.6 Transfer

Language used in one part of a lesson can be transferred (recycled) for use in another part of a lesson in a different activity. Complete items of language can be transferred or items can be transferred in part with, for example, the identifying word or words changed (see 1.2.11).

By transferring (recycling) language, teachers and children manage to use a small amount of familiar language for maximum communication. Young children who have not learned the technique of transferring in

English underuse their ability to communicate. By frequent recycling of English, the teacher provides children with a role model and helps young children realise they can also use this skill in English. Recycling also gets children used to coping with a little English in different and unexpected situations; a good preparation for using English beyond the classroom.

4.4 Creating methods of communication

4.4.1 Dialogue

In the first lesson, as the teacher is the only English speaker in the classroom, it is difficult to start language interaction. Adult learners use their life experience to communicate in a foreign language and can work out a reply to a question from words they already know or have just learned. For young beginners, knowing how to start off and build a conversation in English is beyond their experience, and before they can be expected to initiate communication they have to listen to some examples. In some schools there may be a young child who has lived abroad and the teacher can arrange to borrow them or the teacher can invite an English-speaking parent to help for the first few lessons, so the class can hear English in meaningful dialogues. Where a teacher has access to DVD, YouTube videos or other screen materials, these can also be used to provide examples of dialogues. However, in all these cases the same problem exists. The teacher cannot control the replies to her questions and the questions themselves may be too complex for this first stage of learning. For this reason, many teachers prefer to use a puppet or a soft toy (eg a bear), whose spoken language is controlled by the teacher.

From the first lesson the teacher can use the puppet to create simple dialogues that can initially be between the teacher and puppet, providing the role model, and then between the teacher and a child. Some teachers use two puppets, making them talk to each other without any 'human' taking part. This can be a useful variety of activity, but should not replace the teacher/puppet dialogue, as many young children appear to see themselves in the place of the puppet talking to the teacher or adult. The two dialogues below show how you can repeat basic language in two different situations.

	Situation 1	Situation 2
Teacher	Have you got a pencil?	Have you got number nine?(*card*)
Puppet	Yes, I have. (*holding up a pencil*).	Yes, I have.
Teacher	Have you got a book?	Have you got zero?
Puppet	No, I haven't. (*shaking his head*).	No, I haven't.
Teacher	Have you got a pencil?	Have you got number six?
Child	Yes, I have.	Yes, I have.
Teacher	Have you got a book?	Have you got number three?
Child	No, I haven't.	No, I haven't.

It is possible to build a whole world round a puppet, making it take on the role of a child in the class. For example, the puppet can have a school bag, can play the same games, can have some mini-cards of numbers and so on.

It is also a good idea for children to make their own simple puppets as an activity. Not only is the process fun, but it provides opportunities for the use of language whilst making the puppet, as well as further opportunities for language practice once it is completed. Making a puppet can be done very quickly – the aim is not to produce a fine detailed specimen, but rather something that can communicate. For this reason it is sufficient for a first puppet to consist of only a face or head. This can be made using a wooden cooking spoon or cutting out an egg-shaped head and sticking it onto an ice-cream stick or a wooden chopstick. During the year it is possible to make several types of puppets. Young children enjoy repeating the activity and it gives the teacher a good opportunity to consolidate language as well as introduce new language in a familiar activity.

Figure 9 Some easy-to-make puppets

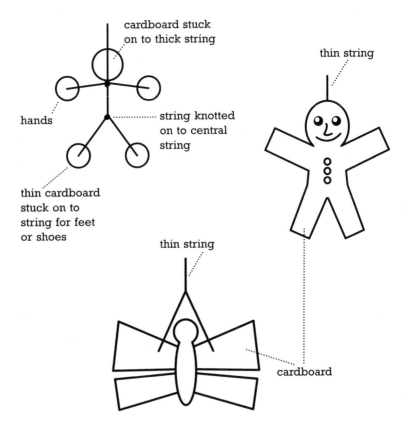

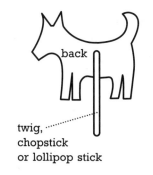

back

twig,
chopstick
or lollipop stick

wool, string
or paper
for hair

toilet roll

thumb

little
finger

thick paper bag

hand (can be
done as
finger puppet)

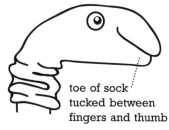

toe of sock
tucked between
fingers and thumb

face drawn
on palm side
of finger
or thumb

nail

blackbird stapled
onto ring of paper

ring of
paper

4.4.2 Language errors and correction

> *It is now well established that the advent of error can be a*
> *sign of progress (which is not to say that all error can be*
> *interpreted in this way).*
>
> (Donaldson 1978)

The idea that it is bad to make a mistake must not be allowed to penetrate into the English lesson. Young children want to communicate and learn about language through trial and error and, if supported, use their innate ability to self-correct. Language errors are a necessary part of language learning and young beginners must be expected to make some as they revise their L1 rule system to approximate to the rule system of English.

The main types of mistake made by young children are:

- **Misunderstanding**: a young child makes a mistake because he misheard or misunderstood the information or the instruction given: *Put the paste on the cupboard/Put the paste in the cupboard* (confusion with prepositions of place – *in/on*).

- **Grammatical**: a young child applies a generalisation to an exception. Language is governed by grammatical systems and children have an ability to analyse these systems. Between the ages of about 3 and 4 years, it is noticeable that monolingual and bilingual English-speaking children are orally working out and experimenting with the systems of English. Adults are familiar with these mistakes, made when children overgeneralise a rule they have acquired. These logical generalisations (mistakes) are sometimes referred to as *interlanguage* as in Corder (1977).

Examples of interlanguage

making the past by adding *ed*	*look – looked*
	took – tooked instead of *taken*
	drink – drinked instead of *drunk*
	ate – eated instead of *ate*
	run – runned instead of *ran*
	fall – falled instead of *fell*
making trades from verbs	*bake – baker*
	cook – cooker instead of *cook*
making verbs from nouns	*jammed my bread* (copying *buttered*)
making plurals	*tooth – tooths* adding *s* instead of *teeth*
	mouse – mouses adding *s* instead of *mice*

These forms are a natural stage in a child's development and should be regarded as landmarks that give adults an insight into individual children's language development. Children learning English as L2, L3 or L4 seem to make similar mistakes as they generalise when applying what they have worked out to be the rules of grammar, not realising, due to lack of experience, that there are exceptions to rules. The child is applying a regularity to an exception.

Some generalisations show the child is trying to use a past tense to talk about what he has been doing. Young children express themselves through narrative (story); they need to tell the story of what they did and thus need the past tense earlier in learning English than many adults realise and earlier than the syllabus may include.

Intonation

A mispronunciation of a sound or word may be due to:

- not listening or hearing properly – check young children's ability to hear. Hearing can be temporarily difficult if a child has a bad cold.
- not observing the mouth movements of the adult speaker correctly. Young children may not have an opportunity to watch adults speak.
- not yet having sufficient control of their mouth movements (tongue and/ or lips) or losing teeth; getting new teeth and wearing braces all interfere with pronunciation.

If young children are given opportunities to see and hear an adult using words in context, they have an enviable ability to pick up the sounds and intonation patterns (tunes) of language and continuously self-correct. They also gradually refine their pronunciation to imitate the role model's pronunciation. Refining their pronunciation to match the model speaker may take a little time or in some cases may be immediate. Children know what is and is not correct pronunciation, and once they begin to create their own language they often begin to correct their parent's pronunciation in English. Adults who learned English as adolescents often do not manage to imitate pronunciation as well as young children, who may be able to speak two dialects of English – one in the classroom and the other when playing outside with their neighbourhood friends.

Intonation (tune)

It is possible to ask a question in Japanese, English and French not by changing the word order, but by raising the tone of voice: *Yours? Tu viens?*

Question words used in the early stages make learning easier: *When are you coming? What did you do?*

Meaning can also be changed in a sentence by stressing a word. *Did you go there?* The stressed *you* implies that the speaker was surprised that you went there. English is a stressed language.

Word order

The degree of interference of the mother tongue in acquiring English remains a matter of debate. Some very young children seem to have little interference if:

> **Input** is regular, structured, correct and at the child's level
>
> **Dialogue** offers regular one-to-one opportunities to recast language
>
> **Translation** is used for getting meaning or emphasising the comparison between English and L1 where there is a marked difference (eg Malay/Indonesian doubling word to get plural *orang* = man, *orang orang* = men).

Mistakes in word order seem to be fairly rare since a young child learns through:

- acquiring prefabricated blocks (chunks) of language without knowing their breakdown into words: *itsme*. Later adding on creatively new blocks or words to part-fabricated language: *itsmyturn*.
- copying the model speaker, whose word order is correct
- acquiring prefabricated language from picture books, rhymes etc.
- transferring language without knowing the grammatical or word content.

Each child is unique and if word order mistakes occur teachers need to find out about the child's background including:

- how L1 and L2 were learned and are used
- the type of follow-up by parents and parents' skills in simple English (it could be that parents' word order in English is strongly influenced by the language through which they learned English)
- the child's ability in L1 and/or the school language.

With more exposure to spoken language, children revise their rule formation to incorporate the correct rule or exception. When their children make 'interlanguage' errors in L1, but the meaning has been understood, most parents make little comment or let the mistake pass without correction. Teachers are advised to do likewise, making sure the children have an opportunity, soon after, to hear the correct usage in some related activity.

Mediating

Adults in the role of mediator need to be flexible, adapting to each encounter as young children, like adults, have their good days and off days, when sometimes for unpredictable reasons, even a rainy day, they are not ready to settle down and concentrate and consequently may make more mistakes. Children cannot switch on readiness to learn without an adult's mediation to help them switch their focus and mood. Lack of focus can often be successfully changed by abandoning any prepared plans and returning to a favourite, familiar activity, game or picture book that is easy to use, more playful and requires little effort on the part of the children.

4.5 Pronunciation

4.5.1 World Englishes

Today children have opportunities to hear many world Englishes on screen, spoken by native-speaker members of the Commonwealth, including Australian English, Malaysian English, South African English, Nigerian English, Indian English as well as the English of members of the EU and other nationalities. So what is the 'Standard English' that some parents request and expect their children to learn? Children have an amazing ability to pick up different pronunciation and intonation, and throughout their learning life they will use this special ability to alter their pronunciation to fit in with their current environment.

Parents who have learned English later in life, in secondary school and beyond, may not have acquired this same ability and this may contribute to their concern about the type of English being introduced to their children. Parents need to understand that young children, who have absorbed language without any tedious learning involved, have an amazing ability to adjust their accent to their surroundings. The most important thing is for them to be motivated and to learn how to communicate in English and use it with confidence. Once children can take part in dialogue, they can pick up more language quickly and become fluent speakers in certain areas. When they have a degree of fluency, they will begin to adjust their pronunciation to meet their needs.

Many of the most effective teachers of English to young children may be trained as teachers of YLs. Such teachers understand child development as well as being sufficiently proficient in young children's activities in English to relate socially and emotionally to very young and young children and help them begin to develop English naturally and enthusiastically, according to their individual potential.

To 'feel good' with the teacher at this age is very important for language learning, as a child's first language was learned from a *significant person* (mother) in the child's life and if this type of shepherding is replicated with English then learning can be similarly successful. **Language is acquired in the course of human development as a means of interacting with those 'significant others' who are most involved in the life of children** (Wells 1981). Some teachers who trained as secondary school English teachers may find it difficult to plan activity-based lessons for very young and young children and to use *teacherese* to develop English unless they have brought up children of their own.

Young children's enviable ability to pick up the sounds and patterns of language has already been mentioned. Unlike most adolescents and adults, they do not need to be taught how to say words. If the role model's pronunciation is good and clear, there is access to recordings and opportunities to use language in real situations, YLs are capable of refining their pronunciation until, in some cases, it is hardly distinguishable from that of their model speaker. This happens with native-English speakers. How often are children of 9 or 10 years of age taken to be their parents when they answer the phone, as their pronunciation is identical?

Mistakes in pronunciation need analysing carefully. It is often mistakenly thought that pronunciation is comprised of sounds alone. Pronunciation is a complex of:

- sounds (consonants and vowels)
- syllables (word stress and rhythm)
- intonation (tunes).

In many cases mistakes are made not in individual sounds or clusters of sounds, but in the stress, rhythm or intonation of a single word, phrase or sentence. When the tune (intonation) is very different from the adult model, what is said can be misunderstood and the feeling of the speaker misinterpreted.

There are differing opinions on the number of sounds that comprise English as well as their division into categories. The following simplified introduction is intended to help teachers when preparing children for *reading readiness*. The more familiar a child is with spoken language, the easier they will follow a programme for learning to read in English (see Chapter 6). Where written language is a natural part of activities in the classroom, many children who can already read in SL work out how to read in English by themselves. Of course, at a more advanced stage they need a more formal reading programme if they are to decode unfamiliar words and become fluent readers (see Chapter 7).

4.5.2 The sounds of English

It is generally accepted that there are 44 sounds in English (*phonemes*) whilst there are 26 letters in the alphabet (*graphemes*). The 44 sounds are based on what is called British Received Pronunciation (RP). The following charts, based on the teaching of reading, writing and spelling in England, are provided by the British Department for Education and Skills (DfES 2007). This basic information is to help teachers in introducing the initial sounds of words; the terminology is not suitable for VYLs and YLs. More detailed information on the 44 sounds is given in *Introducing English to Young Children: Reading and Writing*. The linguistic details given on

Figure 10 The 44 phonemes of British Received Pronunciation

Consonant phonemes, with sample words		Vowel phonemes, with sample words	
1. /b/ – bat	13. /s/ – sun	1. /a/ – ant	13. /oi/ – coin
2. /k/ – cat	14. /t/ – tap	2. /e/ – egg	14. /ar/ – farm
3. /d/ – dog	15. /v/ – van	3. /i/ – in	15. /or/ – for
4. /f/ – fan	16. /w/ – wig	4. /o/ – on	16. /ur/ – hurt
5. /g/ – go	17. /y/ – yes	5. /u/ – up	17. /air/ – fair
6. /h/ – hen	18. /z/ – zip	6. /ai/ – rain	18. /ear/ – dear
7. /j/ – jet	19. /sh/ – shop	7. /ee/ – feet	19. /ure/ – sure
8. /l/ – leg	20. /ch/ – chip	8. /igh/ – night	20. /ə/ – corner (the 'schwa' – an unstressed vowel sound which is close to /u/)
9. /m/ – map	21. /th/ – thin	9. /oa/ – boat	
10. /n/ – net	22. /th/ – then	10. /oo/ – boot	
11. /p/ – pen	23. /ng/ – ring	11. /oo/ – look	
12. /r/ – rat	24. /zh/ – vision	12. /ow/ – cow	

Source: Letters and Sounds: Principles and Practice of High Quality Phonics, Notes of Guidance for Practitioners and Teachers (DfES Publications 2007, p. 11). For additional information on graphemes and phonemes from this publication, please see the Appendix.

consonant and vowel sounds are to help teachers understand and be able to help young children recognise the 26 letters of the written alphabet and their sounds.

In the sections below please note that letters surrounded by slashes – /a/ and /d/ etc. – indicate a particular sound rather than the letter.

The vowels

The vowel sounds are not only made up of /a/ /e/ /i/ /o/ /u/. There are 20 vowel sounds, five are so-called short vowels /a/ /e/ /i/ /o/ /u/. This does not mean that they are short in the way they are sounded, but they are not composed of two vowels fused together, which are called *long vowels* or *two-vowel diphthongs*. The so-called *long vowels* often have the same sound as their name.

Initial *short vowel* sounds	Initial *long vowel* sounds
/a/ as in *at, ant, apple, cat*	/a/ as in *apron*
/e/ as in *end, egg, elephant, bed*	/e/ as in *eel*
/i/ as in *in, insect, sit*	/i/ as in *ice*
/o/ as in *on, orange, hot*	/o/ as in *open*
/u/ as in *up, umbrella, cup*	/u/ as in *uniform*

In lists of sounds there is sometimes confusion between:

- /oo/ in *book* and *look*
- /oo/ as in *hoot* and *boot*.

Consonants

There are many different ways to produce consonants. Consonants can be long or short. It is useful to note that there are many pairs of consonants that are made by using the mouth in exactly the same way, the difference being in whether they are voiced (that is the vocal chords vibrate as they open and close when air passes through the throat [larynx]) or voiceless (when air passes through the throat freely and the vocal chords do not vibrate). If you place your hand on your throat you can feel the vibration of the vocal cords in the neck if you prolong the pronunciation of letters like *mmmmmmmm* or *zzzzzzz*. Then compare this with letter *sssssssss*. Another way to understand the difference is to cup your hands over your ears. It is easiest to understand differences when you compare some voiced sounds with voiceless sounds in pairs.

Voiced	Voiceless
/d/ as in *dog*	/t/ as in *tin*
/b/ as in *bin*	/p/ as in *pin*
/z/ as in *zoo*	/s/ as in *say*
/g/ as in *go*	/c/ as in *come*

In lists of sounds there is sometimes confusion between the two /th/ sounds:

/th/ as in *thin* – voiceless making a windy sound
/th/ as in *this* – voiced making a buzzing sound.

Consonant phonemes: /th/	
/th/ windy sound	/th/ voiced buzz
thin	then
thick	that
thumb	this

The letter *k* sound can be represented by /c/ /k/ /ck/ /ch/ or /q/.
The letters *m* and *n* are both voiced as the air passes out through the nose.

The letter *l* in *loud, louder, loudest* is voiced with the tongue touching the gum behind the upper front teeth. When making the letter *r* at the beginning of words like *run rabbit run* the lips are rounded and the tongue curled up to point to, but not touch, the roof of the mouth.

Figure 11 The difference in making /r/ and /l/

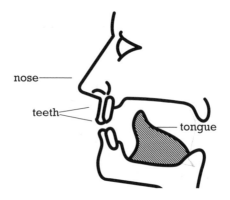

Showing position of the tongue for /r/

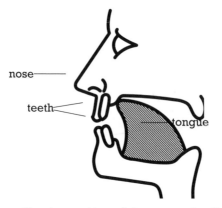

Showing position of the tongue for /l/

Teaching the alphabet

The first step in a *reading readiness* programme is to teach the alphabet, as children need to know the names of the letters in order to talk about words. Children who already read in other classes expect to be introduced to the alphabet in one of their first English lessons. If children's SL is different from Roman script, they need to be given opportunities to look at picture books printed in English before they begin to learn the alphabet.

Very young children, who have not yet learned to read in SL, need to understand the concept of reading. This means they require a longer exposure to oral language play and rhyming language as well as opportunities to enjoy picture books before they are ready to start reading in English. Speaking comes naturally before reading and writing in a child's development and if reading is introduced too early it can become too great a task. Parents may, however, be eager for very young children to learn the alphabet and at this stage the alphabet can be introduced through games.

There are two methods of teaching the alphabet: the teacher can either introduce the names of the letters, or teach the sounds of the letters (phonemes) first. Where some children have already learned the names of some of the letters from their families, CD-ROMs, television, DVDs , YouTube video clips, etc., it is advisable to build on this knowledge, teaching the names of all the letters first. To introduce the sounds of the letters at this stage could be confusing, especially as many parents do not know them and thus cannot offer support at home.

In reading picture books the adult begins to introduce initial sounds of words first and backs this up by playing games like *I spy* (page 161). Sing the *Alphabet song* and give copies to parents.

Introduce the small letters of the alphabet first as these are the letters more frequently used. For young children it is too much to introduce both the capital and small letters at the same time. Depending on the age of the children and their previous experience, two or three letters can be introduced in each lesson. It is easier to learn at least two letters together, as exploring similarities and differences helps learning.

Teach the capital letters (uppercase) once children know the small letters (lowercase). However, use capital letters normally and talk about them, as children will absorb information about them naturally through experience. It is a good idea to obtain two sets of alphabet letter cards, or an alphabet jigsaw, so that children can experience holding letters like *p*, *b* and *d* and getting them the right way up.

At this stage it is better not to teach children to write (handwriting), though writing by the teacher should occur naturally in the classroom eg lists, notices etc. and such writing should be displayed at reading height for young children. Young children who already write SL in roman script often ask to write in English. To be sure they do not slip into reading English with an SL accent make sure their first handwriting experience is copying rhymes which they know orally or copying from a picture book where they are familiar with the short text. This is important as they need to get used to decoding the words with English sounds and if it is language they already know and can recite, they naturally use English to 'sound out' words when reading them. It may be necessary to explain the difference between the written and printed letter *a* and *g* forms.

Initial letters

Talking about alphabet letters should be embedded in activities as the opportunity occurs. Once children are familiar with most of the letters and know the *Alphabet song*, introduce an alphabet frieze for reference. Display it on a classroom wall at a level at which children can, in their own time, point to each letter as they sing or say the alphabet, confirming what they know.

If possible select a frieze with pictures and only small letters until children are familiar with the majority of the 26 small letters. Alphabet picture books introducing initial letter sounds may sometimes include misleading or incomplete examples – here are some to be aware of:

- letter s is not a single consonant but a consonant blend /sh/ as in **ship**
- letter c is not a single consonant but a consonant blend /ch/ as in **chair**
- letter c has two pronunciations – hard /c/ as in **cat** and soft /c/ as in **city**
- letter g has two pronunciations – hard /g/ as in **garden** and soft /g/ as in **gentle**
- letter h is sometimes silent as in **hour**.
- letter x is not the sound for **xylophone**

Some initial sounds

Letter f – say the words *huff and puff* and try to blow out candles on a birthday cake; say *fee, fi, fo, fum*.

Letter g (voiced) – pretend you are drinking from a glass and then say letter c as in *come* (voiceless).

Letter h (voiceless) – pant as if you have run very far and are out of breath *hhhhhhhh* or make a whispered laugh and change the vowel sound to make *hahaha, hehehe, hohoho*.

Letter n – put your fingers on your nose as you say *new nose*.

Letter m – put the lips together and make *mmmmmmm* so the lips tingle then hold the nose whilst the lips are held together and feel how the sound is stopped.

Letter p – make a fish face with the lips pursed together, expel the air, then try making letter b in the same way, feeling the voice passing through the voice box by putting the fingers of one hand on the throat and breathing out onto the palm of the other hand.

Letter s – put the teeth together and make an extended hiss and then say letter z in *zoo*.

Letter w – purse the lips together and make the sound of the wind.

Young children, from their infancy, enjoy playing with sounds and many are interested in discovering how sounds are made. Explain the role of the lips, nose and tongue in making sounds. Tell them about some initial sounds and explain how they are made, perhaps using a hand mirror.

Include other voiced and voiceless pairs. Children find it easier if consonant sounds are introduced in pairs, as exploring similarities and differences helps learning.

Rhyming words

In the beginning stages of learning oral English it is important to build up exposure to rhyming sounds and alliteration (words starting with the same sound) like *a new, noisy neighbour*. Play games asking *What rhymes with Ted? Bed. What rhymes with bat? Cat* etc. Then make oral lists of words that rhyme like *tap*, *mat*, *fat*, *cat*, *bat*, *sat* and add some nonsense words to the list. Children soon follow up themselves playing with rhyming and made-up words, generally starting by changing the initial consonants. Children are used to saying rhyming sounds aloud to themselves from an early age in L1.

Alphabet games

1) Guess the letter

Place all 26 small letters or letter cards in a bag. Children sit in a circle and in turn pick a letter from the bag. They hold it up, say its name and then sound and, if possible, a word beginning with the sound. This involves:

- distinguishing the letter shape
- naming the letter (grapheme)
- saying the sound (phoneme)
- linking the sound to the name of an object beginning with the sound.

2) I spy

Children sit in a circle. Teacher begins, *I 2 3 What can I see? I can see something beginning with the letter 'b' or the sound 'b'*. Children look around and the first one to answer correctly *ball* has the next turn. To begin with the teacher may have to lead, until most of the children are confident to use the initial sound for objects in the classroom. Play the same game spying the same objects over several lessons to build up children's confidence.

Plurals

It is important to remember these basic rules when counting objects aloud with beginners. At this oral stage it is not necessary to point out these rules as children will hear the differences and absorb them naturally.

Most plurals are made by adding s. After the letter s, h or x we add *es* as in *buses, matches, glasses, boxes, foxes*. However, there are three different pronunciations for these 'regular' plurals:

After voiceless sounds add /s/ as in *books*.
After voiced sounds add /z/ as in *boys, games, hands*.
After words ending in letter s, h or x add es – sounds /iz/ eg *buses, watches*.

Add /s/ voiceless	Add /z/ voiced	Add /iz/
books	boys	boxes
cats	cars	brushes
hats	flags	classes
stamps	games	crosses
tickets	girls	faces
	hands	houses
		watches

There are also some exceptions:

- man/men
- woman/women
- child/children
- city/cities
- baby/babies
- tooth/teeth
- foot/feet
- sheep/sheep

Syllables and strong/weak forms

Young children like dividing long words into parts or syllables. Apart from helping them to remember long words it also helps later when they come to read them, *e-le-phant*, *di-no-saur*. Words can have one syllable (*dog*) or more than one syllable (*kan-ga-roo*) and children enjoy clapping the syllables or putting a hand under the chin to feel the number of syllables. Each syllable contains just one of the 20 vowel sounds.

In any word with more than one syllable (a multi-syllabic word), one syllable has greater stress – that is, it is pronounced with greater strength – than others. The stress may be on the first syllable, as in *Monday*, or in the second syllable, as in *today*, or on the third syllable as in *understand*. Within a phrase or sentence there is also a pattern of stressed and unstressed syllables. Many structural words pronounced in isolation are said in their strong form, but when they are said within a phrase or sentence they take their weak form. Verbs are a good example of this. When teaching the verb *to be* a teacher stresses *am*, *is*, *are* and so on. But when these words appear in a phrase or sentence in normal fluent speech, weak forms are usual. For example, *He's in the playground and we're going out, too.*

When teachers speak slowly to help children understand more easily, they need to take great care not to distort their pronunciation model by giving abnormal stress to words and by substituting strong forms for weak forms.

4.5.3 Improving pronunciation

Young children around the age of 6 and 7 years begin losing and growing new upper and lower front teeth, which can make pronouncing some of the sounds difficult and cause embarrassment. The lower front teeth are used in making letters /s/ and /z/ and the upper front teeth in making /th/ voiced and voiceless. When children are at this stage of change it is better for them that any saying of rhymes and letters are done in pairs or groups of children, as they recognise their inability to pronounce clearly and correctly and any cause for embarrassment can thus be avoided.

At the very beginning of English language learning it is better not to lay too much stress on faults in pronunciation as this could demotivate children. In speaking and in reading picture books teachers can repeat mispronounced words, exaggerating the way the sounds are made. Young children are used to self-correcting their pronunciation to get it closer to that of the role-model speaker in SL and they soon begin to reuse the same skill when picking up English.

One of the best ways to help children improve is to let them audio-record rhymes or tongue-twisters. Children are quick to recognise their own faults and want to self-correct immediately. To help young children improve their pronunciation, teachers might find the following points useful.

* Analyse the faults to find out if they are individual sound or language pattern faults.
* Based on the analysis of the faults, increase exposure to either patterns or sounds or both by revising previous work and/or introducing new rhymes or songs focusing on specific difficulties.

It is important to draw children's attention to mouth movements and to let them feel as well as hear the difference between voiced and voiceless sounds by putting their fingers on their throats.

Once children have some fluency in certain areas of language and begin to read and write English, they are ready to find out more about how sounds are made in English and how words can be broken into syllables. (Dunn forthcoming)

Phonetics and phonics

Many teachers are confused by the differences in representation between *phonetics* (the science of the analysis of speech sounds) and *phonics* – a method of teaching reading following the rules of speech sounds (phonemes) and letter (grapheme) relationship. The term 'phonics' was first used in the nineteenth century to refer to reading materials, which helped children to read by learning the rules governing the sound–symbol relationship. New linguistic research has brought about a revision of phonic rules to bring them in line with more recent theories of linguistics.

There are three main systems of teaching reading using phonics:

- **Synthetic phonics** is a teacher-led isolated method where children learn to build up words (write them) *c-a-t d-o-g st-o-p*, blending the sounds of letters to make the 44 sounds of English. Before a child is ready to read English using this method, they need to have an oral foundation in order to match the oral (spoken) word with the written word and get meaning.
- **Analytic phonics** is a teacher-led isolated method where children learn to analyse words they can or cannot already read (decode) using sound–symbol correspondences they know, often breaking the words into syllables to help the analytic process.
- **Embedded phonics** is a holistic approach, where the individual child, who is used to using different skills in gist understanding of oral language, uses his own text-decoding skills including word shape, initial sounds, rhyme, alliteration, syllables, sound–symbol information and context clues in an activity or picture book experience to get meaning.

Phonics are discussed and explained as the opportunity arises within a rich, active language programme. Talking about sound–symbol relationships related to words in activities or games may also be included in Circle Time in Phase One of a lesson. Sounds that some children find difficult can also be focused on in Circle Time as the need arises. Although embedded phonics does not follow a systematic plan with structured instruction, the teacher follows a hidden plan, checking that in lessons children have become aware of the alphabet and initial letters and have found out how their sounds are made.

In learning to read by the phonic method, and especially by synthetic phonics, a change in the teacher of spoken English (where the new teacher has a markedly different accent and especially vowel sounds) often causes confusion as children are learning by matching sound and symbol and not yet reading whole words. Where this happens, children need to revisit the first steps in matching, listening to the new teacher's sound–symbol correspondence before embarking on more difficult sound combinations. In this way they will avoid problems later on.

Research now suggests that children's comprehension in L1 is a positive attribute that enhances their ability to acquire English. If they can already read in another language, learning to read in English is faster as children already know how to decode a different text to get meaning and soon work out how to transfer this skill to English.

Although reading and writing are included naturally in daily life situations, formal teaching of reading is not introduced before children have a good oral foundation. Children find it difficult and demotivating to decode text until they have all the tools (sound–symbol relationships) needed to decode unknown words.

Once young children are sufficiently mature and have been exposed to a varied and rich *ready-to-read* programme, they are ready to begin reading stories, writing creatively (this is different from handwriting skills) and spelling. They are what some teachers refer to as *emergent readers*.

> *Young children do not have the same facility to talk in details and draw on memories. (The best things adults can do is to observe them with care and sympathy). We need to be open, attentive and intrigued by the unique freshness of their communication.*
>
> Julian Grenier

Ready-to-read programme for total immersion or bilingual classrooms

- general awareness of single sounds in English and how they are made
- sensitivity to rhymes, repetitive sounds and ability to recite rhymes, tongue-twisters and other verbal play (see Chapter 6)

- knowledge of alphabet letter names and sounds
- knowledge of sounds in the context of initial letters and some final letters
- knowledge of writing through notices, labels in classroom
- knowledge of what writing looks like through text in picture books (see Chapter 7)
- ability to understand language in familiar and linked new activities
- some ability to speak fabricated language and to attempt to form creative language
- ability to recite some picture books texts and rhymes, pretending to read them.

Children whose parents frequently read with them in their first year of school are still showing the benefit when they are 15. Parents did not have to be particularly well-educated themselves for this impact to be achieved.

OECD Report

5

Oral games

5.1 Selecting games

Games are play activities that become institutionalised (Garvie 1979). Games are structured, organised play with rules that have to be followed. The rules that govern a game give it a form with a definite beginning and end. The rules also ensure that the play takes more or less the same form each time, which gives children a feeling of security and contributes to a 'feel-good' factor necessary for all learning. As a game evolves children know, more or less, what to expect. This consistency and predictability makes understanding easier for children as they can predict what is going to happen and what language is likely to be used.

Games add excitement and fun to learning English at school, and also to family life, as most children like to play the same games at home as they play in school. Playing together in a group, either at school or later at home when children know how to play the game, not only increases children's English ability, but also their holistic learning and development and their interpersonal skills (social intelligence).

Games are a social affair: through them children can learn about fair play and how to follow rules. Not only do young children learn the rules of the game, they learn the social rules of how to play with others in a formalised setting. Playing games together can help bonding. If young children know and understand socialising game rules and yet they break a rule, it might be a result of overexcitement. Often a glance from the teacher is sufficient to maintain control, as young children respond to eye contact and basically want to please! Games often help teachers to know young children better as, immersed in the excitement of playing, children often reveal their emotions and attitudes to others. Through playing games, children have opportunities to work out their self-image and self-worth

Playing games within a lesson may also help children develop positive attitudes to learning English. Playing games can even change the attitude of some young boys, who can find learning English difficult and even frustrating. Games give boys the challenges they enjoy and chances to take risks in concise, controlled and meaningful competition. Games also

Socialising game rules

Don't interrupt.

Don't talk when someone else is talking.

Listen to the others.

Wait for your turn.

Don't be a 'snitch' ('tell tale') (a child who tells the teacher when some other child cheats.)

give children an opportunity to win and feel successful. Games are different from many other activities in English in that success is not only measured by how well you can speak English!

Games can be broadly divided into families of similar types of games, such as starting games or board games, with each game family using more or less the same organisation and management language to play. Young children seem to become absorbed in playing games that are appropriate for their stage of development and linguistic level, without being conscious of the meaningful and sometimes drill-like repetitive language involved. Once children become familiar with the game management language, they are ready to concentrate on the content language of each individual game and cope with new content as the level of play is gradually increased.

Playing the same game over and over again may seem boring to adults, but not to young children, providing the adults have added suspense and excitement into the play. Children welcome opportunities to improve their own language as well as their game skills. *Can we play it again? One more time. I want to win.*

Group games involve taking turns, which apart from acquiring social skills, give opportunities for one-to-one dialogues. *Is it my turn?* **No. No it isn't. It's mine.** *Well, hurry up. We are waiting for you.* **OK, give me the dice, please**.

5.1.1 Selecting suitable games

Not all games are suitable for young beginners and not all games give suitable language experience. Those played with little or no language participation are only time-fillers, unless the adult adds their own language.

Games are most useful if they are integrated with teaching, consolidating the use of language items. However, for games to be rich English language experiences, adults need:

- to create additional opportunities to repeat language, often in a fun way, as each child has a turn
- to give a running commentary on play using language at the children's level of understanding, bearing in mind that children always understand more than they can say.

Many games are not appropriate for young children as they require player participation that is too advanced for their stage of holistic development. Games in English that have similar cognitive, physical and emotional levels as the games the children already play at school are the most appropriate. A short visit to a local playground is a quick way of finding out about the type of games children are used to playing; game skills differ from culture to culture.

Very young children enjoy co-operative games, for example, *Farmer, Farmer, Can I cross the water?* (see 5.1.7), which involve the whole class and allow children to participate as much or as little as they feel able. Games that are based on individual competition to see who wins, or who gets the most cards, seem to be popular with children about 6 or 7 years old or older. Younger children may be still at the age when they find it difficult to lose. However, as children get more experience in playing games, and especially as they grow older, they seem to grow to accept winning and losing, provided neither state is given too much importance. For many very young children, having a turn in a game is more important than who actually wins.

Boys respond well to chasing games in which there is a small element of fear and they can take risks. When selecting chasing games it is important that very young children know what to expect in advance, otherwise they may be too frightened to participate. For this reason, it is advisable to explain the chase and play the game the first few times omitting the chase. Once the initial fear is overcome, many even ask to play this type of game as they get some satisfaction in being able to manage their fear, which they know is contained within the game. Before they introduce chasing games, teachers need to check that the area in which they are to be played is safe and children understand that they must not get too excited or too noisy as other classes are working. Some teachers use the yellow card or even red card football system in chasing games, as most young boys understand this!

5.1.2 Fitting games into a programme

Oral games for young beginners can be divided into three groups:

> **Starting, selecting or counting-out games**: played at any time in a lesson. A quick game played before another game to find a leader or catcher or to decide who will play first or to select a child to be responsible for something in the classroom like giving out pencils, leading the line to go out to the playground.
>
> **Phase One quick games**: played in the first phase of the lesson. These games only last a few minutes and are played to consolidate a point or change the atmosphere. They are often created by the teacher to fit an immediate need.
>
> **Phase Three games**: longer games played in the third phase of a lesson, which can involve more movement, such as running or hiding. Others are card and board games to consolidate a language point taught in Phases One and Two. Before playing a longer game like a chasing game, select the chaser by playing a starting game.

5.1.3 Monitoring or documenting

Children are competitive, especially boys, and they like to know who is the winner, although it is always best not to make winning important. It is important to document who won, who did not participate, who was a leader etc. so that next time other children have a chance to participate more.

Visual documentation by a camera or an easy-to-use video recorder of children playing is an interesting record for children and parents, too. Children like to discuss who was doing what in the photos/film. It is fun, as children begin to read, to add speech bubbles to the photos. Children enjoy discussing what they were saying and commenting on what they should have been saying.

Once children know how to play a game, if possible arrange for them to take the game home. Through playing together, parents can see what the children have learned. However, when games are taken home be sure to send home the rules of play so that parents understand how to play. Add a list of useful phrases in English, too!

5.1.4 Game families

Games can be loosely grouped into these families:

Starting, selecting or counting-out games – quick games used to select one person to be a leader or have the next turn.

Physical games – games that involve meaningful movement and space.

Card games – games played with home-made or bought cards.

Board games – games based on a board or boards.

Chasing games – games that involve chasing and being chased and caught.

Games in the same family use more or less the same organisation language.

Some games from the same family fit together to make a series, providing a natural sort of grading, for example, *What's this?* leads on to *Memory Game* and *Memory Game* on to *Bingo*.

Many children enjoy playing their own national games in English. Since children already know how to play these games, they need only learn the management and content language in English. It is also interesting to teach games played by children in other countries, taking the opportunity to tell the children a little about the other country. The game, *Up and down*, is a starting game from Pakistan, *Big and little* is from Thailand and *Ram, ram, rip* from Malaysia and Indonesia (Dunn 2000).

5.1.5 Starting, selecting or counting-out games

These types of games exist in many languages and are played by children in most continents. They

- are quick to organise and get a result (ie selecting a leader, someone to start a game or person responsible for a task)
- may need no equipment
- can be played anywhere, anytime
- are fun, useful for changing an atmosphere
- offer quick opportunities to have fun in English
- are easy to pick up and transfer to own play outside the classroom
- may, in the case of rhyme and alphabet games, give practice in saying English sounds.

(When playing some short rhyme counting-out games, smart children work out the number of counts and position themselves in the right place to win! If this happens teachers have to organise the circles themselves, before they begin counting out.)

1) Rhyme starting games

Counting between two people or round a circle. Point to a different child on each count. The last child counted wins or is out of the game and the game restarts.

Tom Tit
You are IT! (*5 counts*)

Ickle ockle
Black bottle
Ickle ockle OUT! (*7 counts*)

Red, white and blue.
All out but YOU! (*8 counts*)

Counting round the circle. One count usually to each word. The last counted is out and counting begins again from the next child. The remaining child wins.

Acker backer soda cracker,
Acker backer boo!
Acker backer soda cracker
Out goes YOU! (*14 counts*)

Inkey Pinkey Spider
Climbing up the spout.
One, two, three, four
And then you are OUT! (*16 counts*)

Eeny, meeny, miney, mo,
Catch a tiger by his toe,
When he roars, (ROAR) let him go,
Eeny, meeny, miney, MO! (*20 counts*)

Dip, dip, dip.
My blue ship,
Sailing on the water
Like a cup and saucer.
Dip, dip, dip
You're not IT! (*20 counts*)

2) Alphabet starting games

Counting between two people or counting round a circle; one count to each letter or word; the last child counted wins.

A E I O U   (5 counts: letter U equals 'you' and the selected person).
A B C D E F G H I J K L M N O P Q R S T U
You, you, you are it. (26 counts: *U You, you, you are it* – the last six
counts are said as you tap the same child).

3) Multicultural starting games

Ram, ram, rip (Indonesia/Malaysia)

> Ram, ram,
> RIP

One very young learner holds out the palm of their hand. Another two place their first fingers on the child's hand. This child then says *Ram, Ram*, and on *RIP* closes his hand quickly hoping to catch a finger. The child whose finger is caught is out and the other child wins. If both fingers are caught, the game is played again.

Big or little (Thailand)

One YL takes two pencils or pieces of wood of different lengths and clasps them in his fist so that the two protruding ends look the same length. He then asks *Which is big? Which is little?* The other player points to one and replies *This is big*. If he is correct the reply is *Yes. It's big.* with a show of the pencils. If he is wrong the reply is *No. It's little*. This game can be used for choosing between two children or two teams.

Up and down (Pakistan)

Three YLs hold hands and swing them in rhythm, counting to *five*. After they say five, they drop hands and place either their right hands with the palm facing down *This is facing down* or their left hands with the palm facing up *This is facing up*. If two players place their hands the same way and the third player places his hands differently, the player who placed his hands differently becomes the leader, *You are the leader*. If all three players place their hands the same way, the game is repeated. *Everyone is the same. Let's play again.*

5.1.6 Physical games

1) Where's the monkey?

Game

VYLs shut their eyes and count to 10, whilst the teacher hides the toy monkey, or some other soft toy, anywhere in the room and then shouts *ready*. They then open their eyes and the teacher says *Where's the monkey?* The children repeat *Where's the monkey?* and run to look for the monkey. The child who finds the monkey holds it up and says *Here's the monkey.*

The game begins again with the finder hiding the monkey.

Whilst children look the teacher can ask *Is the monkey on the chair? Is the monkey near the door?*

Development

Children can take it in turns to bring in one of their soft toys to hide.

Two toys can be hidden together and teacher asks *Where are the . . . and the . . . ?* The finder replies *Here they are.*

2) Listen and do

Game

The teacher chooses a VYL or YL and says *Stand up* and the child stands up. The teacher continues giving commands *Turn round, Touch the floor, Point to the door* until she says *Sit down*, which ends the turn. If the child makes a mistake and does not carry out an instruction correctly, he has to sit down straight away and the game begins again with another child.

Development

Instructions can be extended to *Jump three times/Hop twice/Clap four times*. Instructions can then be further extended to *Stand up quickly/Run to the door/Hop to the window/Come here slowly/Sit down*.

3) What are you doing now?

Game

One VYL stands in the middle of a circle. The teacher whispers to the child an instruction, for example *Laugh*. The other children walk round the circle saying

> What's he/she doing?
> What's he/she doing?
> What's he/she doing now?

whilst the child in the middle mimes the instruction. The child continues to mime whilst the teacher asks another child to guess what he is doing eg *sleeping*. If the guess is correct the child says *Yes. I'm sleeping* and the two exchange places. If the guess is incorrect *No, I'm not*, the game starts again with the same child in the middle. If children reply correctly in home language, reflect back in English and after they have tried to say it in English allow them to change places. *Yes, he's laughing. He's laughing. Well done. Now it's your turn. Stand in the middle*.

Development

The instructions are more complex: *Eat an ice cream. Play the piano. Ride a bicycle. Drive a car.*

4) Touch your nose

Preparation

Make self-portraits or puppets to make sure VYLs and YLs know the names of parts of the face.

Game

The teacher says *Touch your nose* and all the children touch their noses. The teacher continues *Touch your ear* and the children touch an ear. The game continues until the teacher says *Don't touch your mouth*. When the children hear *Don't* they freeze where they are and any child who makes a mistake and touches his mouth is out of the game. The game continues until all or nearly all the children are out.

Development

Once children know the parts of the face, introduce parts of the body. Then add plurals – two eyes, two ears, two feet etc.

Children can take over giving the instructions if they begin by sharing the role with the teacher.

5.1.7 Chasing games

1) How many teeth have you got Mr Bear?

Materials

A hand mirror for Mr Bear.

Preparation

Explain and mark the 'home' area.

Game

VYLs skip around Mr Bear, who is in the middle of the circle pretending to look into a mirror to count his teeth. As they skip they chant,

> How many teeth have you got, Mr Bear?
> How many teeth have you got?
> How many teeth have you got, Mr Bear?
> Can you tell me, please?

When Mr Bear replies *One tooth* he chases them and tries to catch them before they reach 'home'. If Mr Bear said any other number of teeth, for example, *10 teeth* he does not chase them and they have to repeat the chant. The first times the game is played, the teacher plays Mr Bear and mimes his actions but does not say *One tooth*. When she finally says *One tooth* she lets the children run 'home' without chasing them. The next time the teacher chases them and the child caught becomes Mr Bear. (NB Children at this age are interested in teeth as they are getting new front teeth and molar teeth.)

2) What's the time Mr Wolf?

Preparation
Make sure YLs know about clocks and hours.
Explain and mark Mr Wolf's 'house' and sheep's 'house' areas.

Game
Mr Wolf (the teacher takes this role for the first few times) stands in his 'house' at one end of the room behind a line. The children, who are the sheep, stand in their 'house' behind a line, at the other end of the room. The sheep ask Mr Wolf *What's the time, Mr Wolf?* and Mr Wolf replies *One o'clock*. The sheep walk a little closer to Mr Wolf and again ask the question. Mr Wolf replies *Two o'clock*. They again walk a little closer and ask. Mr Wolf replies *Three o'clock*. The game continues until Mr Wolf replies *Dinner time* and chases the sheep back to their 'house'. If he catches any before they reach their house, they stay at Mr Wolf's house for a turn.

Development
Once the children are familiar with the game, Mr Wolf can introduce other meal times like 'breakfast time', 'tea time', but Mr Wolf still chases only when he says '*dinner time*'.

3) Farmer, Farmer, can I cross the water?

Preparation
Explain and mark the river and two lines on either side of the river – the river banks, which are both safe areas.

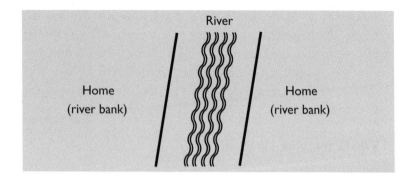

Game

VYLs or YLs ask *Farmer, Farmer, can I cross the water?* standing on one marked riverbank as they want to cross the river to the bank on the other side. The farmer standing in the middle of the river replies *Yes, if you have got something yellow.* Anyone with something yellow replies *Yes, I have got something yellow* (shows yellow clothing) and safely walks across the river. Anyone who has not got something of the right colour, races across the water trying not to be caught by the farmer before they get to safety on the other riverbank. Anyone caught has either to drop out or help the farmer. When the farmer has caught everyone, the game restarts. Each time the question is asked, the farmer selects a different colour. When everyone has been caught, the farmer then selects the next farmer and the game restarts. The teacher plays the farmer initially until children understand the game, which may take several lessons.

5.1.8 Board games

1) Snakes and Ladders

Materials

Board (see 5.5 for how to make the board), counters, dice.

Preparation

Make sure YLs can count to 16 and can read the numbers on a dice. Play a starting game to see who plays first. Teach the chant.

Up the ladder
And down the snake SSSSSSS

Game

Children select their colour counters *What colour counter do you want? Green, red or blue?*

Blue, please. *Here you are. Put them here, on 'Start.'*

Starting game already played to see who begins. *You begin. Throw the dice. How many? Let's count 1 2 3 4 5.*

Look, up the ladder. Well done.

Oh dear. SSSSSS! Down the snake – down, down, down.

All the counters are put on START. The first child throws the dice and counts the numbers on the dice. Although the winner is the first child to reach HOME, having jumped over each of the 32 squares, the way home is not straight nor easy, as a counter may land at the bottom of a ladder, which takes it up and nearer to HOME or it may be eaten by a snake *SSSSSS!*, which takes it down to end of the snake's tail. *Up the ladders and SSSSSS! down the snakes.*

Development

Once children know how to play make bigger boards with more numbers and include more snakes and more ladders.

Picture bingo

2) Materials

Board and picture cards (pictures for these are available in toy catalogues or on the Internet).

Figure 12 Bingo board and cards

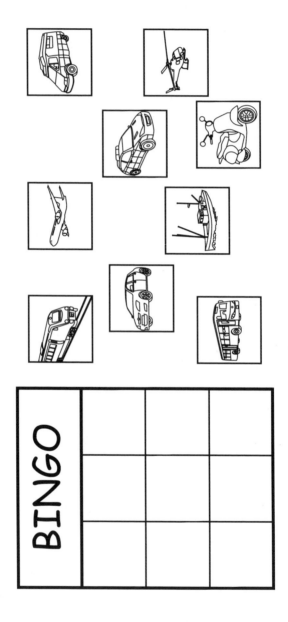

Preparation
Children should know the names of things on the picture cards.

Game
Give out the boards to YLs – individuals, pairs or groups, with six items of transport per board – a car, a bus, a train, an airplane, a tractor, a scooter, a boat, a bicycle, a taxi, a helicopter, an ambulance, a police car (NB call out the article plus noun). Initially the teacher is the caller and holds up a card and says an airplane. If a board has a picture of *an airplane* the children say *We've got it, an airplane. Give it to us, please.* If they say it correctly they get the card. The first to complete their board says *We've got them all. BINGO.* They win and can become the next callers.

Development
Once children know the vocabulary, introduce a new set of cards and boards with nine places on each board.

5.1.9 Card games

1) Snap
Preparation
VYLs and YLs make six hand-sized cards: 1, 2, 3, one dot, two dots, three dots.

Game
Two children or a small group play together round a table. Each child mixes up their cards and puts them face down in a pile in front of them. In turn each child picks up a card from their pile and as they place it face upwards in a pile in front of their other cards, they say what is written on the card. When there are two cards on top of the piles with the same number, the first child to shout out the word *SNAP* can pick up and keep the two piles of cards. The winner is the child with the most cards. When a child has no more cards they can watch and still call out *SNAP*, like this they continue to play and have not lost.

Figure 13 Snap cards

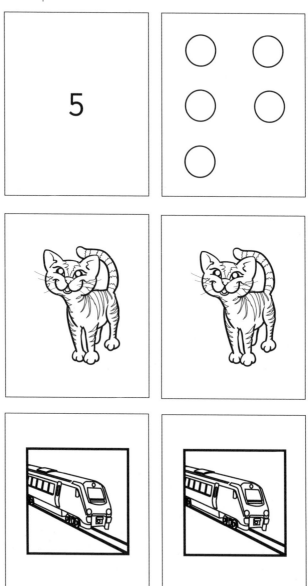

Development

Add more numbers gradually and fade out the cards with dots.

The same game can be played with animal cards (*a cat, a kangaroo, an elephant*), transport cards (*a tractor, an airplane, a bus etc.*).

2) How many?

Materials

Cards with numbers.

Preparation

VYLs and YLs should know number symbols 1, 2, 3.

Game

Fifteen cards (including five cards with number 1, five cards with number 2, and five cards with number 3 on one side) are placed number side down on a table. The teacher points to one card and says *How many?* looking at a child. The child guesses and replies – either *one, two* or *three*. The teacher turns over the card. If the child has guessed correctly, the teacher gives the card to the child. If the child guesses incorrectly, the teacher replaces the card. The teacher then asks another child and the game continues until all the cards have been picked up. The child with the most cards wins.

Development

Cards with numbers 4 and 5 are added, then cards with numbers 6, 7, 8, and finally 9, 10.

This type of game can also be played with picture cards of objects *What's this?*, where the reply should be *a book* not just *book*.

The same game can be played with colours and the question *What colour is it?*, where the reply is *Red, it's red*.

When children begin to read, words can be added to the cards and eventually cards with only words replace the picture cards. This game leads on to *Memory Game* or *Pairs* and also *Bingo*.

3) Picture memory game or Pairs

Materials

Twelve identical pairs of picture cards of transport.

Game

Place the 12 pairs of picture cards face downwards on a table. The first YL turns over a card and says *a bus* and then turns a second card. If the second card is the same, the child adds *and a bus, two buses* and keeps the two cards. If the card is different the child says *and a bicycle* and replaces both cards from where she took them.

The aim is to find two cards (a pair) with the same picture. When no more cards are left, each YL counts their pairs. *How many pairs have you got? I've got 5 pairs. And how many have you got? I've got 7. You have the most pairs. Well done.* Gradually new pairs are added.

Development

Change the theme of the cards, for example, to clothing (a pair of socks, two red T-shirts etc.). Before making the picture cards make a funny washing-line picture of the different items of clothing by cutting photos from magazines.

4) I went on safari

Materials

Twelve animal picture cards.

Preparation

Cut and paste photos from travel magazines to make a big safari picture. Talk about the names of all the animals. At the same time make 12 picture cards of single animals.

Game

Imagine all the YLs went on safari to Africa. Each YL in turn has to say *I went on safari and I saw* as they turn over a card and say what is on the card *an elephant.* They put the card, picture down, on another pile. The next player says *I went on safari and I saw an elephant and* turns a card and adds the name of the animal. Each player, in turn, adds the name of an animal. If they forget to say any of the animals in the list, they are out of the game. If the list grows to more than eight animals, the game begins again and anyone who is already out can rejoin it.

Development

When children know the names of the animals and how to play, add two more animal cards each time, so increasing the number of animal names they will know.

5.2 Language for games

When organising and managing games in the early stages, teachers need to rely heavily on prefabricated chunks of language and use them more frequently than they would in playing the same game for the first time in the child's L1. The first times a game is played, children are often tense as they are not sure what to expect. Some may not ever have played this type of formalised game. To make the experience comfortable and enjoyable teachers have to insert fun by dramatising and adding suspense. To help sustain interest the children need the teacher to give a running commentary.

Games include three types of language:

- organising language to get ready to play and tidy up after play
- management language for mediating and sustaining the game
- content language related to each game.

As simple games have the same basic beginning and ending and have to be sustained in a similar way, standard routines can be used for all games played in the early stages of learning English. For example, some card games involve giving out the cards, counting the cards individually at the end to find the winner and then collecting them to tidy up. During the game children need encouragement to sustain interest and enthusiasm. Once a type of game is familiar, it is easier and quicker to teach a second game of the same family.

Continual repetition of organisational and management language makes picking up English easier. Once children are familiar with many of the common organisational and management phrases, they are ready to concentrate more on the different content language of each game.

When children begin to use some of the organisational and management game language they are ready to share the teacher's role with the teacher and eventually take over the teacher's role. At this point the teacher should stay in the background for the first few times ready to guide with a few whispered instructions. Next the teacher takes the role of a player, interacting with the 'new teacher' and showing the children how to develop language, for example, by asking questions to stimulate replies like *How many? Is it your turn?* In this way children can understand the role both of the asker and the answerer and use it as a model on which to base their own interpersonal communication.

By this stage it is possible to build on known prefabricated language and introduce new language.

Checklist of language for starting a game

Stand here/Stand behind here.
The line is here/Stand behind this line.
This is home/Behind this line is home.
Make a circle/Join hands.
Sit down/Cross your legs.
Follow me/Do it like me./Copy me.
Give out the cards/Give one to everyone/Give two to everyone.
Have you got a board?
Are you ready?
Get into twos.

Let's start/You start.
Shut your eyes/Don't look.
Count to five/ten.
You're first /You're second.
You're last.
Look everyone/Do it like this.

Checklist of language for sustaining a game

My turn/Your turn/It's your turn.
Who's next?

He's next/She's next.
Look! Your card/It's your card.
Take a card /Take two cards.
Put the card on the board.
They are your cards/Take them.
Put them back/Put them back on the table.
Put them in a pile in front of you.
It's your turn again/Have another turn.
Again/Try again.
Show him/Show him what to do.

Checklist of language for ending a game

Stop/It's time to stop.
Have you finished?
Count the cards/One card, two cards etc.
How many cards have you got?
You're the winner.
Tidy up, please/Put the cards away/Put the things away.

5.3. Introducing new games

Here are some useful tips before introducing new games or reintroducing an old favourite.

- Check that children are familiar with most of the content language.
- Be ready to do most of the talking, pointing to confirm meaning, using *teacherese* language skills.
- If some children have not understood, let a child who has understood explain. (Young children love to be interpreters and teaching someone else helps confirm their own learning!)
- Each time you play use the same management language for:

---

starting the game *Are you ready? It's your turn, first, off you go.*

sustaining the game (keeping up the pace and interest) *Well done, Michel. Next time you may get a 6. Yes, that's right. Have another go.*

ending the game *Time to stop. Let's see who has the most. You are the winner. Never mind, next time you may win!*

5.4 Organising games

The first few times a game is played, the teacher organises the game and manages it totally using simplified *teacherese* to facilitate understanding and encourage children to take part in dialogue. Gradually the child's input increases in the one-to-one dialogue that take place with the teacher when it is the child's turn. Other children watch carefully as each child has a turn and YLs probably pick up language second-hand from the teacher's dialogue with another child.

Playing a game is exciting and some children in the group may try to say what they think or feel using incomplete phrases or single words *Me*

Figure 14 Introducing the game *How many?*

| Frequency of game | Organisational/Management language | | | Game language | Teacher's role | Child's role |
	Starting	Sustaining	Ending			
First time	Sit down Look (pointing to cards)	Yes No (shaking head)	Finished?	How many? one two three	All management and game language	(Listening) one two three
Second time	Sit down Are you ready? Look	Yes, good No	Finished? Count (pointing to cards) one two three etc.	How many? one two three four five	All management and game language	(Listening) one two three four five
Third time	Sit down Are you ready? Look Yes Your turn, John	Yes, good No Your turn next Quickly	Stop Finished? Count (pointing to cards) one two three four five etc.	How many? one --> ten	All management and game language	Yes one --> ten Counting cards in response to teacher's question 'How many?'
Fourth time	As above No new language Concentrating on building up interaction				Teacher plays child's role	A child plays teacher's role Other children as above

won (for *I've won*). These are not mistakes; these children have not yet acquired the language to say what they want. Teachers should encourage them *Yes, Marie's right* and then reflect back what they said in correct English, so they hear a role model, which they will hopefully imitate. *It's Lily's turn. Now, play Lily. It's your turn.* Taking part in a group dialogue needs to be encouraged, as apart from the use of language it also tells us more about the child and reveals the relationships between the children.

Children need to know exactly how to play a game; they need to know all the rules because children, especially boys, have a keen sense of justice. If boys perceive an injustice, they tend to feel picked on and lose trust. Sometimes a misunderstanding can arise where a child thinks he has won, but in actual fact he has broken the rules inadvertently and has been accused by the others of cheating. For this reason it is always better if the teacher plays first and whilst playing she shows and explains the rules. Some boys can be mischievous in the way they try to win; it is part of risk-taking, which they enjoy. If rule-breaking occurs, explain and show the rules again and give the child a second chance. To be accused of cheating when innocent can hurt a child so much that he can refuse to join in future games.

As children get used to playing a game, the speed of playing increases and it becomes more fun. It is then possible to extend the length of play. However, it is important to always stop play before children get tired as they then lose interest; the ideal time to stop is when the children still want another turn.

Games need to be fun. Teachers will often find that, apart from sustaining interest in a game, they will also have to add some fun by:

- a well-timed hesitation
- a surprise
- playing a card slowly
- making a guess
- changing the tone of voice to be mysterious
- playing the wrong card on purpose to raise a laugh.

Teachers may also find that, where a game is a bit slow, they have to speed it up by temporarily intervening. If games get a bit too noisy, teachers can encourage children to think of other people and use loud whispers. If this does not work, it may be best to move outside to the playground or stop the game explaining *We can play again tomorrow.*

Some young children do not want to participate in games, especially in chasing games. It is better not to insist, but to let them watch or help the teacher until they feel ready to join in. This may take time and encouragement.

Discipline troubles generally arise when a child does not understand the game and cannot participate fully. In these cases, it is a good idea for the teacher to play in partnership with the child for one or two turns. If this is impossible, a child who is good at the game can be asked to help.

In some games children have to drop out – for example, after being caught. There should be some special place in the classroom where children know they should stand and wait, watching the game until it is finished. Children appear to learn whilst watching. Although most children like watching, some become restless. These children can go back to their places and get on with finishing some work until the game is over. It is important that they have something definite to do otherwise discipline problems can arise.

If some children are not getting sufficient opportunity to use English even though they have a turn, teachers can stimulate the use of English by asking children a few questions during the game, for example *How many cards have you got? Is it your turn next? Who is next?*

Where classes are large, children can work in pairs or in small groups rather than as individuals. An alternative in large classes is for one group to help the teacher whilst the other groups play. In most of the games described, a pair or group can be substituted for the individual.

The first time a game of a specific family, for example a card game, is introduced, teachers may find it necessary to repeat how to play it in school language (SL). However, once one game of a family has been played, it is usually no longer necessary to use SL when introducing another game of the same family, as most YLs will use their personal gist understanding skills to decode how the game is played.

Many teachers find it better to introduce a game to children by starting to play it and explaining the rules during the game as the situation arises. At the end of the game the teacher can then explain that it was only a 'trial' and that now they are going to start playing properly. To explain all the rules of a game at the beginning without concrete examples is often too confusing for young children.

5.5 Collecting, adapting and making games

Teachers will find it a good idea to keep their own record book of suitable games. Many games are too advanced linguistically for young children, but with some adaptation can be made suitable. The most effective games are often those made by a teacher or where the content is adapted to fit the needs and local conditions of the children she teaches. Some teachers are hesitant to make their own games because they think their skills are not sufficiently good. Today there is artwork available on the Internet and plenty of coloured artwork and photographs to cut out in magazines.

Making your own boards and cards for games is a meaningful and developmental activity for YLs. It also means that teachers can control the language, making sure it matches children's learning needs. As English ability increases, cards and boards can be changed to meet the increasing ability. Teachers may find they have to help children more than usual with the handiwork side of the activity, as children's attention span is limited. It is important to remember that the main aim in the English lesson is language development not handiwork skills. Young children get great satisfaction from seeing that what they have made can be used by adults and especially family members. Some even repeat the same activity at home.

Making things to play games with can be meaningful and satisfying and contributes to developing positive attitudes to learning English! 'Home-made' games also provide a bridge to commercially published editions of the same games, which are usually more difficult as the language content is not structured.

Snakes and Ladders: how to make your own board

Fold a piece of A4 lengthways in half, and in half again to make four lines. Then fold the other way in half, and in half again to make a total of 16 squares. Lay flat with the large side towards you and label the first square 'Start' and continue numbering 1, 2, 3 to the end of the line. Then begin the second line, numbering above the 4, 5, 6, 7 to the end of the line. On the line above 7, start 8 and continue to 11. On the last line, above 11 begin with 12 up to 14 and mark the last square 'Home'.

From square 4 to 11 draw one ladder, and from square 9 to square 13 a second ladder.

From square 7 draw one snake with an open mouth wriggling down to square 1, from square 12 draw a snake wriggling down to square 10 (See Figure 15 for an example).

Development
Make larger boards with 32 squares and include more ladders and snakes.

> *Don't tell your kids that they are smart. More than three decades of research shows that a focus on effort – not on intelligence or ability – is key to success in school and in life*
> Dr Carol S. Dweck

Figure 15 Simple *Snakes and Ladders* board

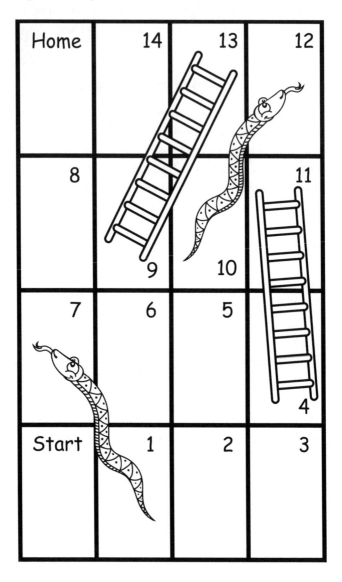

6

Verbal play – rhymes, songs, chants, tongue-twisters, riddles and puns

6.1 Playing with language

A central concern of teachers should be to find ways of unlocking children's linguistic potential: stimulating a wider extension of active vocabulary resources and supporting more complex language performance.

(Whitehead 2002)

6.1.1 Child-led play with language

Most very young and young children seem to initiate their own play using the sounds of the language they are learning. They have been doing this since they tried out their first babbles before they were one year old. As they begin to use words and short phrases, they can be heard playing with doubling word sounds they hear in stories – *Silly-Billy, rat-a-tat-tat, Henny-Penny*; or in rhymes – *Diddle, Diddle, Dumpling*; or experimenting by making up their own, like *willy-wally*. Sometimes such doubled words are friendly, sometimes they are poking fun, but are all easily picked up and remembered.

To pick up, play and have fun with language appears to be innate to children in most cultures, as is child-led play with language, either individually or in groups. Most children seem also to have an innate facility to pick up rhymes from interaction with caring adults and, from an early age, get joy and motivation from 'showing off' their ability to recite nursery rhymes to adoring adults. Later, around 7 and 8 years old, young children can be heard in the playground repeating game rhymes, jokes and tongue-twisters amongst peers without any adult suggestion or intervention.

Playing with language (verbal play) in the form of simple rhymes, jokes, tongue-twisters, chants and riddles, is common to English traditional and even contemporary culture, but not sufficiently included in acquiring-English programmes for very young and young children. This may be because many non-native-speaker teachers are not aware of English-speaking children's store of these fun, easy-to-pick-up language games (which are sometimes a little subversive or mischievous or involve risk-taking).

Verbal play can be an added bonus in building up oral skills; language games are portable, can fill odd minutes, change an atmosphere and inject fun – often the type of fun appreciated by boys. Once children realise they can play language games in English, they are quick to transfer their LI skills and have fun playing with simple language. Verbal games are quickly absorbed and often remain in adults' minds when taught 'textbook' phrases can no longer be recalled. Ask any English person for a *Knock, knock, Who's there?* joke. They will probably laugh and tell you one or two! This form of joke also exists in other languages, like French, Japanese and German.

6.1.2 Language values of verbal play

Verbal play in general consists of:

- a complete structure with a beginning and end, making prediction possible
- chunks of prefabricated language
- repetition of prefabricated patterns (language) plus added known words
- a satisfying rhythm and melody (intonation)
- short, but understood meaning
- focus on the sounds of English as in tongue-twisters
- an opportunity to work out (unconsciously) the mechanics of English (grammar rules)
- learning fun rather than instruction
- consolidation through play (repetition), cultivating a 'love of language'.

6.2 Rhymes

Typical English rhymes learned by very young and young children are the equivalent of adults' short stories, as within the short text they form a complete piece of meaning. They include some traditional nursery or Mother Goose rhymes as well as more modern rhymes and rhyme games. However, rhymes need to be carefully selected for young beginners as some traditional rhymes (for example, *Solomon Grundy*) are part of English culture but include language that is difficult to transfer in the classroom and cultural concepts which are not sensitive to multicultural beliefs.

Young children pick up rhymes easily and quickly and they appear to enjoy learning them and reciting them, often over and over again. When young beginners recite a complete rhyme, they feel that they can 'speak a lot of English quickly like an adult', a challenge many long to achieve. Rhymes are portable play experiences; once learned, they are easy to browse or reflect on, as children can and do repeat them aloud to themselves anywhere, anytime.

Rhymes consist of prefabricated language. If rhymes are specially selected, they can be used to introduce new language or consolidate language already introduced in the classroom.

6.2.1 Selecting rhymes

If rhymes are to be easily acquired they need to:

- be short with a snappy rhythm and some repetition or a refrain
- be easy to pick up
- include useful language for transfer (recycling)
- contain a complete story/piece of meaning with a beginning and end
- be culturally understandable and acceptable.

Rhymes are an added bonus in language learning. Although they should be integrated in a lesson plan, since they can be learned quickly they can be included in addition to a syllabus. They are a quick way of giving children a complete text (a story) from the very first lessons, when children are impatient to learn and get results. Isolated items of language (phrases and words), especially if not linked to activities, are often much more difficult for young beginners to understand, use or remember.

Rhymes introduce children naturally and effectively to:

- English sounds
- rhyming words/sounds
- stress

- intonation patterns (rhythms)
- prefabricated phrases useful for transfer
- new vocabulary
- different genres of English usage.

Very young children's sensitivity to language is referred to as *early phonological awareness* by Bryant, Bradley et al. (1989). Phonological patterns can be heard in alliteration when words all beginning with the same sounds are repeated: *A beautiful, big, brown butterfly.* Similar sounding endings are also referred to as rhyme (rime) and it is the ending that children generally join in with first, followed by the initial sounds of words (onset) at the beginning of a rhyme. **Children with an interest in the sounds and poetry of language may well be on the road to reading, writing and spelling successfully** (Whitehead 2002).

6.2.2 Rhyme Time

It is useful to include a Rhyme Time as part of a Circle Time at the beginning of every lesson when children are sitting on a mat in a circle. Children soon understand what to expect in a Rhyme Time and can predict the activity, which gives them confidence.

Rhyme Times also provide a warm-up time or transition that helps children switch to using and thinking in English. This is especially necessary when there is no separate English classroom and/or English is led by the non-native-English-speaker classroom teacher, who herself has to switch in order to use English (see 1.2.9).

Rhyme Time can begin by running through one or two familiar rhymes or even a rhyme game. After this 'warming up' period children are ready to move on to new and unfamiliar language. Some classes of very young children begin singing or saying *Hello everyone* as they make their way to sit down for Rhyme Time:

Hello everyone,
Hello everyone
Hello everyone
It's time to say Hello. *(Tune Goodnight ladies)*.

At the end of the lesson the rhyme changes to:

Goodbye everyone,
Goodbye everyone,
Goodbye everyone
It's time to say Goodbye.

This can also be sung as:

Tidy up everyone,
Tidy up everyone,
Tidy up everyone,
It's time to tidy up.

Language learned in a rhyme can often be transferred to other situations in the classroom. In the last line of the above rhyme, the phrase *It's time to* can be transferred to add on to prefabricated phrases like *It's time to sit down, It's time to go outside, It's time to have a snack, It's time to play a game.*

Different classes of beginners have been able to remember the actions for all of the following rhyme when it is repeated at the end of the first lesson, having initially heard it repeated three times. Of course some children might already know the numbers one, two, three. However, even for those who knew the numbers, the feeling of success and motivation was not reduced!

> **Look *at* me.** *(teacher pointing to herself).*
> **Clap, clap, clap.** *(teacher claps three times).*
> **One, two, three.** *(children follow teacher holding up one, then two, then three fingers).*
> **Clap *like* me.** *(everyone claps their hands together three times).*

In the next lesson, after repeating the rhyme twice, together with the teacher, many children were able to say the complete rhyme in twos, in groups or by themselves. Learning is undoubtedly helped if the new rhyme is repeated again once or twice, in chorus with the children, when they come together at the end of the lesson, just before saying goodbye.

Many teachers find that, except for very gifted children, who often learn complete rhymes straight away, most children learn only certain words of a new rhyme in the first lesson. These are generally information words. As young children get more practice in learning rhymes, they appear to be able to learn new words more quickly as long as the presentation engages them. Without concentration it is impossible: watch actors – if they lose concentration, they are lost!

6.2.3 Organising Rhyme Times

Rhyme Time may be part of a Circle Time (see 3.1.2) at the beginning of a lesson; where older children no longer need a regular Circle Time it can be organised as a separate activity. To plan Rhyme Times, it is easier for organisation if each rhyme has a title.

Although teachers need to be flexible adapting to young children's mood as they settle into an English lesson, children like to follow the same Rhyme Time routine, which they know and which older children can eventually lead themselves.

Rhyme Time routine

- Warm up by repeating one or two familiar rhymes (each rhyme repeated twice by children, led by teacher).
- Introduce a new rhyme (or last time's new rhyme) once children have warmed up:
  - explain, supported by actions, realia or picture
  - teacher repeats again
  - teacher leads, children join in with actions.
  - end Rhyme Time by repeating a well-known favourite rhyme, rhymes or rhyme game.
- Next Rhyme Time, reintroduce the new rhyme and let children who seem ready join in with the actions or say some words or phrases.
- Future Rhyme Times build up children's ability, step-by-step, to say the new rhyme by encouraging them to add:
  - the final word to a line
  - then the final phrase
  - then a line
  - then another line, until most children can say the complete simple rhyme with a little prompting.

Children who know a whole rhyme need an opportunity to recite in pairs or small groups to the rest of the class. This gives them a chance to show off their skills as well as providing a role model for other children.

Some teachers build up Rhyme Time favourites to make a type of choral Rhyme Concert as a short performance for parents at the end of class or on some other occasion. A Rhyme Time performance requires very little organisation as it is part of an English lesson, but provides parents and children with a visual record of what the children have learned and the progress they have made. These Rhyme Concerts can be developed throughout young children's learning from the first very simple concerts to concerts with programmes or accompanying rhyme books.

Teachers who are uncertain of their own pronunciation when saying rhymes can record material from YouTube, British Council websites or ask native-speaker adults to make recordings. However, the results are better if a teacher, after working with recordings if necessary, teaches the children the rhymes herself, as personal interaction and relationships are very important in learning.

Once children have learned the rhyme with the teacher, children can listen to the recording themselves. They are often self-critical and soon try to refine their own pronunciation to match the recorded model if possible themselves, recording and listening several times until they are satisfied. Young children seem to be fascinated by making their own recordings and have an inner drive to self-correct. With new technology there are different ways of making this type of audible documentation, which is valuable for the teacher, learner and parents (see 3.6).

6.2.4 Collecting rhymes and rhyme books

In most cases there are only a few English rhymes that fit very young and young beginners in each published book or on individual Internet sites. Teachers are recommended to collect rhymes, traditional and new, from books and websites to gradually build up their own collection of rhymes that they enjoy, think are useful and feel comfortable presenting to young beginners.

6.2.5 Rhyme cards

In the early stages of learning it is fun to make rhyme cards of rhymes presented in Rhyme Time. Write out or print out the rhyme on a card (A4/5 size) and let all or some children add an illustration (See Figure 16 for an example.) Store them in the English Corner so that, in their own time, children can take one out and look at it as they say the rhyme aloud to themselves. This is a form of browsing. If a child cannot read yet, they may identify the rhyme from the illustration and possibly recognise a few words. This self-initiated activity contributes to children working out by themselves how to read in English.

Figure 16 A rhyme card

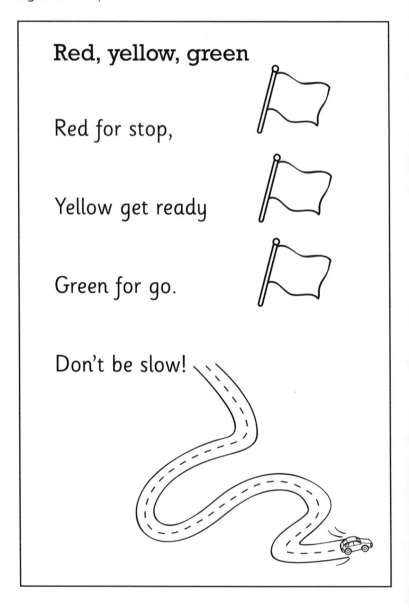

6.2.6 Rhyme books

When a child has made five or six rhyme cards, photocopy them to make a book of rhymes. For a child it is often special to own a book of rhymes that he can recite. A book is easier to carry around than a set of A4/5 cards, especially as a child may want to take the rhymes they know home – a form of visible documentation and portable browsing.

6.2.7 Learning to read through rhymes

If children have watched the teacher point to the words as she reads and if they can recognise some of the letters of the alphabet, they often work out by themselves how to read the rhymes they can recite.

Children need some information on the shapes of the standard forms of the alphabet – small and capital letters – as this will be the reference for comparison necessary for later decoding. Without a solid knowledge of the *standard alphabet shapes* decoding takes longer and can be frustrating and so demotivating.

Many teachers find it easier to introduce the small letters first and only introduce capitals once children can recognise the small letters with confidence. Young learners begin by recognising individual words from the first letter of the word. They continue to recognise the more important (stressed) words and then finally the small linking words. Children who do not manage to do this by themselves can be helped later when they show signs to be ready to read rhymes they know by heart. Reading rhymes that young learners can recite is an important first step in the reading journey. The same type of reading occurs in reading picture books with short texts that children have memorised.

Some rhymes for VYL and YL

1 Red, yellow, green

Red for stop,
Yellow get ready,
Green for go.
Don't be slow!

(Make card circles of the three colours and give them out to three different children before you say the rhyme. As you say the colour name they hold up the appropriate card. Before you say it a second time let the children give the cards to three other children. At the end of the rhyme collect in the cards saying *Give me red. Give me yellow. Give me green.*)

2 One, two, three, four

One, two, three, four   *(everyone counts)*
Can you jump   *(one child/team asks)*
On the floor?
Yes, I can.   *(one child/team replies and demonstrates)*
One, two, three, four.   *(everyone counts)*

(Children can be divided into two groups, one asking the other answering. The activity can change to *skip, hop, stamp*).

3 **Two, four, six, eight**

Two, four, six, eight,   *(counting and showing fingers*
                                        leaving out thumbs)

Hurry up it's getting late. *(clapping)*

4 **Three, five, seven, nine**

Three, five, seven, nine,
How are you doing?
I'm just fine.

(In pairs, counting, showing fingers then one asking, the other answering.)

5 **Easy peasy**

Easy peasy,
Lemon squeezy,
I can do it,
Look it's easy.

6 **What are you doing?**

What are you doing?
What are you doing now?
Can you tell me, please?   *(one child is asked to guess)*
You are dancing.
Yes I'm dancing.

(One child in the middle acting, dancing or eating, drinking etc. The child
who guesses the right answer can be in the middle next time.)

7   Have you seen the bear?

Have you seen the bear?
Anywhere here,
Anywhere there?
Where's the bear?
I've looked everywhere.

(A small bear is hidden and as a few children look for it, the rest say the rhyme. The child who finds the bear says *The bear is there* pointing and as the child picks the bear up and holds it she says *The bear is here.*)

8   All the monkeys in the zoo

All the monkeys in the zoo,
Had their tails painted blue.
One, two, three,
OUT goes YOU.   *(18 counts)*

(A starting, selecting or counting-out rhyme (see Chapter 5). Count round to select a child – one word equals one count. Children can make pretend tails by placing one arm behind them and waggling it.)

9   10 fingers

1, 2, 3, 4, 5, 6, 7, 8, 9, 10 *(count to 10 holding up the fingers one by one)*

Ten fingers,
Ten toes,
Two eyes,
And one nose.

(Show fingers and point to the other parts of the body. Later draw outlines for the face for self-portraits or make puppet faces as in Figure 9.)

10 It's raining

It's raining on the blue roof,
It's raining on the tree,
It's raining on the sunflower,
But it isn't on me.

It's raining on the big ship,
It's raining on the sea,
It's raining on the whale's back,
But it isn't on me.

It's raining on the butterfly,
It's raining on the bee,
It's raining on the blackbird,
But it isn't on me.

(As you say the rhyme pass a child's umbrella from child to child.)

11 I am walking through the jungle (see 8.2)

I am walking through the jungle
What can I see?
I can see a snake
Looking at me. Sssssss.
Walking through the jungle
What can I see?   (pretend to look through a telescope)
I can see a tiger
Looking at me. Roarrrrrrrr.

(Add animal noises. Later let individual children select the animal they
can see.)

12   Ice cream

I scream,   *(one child screams **ice cream**)*
You scream,   *(three children scream **ice cream**)*
We all scream   *(everyone screams **ice cream**)*
For ice cream.

13   Jelly on a plate

Jelly on a plate,
Jelly on a plate,
Wibble wobble,   *(children move to wibble, wobble)*
Wibble wobble,
Jelly on a plate.

14   What am I now?

What am I now?
Sometimes I'm very, very small,   *(children crouch down)*
Sometimes I'm very, very tall.   *(stretch up high)*
Shut your eyes and turn around
And guess what I am now.

(One child shuts their eyes whilst everyone says the rhyme. The child hiding eyes calls out a name and says either *Tall* or *Small*.)

15   Sippity sup

Sippity sup, sippity sup,   *(pretend to drink)*
Bread and milk from a china cup.
Sippity sup, sippity sup,
Sippity, sippity sup.

16 Porridge

Porridge is bubbling
Bubbling hot.
Stir it round   *(stirring round)*
And round in the pot.
The bubbles PLIP
The bubbles PLOP
It's ready to eat   *(eating)*
All bubbling hot.

(Change *porridge* for some other food known by the children eg *My soup*.)

17 Any more?

1 cookie,
2 cookies,
3 cookies,
4.
5 cookies,
6 cookies,
7 cookies,
Any more?

(Change the object counted and if possible say the rhyme with realia as you give out cookies, sweets or even pencils.)

18   Diddle, Diddle, Dumpling

Diddle, diddle, dumpling,
My son John
He bought a cake
Big and long.   *(mime big and long)*
He bit it once,   *(mime one bite)*
He bit it twice   *(mime another bite)*
And do you know
It was full of MICE!

(Divide into two groups. Group One says lines 1/2 and 5/6 and Group Two says lines 3/4 and 7/8. Before you say the rhyme secretly pick about five children to pretend to be the mice and run away and hide. As they run say:

One mouse, two mice

Look, one mouse, two mice
Three mice, four.
Can you see them running?
They're there on the floor.
They're there by the door.)

Rhymes for YL

1 Two and two

Two and two are four,	*(hold up two fingers from each hand and bring together.)*
Four and four are eight,	*(hold up four fingers from each hand and bring together.)*
Eight and eight are sixteen	*(as above then shut fingers and repeat to show eight more)*
Add eight more	*(as above then shut fingers and repeat to show eight more)*
Makes twenty-four.	

2 1, 2, skip a few

1, 2, skip a few,
99 a hundred.

(Make cards for one, two, 99. Later let children make their own three cards and challenge someone else to read them as they say the rhyme.)

3 Left, right

Left, right, left, right,	*(make actions on the spot or march round the room)*

Left, right, left, right,
Marching down the street.
Left right, left, right,
Who will you meet?

(Take turns to reply *I'll meet my Grandma/Dad/friend/you!*)

4 Can you sing?

A man said to me
'Can you sing?'
I said, 'Sing?'
He said, 'Yes.'
I said, 'Who?'
He said, 'You.'
I said, 'Me?'
He said, 'Yes.'
I said, 'When?'
He said, 'Now.'
I said, 'Now?'
He said, 'Yes.'
I said, 'NO.'
He said, 'Oh.'

(The whole class is the story narrator, individual children take the parts of *I* and *He. He* can be changed to *She* or *They.*)

5 Once I caught a fish alive

One, two three, four, five,
Once I caught a fish alive.
Six, seven, eight, nine, ten,
Don't think I'll do that again!

(Said by whole class except for lines two and four, which should be said by individual children.)

216

6 What do you think?

What do you suppose?
A bee sat on my nose.   *(mime)*
Buzz Buzz
Then what do you think?
He gave me a wink   *(show children how to wink)*
And said, 'I beg your pardon,
I thought you were the garden.'

(This story can be acted as a dialogue between the child and a bee. *I beg your pardon* teaches children a very polite adult way to say *Excuse me*. Some children like to cut out their own bee, which they can place on their nose.)

7 Algy

Algy met a bear,
A bear met Algy:
The bear grew bulgy;
The bulge was Algy.

(Fun to illustrate in comic style with two or more pictures. Children have their own ideas of before and after the meeting of Algy and the bear.)

8 Fuzzy-Wuzzy

Fuzzy-Wuzzy was a bear,
Fuzzy Wuzzy had no hair.
If Fuzzy Wuzzy had no hair then
Fuzzy Wuzzy wasn't fuzzy, was he?

(Divide into two groups; Group One: line 1; Group Two: line 2; both groups: lines 3 and 4.)

9 Little Tee-Wee

Little Tee-Wee
He went to sea,
In an open boat;
And while afloat
The little boat bended.
My story's ended.

(This is a good story to illustrate in four pictures in book form, writing in the words but leaving the child to decide how the story ended.)

10 A whale

If you ever, ever, ever, ever, ever,
If you ever, ever, ever meet a whale.
You must never, never, never, never, never,
You must never, never, never touch its tail;
For if you ever, ever, ever, ever, ever,
If you ever, ever, ever touch its tail,
You will never, never, never, never, never,
You will never, never, never meet another whale.

(Before introducing this discuss whales especially blue whales and how to distinguish them from fish. It is fun to have a child count the *nevers* and *evers* and check that as you say the rhyme you include the correct number.)

11 Fire! Fire!

'Fire, Fire,' said Mrs Dyer.
'Where? Where?' said Mrs Dare.
'Down the town,' said Mrs Brown.
'Any damage?' said Mrs Gamage.
'None at all,' said Mrs Hall.

(The class do the narration (*said Mrs …*) and five children take the role of the women. In a mixed class the names can be changed from *Mrs* to *Mr* for the boys.)

12 You do it

I do it,
You do it,
He does it
And she does it.
We all do it
Just like they do it.
So why don't you do it
Like I do it – NOW?

(The teacher is the role model conducting this rhyme, which is good for choral speaking. She points to children as she says it and expects them to show the action eg waving, clapping, whistling etc. Once the children have got the idea, one of them can take over being the 'conductor'.)

13 The sneeze

Sneeze on Monday, sneeze for danger,
Sneeze on Tuesday, kiss a stranger,
Sneeze on Wednesday, get a letter,
Sneeze on Thursday, something better,
Sneeze on Friday, sneeze for sorrow,
Sneeze on Saturday, joy tomorrow.

(Divide into two groups, first group say *Sneeze on Monday* and the other group finishes the line. One child is selected to surprise sneeze anywhere in the middle or end of the rhyme to add fun: *Oh dear. You sneezed on Wednesday. You are going to get a letter.*)

14 Double, double

Double, double	*(two fists banged together twice – single child)*
This, this.	*(right palms clapped twice – pair of children)*
Double, double	*(two fists banged together twice – single child)*
That, that.	*(left back of hands clapped twice – pair)*
Double, this	*(two fists banged together once – single; right palm clapped once – pair)*
Double, that	*(as above but with left back of hands)*
Double, double	*(two fists banged together twice – single child)*
This, that.	*(right hands clapped, left palms clapped – pair)*

(A clapping rhyme to be played in pairs facing each other. The palm is nearer and so it = *this*, the back of the hand shows distance = *that*. The aim is to complete without a fault and develop speed.)

6.3 Songs

6.3.1 Supportive recordings

For teachers who are not confident of their singing ability, there is a wealth of supportive recorded material on the Internet including traditional songs and suitable modern songs with which many young parents may be familiar. A few songs or singing games can be included in Rhyme Time.

As in the choice of rhymes, songs and singing games should be selected for their suitable language content. Traditional songs with difficult language and vocabulary or complicated music are best left until later.

Recent research at Auckland University, New Zealand, pointed out that there are huge differences between sung and spoken pronunciation in some words of songs in some Englishes. Songs that distort intonation patterns or pronunciation are best avoided at this early stage of learning. It should be remembered that it is more difficult for children to transfer and use language from songs than from rhymes, as they have first to put the language into spoken form and then transfer it. To help children over this difficulty, it is a good idea to sometimes 'say' songs instead of singing them as most songs for young children can be said or sung as rhymes, for example *Twinkle, Twinkle Little Star or Incy Wincy Spider*.

Some teachers set their own words to well-known songs, which makes learning the words easier as the children already know the music.

Teachers can introduce new songs in English lessons either when they introduce new language or linked to an activity. In this way children gradually build up a selection of songs they can sing in lessons or in a sing-along to a CD-ROM or iPod/MP3 or website. Karaoke can be great fun!

Many traditional songs can be adapted to fit different activities and circumstances in the classroom. Adapting is fairly easy to do once children know the tune. For example *If you are happy and you know it* can be changed to *If you are hungry and you know it, eat an apple* or *if you are dirty and you know it, wash your hands*. Adaptations like these can add some fun.

In English lessons, try to include some traditional and some new songs:

- with or without actions
- with props
- with a teaching aim eg the *Alphabet song.*

Include some adult songs with easy words that you enjoy (eg the Beatles' chorus to *Yellow Submarine*), which most parents know and with which they usually will happily join in. In all cases, select songs that you feel confident singing together, as children can be critical.

6.3.2 Alphabet song

The *Alphabet song* can be sung to the tune of *Twinkle, Twinkle Little Star* (see Chapter 4 for music).

Alphabet song game

Make cards for the 26 capital letters and 26 small letters.

Before you sing, put the small letter cards, written side upwards, on the table. Sing the song once and then, the second time, as you all sing a letter, ask one child to pick up the matching small letter card. Later do the same for the capital letters and finally both capital and small together. Then sing the song again asking the children to put the cards in a line as you all sing the letter name. This is a fun way to include more repetition.

Figure 17 Alphabet cards

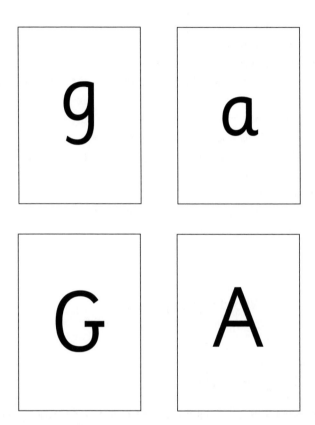

6.4 Chants

Some English families use chants naturally within the running commentaries they keep up with their young families. The chants may be phrases transferred from songs eg *Time to tidy, time to tidy up* or *5 minutes to go, 4 minutes to go* etc. Personalising or making up a chant is more effective and closer to very young and most young beginners' language needs and understanding than many prefabricated chants suggested in books to practise a specific language item. Although a prefabricated chant is close to a rhyme, at this young beginners' stage, rhymes and jokes, which are short stories and thus a complete piece of meaning, appear to be easier to pick up and use.

Many native-speaker adults have grown up knowing this chant, which can be turned into a simple game.

> ## 2 – 4 – 6 – 8
> ## Who do you appreciate?
> *(break into syllables – a/ppre/ci/ate)*

6.5 Tongue-twisters

A tongue-twister is a difficult-to-say phrase or group of words consisting of alliteration or a sequence of nearly similar sounds such as *thin sticks, thick bricks*. The book *Fox in Socks* by Dr Seuss consists of rhyming tongue-twisters. Saying a tongue-twister is a form of language play that in some ways is like a continuation of a baby's babbling. The aim is to say the tongue-twister correctly, faster and faster, either by yourself, in pairs or in a group. To become skilled entails practice in verbal gymnastics. Once achieved, the skills seem to remain for life: many adults enjoy saying tongue-twisters with children, in this way showing off their verbal skills. Such tongue-twisters exist in many cultures.

1) Tongue-twisters for VYLs

Some tongue-twisters can become *in-class language*, for example, if someone is making too much noise the teacher can say '*Sasha, you are Mr Walker. Mr Walker is a Talker!*' or '*Snap, crackle, pop, what have you got? Tell me, please*' when a child brings something new to school.

When introducing tongue-twisters to make understanding easier, it is better if you can back them up with mime or realia.

Busy buzzing bumble bee

Mr Walker is a talker but Mrs Walker isn't a talker.

Three free flies

Fee fi fo fum. Tell me quickly where you're from?

(answer: name of the town or country)

Two tiny tigers take taxis to town.

She threw three balls. Can you catch three balls?

Snap, crackle, pop, what have you got?

Lovely lollipops to lick
Lucy likes red lollipops
Lovely round lollipops
Do you like lovely round lollipops? Yes, I do.

(change the colour and repeat)

2) Tongue-twisters for YLs

Plain bun, plum bun, bun with a plum

Three free throws

Flies fly but one fly flies

A real, rare whale

A sailor went to sea and all that he could see, was sea, sea, sea (difference in meaning of sea/see)

Fresh French fries first, please

Round and round the rugged rock, the ragged rascal ran.

6.6 Riddles and puns

Around the ages of 6, 7 and 8 years, children, especially boys, who sometimes enjoy subverting situations a little, become interested in asking adults and older children riddles. Riddles and puns are both verbal games and have been found in literature since Greek and Roman times.

Riddles and puns are closely related. Riddles are a complete story, a verbal trick and part of a ritual of storytelling. Riddles sometimes include a pun. A pun is a deliberate form of word play; many may exploit the fact that a word or phrase has the same sound (*homophonic*) – *a rose* (flower) and *he rose up* (verb) – or two different words have the same pronunciation, but different spelling and meanings (*homographic*) – *sun and son*.

Children love the fun of riddles, they absorb them as prefabricated phrases and enjoy the ritual of asking them to willing listeners. Later, when children can read, it is a good idea to reintroduce both riddles and puns in written form to make a 'joke' book. These are a few selected examples. Try to collect other suitable riddles and puns from L1 English adults.

1) Riddles for YLs

What goes up when the rain comes down? *An umbrella.*

What do cats like to eat? *Mice-cream* (not ice-cream!).

What do you call a sleepy dinosaur? *A dino-snore* (Do you snore when you are asleep?)

What animal goes OOOOOO? *A cow with no lips who can't make the letter m.* (Cows say moo.)

What's a dog's favourite colour? *Grrrreeen* (a growl).

What did the banana say when the elephant stepped on it? *Nothing, bananas can't talk!*

What do snakes use to cut paper? *Sssscissssors* (scissors).

What is a snail? *A monster with a crash helmet.*

What dog smells of onions? *A hot dog.*

What do you call a man with bananas in both ears? *Anything you like. He can't hear you!*

Why is there's a fly in my soup? *Oh dear, the spider's on holiday.* (Spiders like to catch flies in their webs.)

Why do old beekeepers never die? *They just buzz off.* (Buzz off = go away, a bee says *buzz*.)

2) Knock-knock jokes

These are some of the best-known jokes that involve a punning response or the misuse of a word or phrase. The same ritual of this kind of joke exists in other cultures: *toc toc* in French and *kon kon* in Japanese.

Knock, knock,
Who's there?
Amos.
Amos who?
A mosquito just bit you *(pretend to bite by pinching the skin on the arm or leg)*. Ow!

Knock, knock,
Who's there?
Plato.
Plato who?
A plato' French fries. (*A plate of French fries.*)

Knock, knock,
Who's there?
Red. *(colour)*
Red who?
Redanygoodbooks lately? (*Red has the same pronunciation as read a book [past]*)

Knock, knock,
Who's there?
Ken.
Ken who?
KenIcome in? It's raining. *(Can I come in?)*

Knock, knock
Who's there?
Boo.
Boo who? *(Boohoo = crying)*
Why are you crying?

By showing children that we value their learning processes, we help them to reach confidently for the opportunities to learn.

Nancy Stewart

7

Introducing picture books

Reading a picture book at any age should be a pleasurable and satisfying experience that stimulates the emotions, stretches the mind and inspires creativity.

(Dunn 2001)

7.1 What is a picture book?

Picture books have been – and still are – under-utilised in teaching English in the classroom and extending the English experience into the home. Introducing and mediating a favourite picture book to a young child or children can be a magical experience. Enthusiasm is infectious and most children sense it and soon join in with the text as it is read, providing the book has been selected to meet their learning needs and interests. If given time to book browse (a self-initiated, child-led form of play), some children may add a simple spoken text to each picture themselves as they turn a page, even imitating the different voices, if the adult's reading had been dramatised. Others may have picked up the text, word for word, and may recite it, pretending they are reading it, as they turn each page.

> *Recreational reading is the most powerful tool available for language and literacy development. It is especially important for helping second and foreign language acquirers develop the ability to use language for more than simple conversation. The amount of pleasure reading done in the second language is a strong predictor of performance in tests of writing, reading, grammar and vocabulary.*
>
> (Krashen 2004)

Although adults cannot see into a young child's mind, they know that a focused, good picture book experience, even when a child is very young, leaves some lasting impression at both a conscious and subconscious level.

A beginner's picture book experience is generally a dual one in which the simple text carries meaning, but the sequence of the here-and-now narrative pictures supporting it carry more detail, from which a child can decode deeper meaning and additional stimulation. The breadth of a picture book experience is increased where a child has an opportunity to hold the book and pore over the text and pictures – or only pictures, in the case of VYLs who cannot yet read text – at their own speed. Book browsing is a vital and agreed often overlooked part of a picture book experience. It allows a young child to reflect on their experiences, so taking them to a deeper level of thought.

> *A man ought to read just as inclination leads him, for what*
> *he reads as a task will do him little good.*
>
> (Dr Samuel Johnson 1709–1784)

A colour picture book is written for children's enjoyment by an author and an illustrator working together, or an illustrator who also writes his or her own text. It is a total design experience and, unlike a syllabus-based textbook or graded reader, designed with no planned educational aim. A picture book is not a teaching tool.

During what was described as 'the golden age of children's publishing', the 1980s to the turn of the century, thousands of new picture books were published each year. Work by some of the best world illustrators, many trained at British university art departments, can be found in picture books. Picture books enable children to hold, examine and self-mediate, as they decode at their own speed not one but a sequence of quality illustrations that challenge understanding and extend experiences beyond children's own environment, and sometimes beyond their dreams. Picture books are part of children's culture, especially in developed countries. Teachers in Europe often report that children are happier, calmer and more positive about English lessons when picture books are introduced into their programme.

7.1.1 Telling or reading stories?

Adults often interchange the English verbs *telling* and *reading* stories without realising that very young and young children, who are logical thinkers, see them as two different activities. *Reading* a picture book is linked to a book, something physical and permanent that can be held, even hugged, with pictures and texts that can be decoded. In early years' situations the book experience is mediated by an adult or older person who reads aloud.

Telling a story is a recognised skill linked to a person's talk (language), which is sometimes supported by realia. In the VYL and YL context, the child's role in the telling is largely that of a listener. *Telling* ends once the storyteller stops talking. The storyteller may *retell* the story at some other time, but, since *telling* depends on human creation, the manner of *telling* can alter each time the story is told. This variety of presentation can make it difficult for young children to pick up more than repetitive refrains.

Reading aloud a picture book is a holistic, tangible, physical experience. The story text and illustrations remain constant and are thus available, in the same form, for children to revisit and browse through. This is important for most very young and young children, who need to match and rematch thought and meaning to the language (verbal experience) and pictures (visual experience) if they are to decode both experiences successfully. In story-*telling* young children beginning English may find the changing language (unsupported by challenging illustrations) more difficult to pick up as they cannot work out when and how to use their language-acquisition skills.

> *The first quality of a real book – it reads well aloud. The second quality is that, however simple, the text must have natural language rhythms and furthermore must interest both the child and the adult.*
>
> (Waterland 1985)

Storytelling has its place but for very young and young beginners it seems that acquiring English is easier if the story is linked to a picture book that provides:

- fixed, easy-to-pick-up language (verbal experience)
- detailed illustrations (visual experience)
- reference for browsing (playing/reflecting)
- a ready-made shared activity always available in class
- a ready-made activity to share at home.

Mediating a picture book to a young child is a more personal, longer-lasting interactive experience in most cases than share-watching a TV/DVD/YouTube clip of a children's programme or film, where the screen pictures change rapidly and automatically and browsing may be less available. From positive experiences with picture books, many children develop a lifelong love of reading books.

Many children learning English may never have had the experience of reading a full-colour picture book in their own language. For them, and their families, a picture book is a completely new and exciting experience, especially if the children's and parents' only book experience has consisted of traditional syllabus textbooks. Possessing a picture book may not be a realistic experience for some of the world's children for many reasons including climatic ones (books deteriorate rapidly in tropical climates and get eaten by termites). However, through new and rapidly developing technology, stories are becoming available on the screens of computers, smartphones, iPads etc. so even in the African bush it is now possible for a child to have an on-screen picture book experience and get to know some of the classic picture books of English children's culture.

Picture books are sometimes referred to as 'real' picture books or *organic books grown from the author's desire to write that particular story in that particular way; the natural wholefood approach to writing* (Waterland 1985). This term was used to make a clear distinction from the inorganic picture books written as part of a reading scheme, which are word-graded to help children learn to read text in English. Reading schemes like Janet and John, used in 1960s, and the *Ladybird Key Words* scheme, both recently revised, start from the simplest text of a few easy-to-read words in unauthentic children's language, supported by illustrations on each page aimed to help the child guess and get added meaning from the text. By the end of the scheme a child was considered to be a fluent reader. Most children's reading experience, until they reached the top level, included no real picture books. Readability and word counts were based on whole-word recognition (termed *Look-and-say or Gestalt*) or phonic sounds (26 letters/44 sounds: 20 vowels and 24 consonants). Phonic first reading was often jokingly referred to as _The cat sat on the mat, the_ being the only difficult word to read phonetically. Today the term _authentic_ is gradually replacing _real_ in being applied to picture books. The division between 'real books' and reading schemes is also less marked as schemes like the _Oxford Reading Tree_ have tried to emulate the style of real picture books.

> **_Real books are good reading texts for learners because they introduce children to the discourse styles of various genres._**
>
> (Meek 1988)

Textbooks for learning English as a foreign language fall into another category. Such textbooks follow a syllabus and are now more often written for specific countries or regions. Children are quick to recognise the differences in text and quality of artwork if they are used to the pictures in real picture books going beyond confirming the text and firing their imagination. Many picture book artists accept no instruction from the author of a text, as this would compromise their creativity.

Picture books are part of a child's experience in English-speaking cultures and many English-speaking children grow up with favourites they own, have read at school, seen on screen or borrowed from the school or local library. Sharing a picture book with a child offers the adult a glimpse into the child's world and the way in which they interpret what they see, feel and imagine. A picture book can become a lifelong friend; some adults confess to keeping childhood picture book favourites on their bookshelves.

7.1.2 Types of picture books

Published children's books

Picture books can be divided into the following main categories:

* story books with rhyming text
* story books with narrative text
* rhyme, poetry and song books

236

- information books
- novelty books, which may include any of the above categories
- books in SL, LI or dual language (identical texts in both languages)
- home-made picture books – story, rhyme, information etc.

Some books in these categories are written as novelty books with interactive additional flap-ups, buttons to press and push–pull devices making them into 3-D experiences. Some classic children's books have been reprinted in 3-D. Today's children and their parents (who are the book buyers) may believe that the novelty interactive experiences make picture book experiences easier as children need less adult mediation. After initial mediation, children generally become engaged in the play-like game experiences that exist within the book and the story language takes second place. Some of these picture book experiences with giants, ghost trains etc. are very realistic and even fearsome, yet are within young children's control as, with a bang, the book is closed and the experience is contained – the giant cannot escape!

Some novelty books provide children, especially boys, with contained, portable, easy-to-access, imaginative springboards and emotional challenges way beyond what they can experience within their own environment, such as *Come for a ride on a Ghost Train*. Mediators, however, need to be sure that listening to the story text is part of the experience, so that eventually the child has absorbed sufficient text language to add, often aloud to himself, his own edition of the text as he turns the pages and activates the novelties. Novelty additions or pop-ups, mostly handmade, are fragile and easily torn, so teachers have to be ready to repair them and also to explain that books and especially novelty books need to be *handled with care!*

Apart from widening children's English language experience and especially vocabulary, a picture book brings a holistic experience to a lesson, which is extremely important for the emotional well-being ('feel-good' factor) of a developing child.

Learning how to recognise and manage personal emotions is an important part of growing up (Emotional Intelligence). This is especially so in the pre-puberty years, when children become more self-conscious. In some cultures, although children may be exposed to many forms of stress, the formal school curriculum may give little help in emotional management.

Picture books can help children work out how to manage their emotions as many provide focal settings beyond daily life occurrences. Through sharing the pictures and text of selected picture books, adults can provide opportunities to talk about how to manage stress. Through story picture books children can:

- explore emotions and acquire the language needed to express them
- share emotions confidently and freely in a sympathetic, warm, caring atmosphere
- reflect on experiences and relate them to their own life, which leads to greater understanding, security and self-confidence
- relate to the emotions of the characters in stories
- come to terms with their own feelings in a safe, caring situation
- find out about fear in a way that is exciting without it being a threat or real danger as the experience is contained (a book can be shut and put away!).

A picture book can challenge each child differently; each boy and girl interprets it at their own level, getting different images and feelings from it, depending on the quality of the mediation. Adults have to be well 'tuned-in' to judge this level as they need to think about the child of today's holistic needs if they are not to underestimate young learners' English potential. Children understand and can relate better to well-selected picture book experiences than many adults imagine. *Literature provides meaning in our lives. Finding meaning is the greatest need and the most difficult achievement for any human of our age (time)* (Bettelheim 1991).

7.2 Selecting picture books

We are talking about picture books – not books with illustrations, but books in which the story depends on the interaction between written text and image and where both have been created with a conscious aesthetic intention (not just for pedagogic and commercial purposes).

(Arizpe and Styles 2003)

Selecting the right book for children's development needs is important if children are to be motivated from their first experiences in English. Although adults have their favourite picture books, they need also to select books by relating them to young children's language needs. Their favourite may not be right for young beginners. *The Very Hungry Caterpillar* (published in 1969 and one of the first modern novelty books) is a great favourite; children love the holes, but the full text is difficult to present to very young children as it includes the butterfly's life cycle and classifiers for things to eat etc. The result is that very young children play with the holes, adding their own language. However, the phrase *he was still hungry* is repeated five times, and children may pick up this phrase and even recycle the phrase *still hungry* to use at snack time! Where the first picture books have simple text, children are more likely to get the feeling of 'I can' and thus be more positive and motivated.

What texts teach is a process of discovery for readers, not a programme of instruction for teachers.

(Meek 1988)

Selection criteria for story picture books

- Is the language easy to read aloud and mediate?
- Is there plenty of natural repetition to aid in picking up language?
- Is there any rhyming language as this helps in introducing and working out sounds of English?

239

- Does it have colourful, fun illustrations?
- Is there a standard and a novelty edition?
- Is there an accompanying CD-ROM or DVD?
- Is it suitable for boys as well as girls (many books are very pink and feminine and off-putting for boys)
- Does it include emotional experiences as these help children to understand themselves and society?
- Is the text font clear for beginners (some texts insert emotions using words in capitals, added exclamation marks etc.)?
- Does it offer an enriching experience in English (useful phrases and vocabulary) that is different from a textbook experience?

The selection should also include some information books. Some of these may be related to project work (see Chapter 8).

7.3 Mediating picture books

The teacher is the mediator between the book and the child and through their mediation the child becomes engaged in the book. The better the match between the mediation and the child, the more the child becomes engaged. *Teacherese*, together with personal dramatisation, should create a personal 'mini-theatrical performance' loved by children. How often do children of all ages ask teachers *When will you do it again for us?*

> *The adult's voice creates the book for the child. It brings it to life between the speaker and the hearer, as a shared possession both can enjoy … When the adult voice performs the story, it is doing some of the work of deciding what the world of the story is like.*

(Karpf 2006)

The success of picture book reading and related activities (as with any activity) depends on the quality of the mediation. Teachers need to be aware of the following, which can affect that quality:

- the teacher as the sole enabling mediator (in the beginning stages)
- the teacher's attitude to a book (this is felt and is usually contagious)
- the teacher's book selection (vital for matching individual children's needs and interests)
- the teacher's style of reading and dramatisation
- the teacher's organisation of a time and place for book browsing (this should allow for reflection – vital for consolidation)
- the teacher's related follow-up activities.

7.4 Introducing picture books

From the first lesson introduce a well-selected easy-to-read picture book. Although the teacher reads the simple text aloud, children will 'read' (ie decode) the pictures.

A book in English needs more careful presentation than a book in the SL if it is to be successful. Children need to understand some of the English text before the book is introduced, otherwise they may quickly think 'I can't understand', become overwhelmed and switch off. Children need to feel confident in order to use their problem-solving skills to tackle something new successfully.

Oral understanding of language should come before children are ready to recognise the print form of a word. Even if the reading of text is not yet being introduced formally, some children who write in different scripts are curious to find out about the Roman alphabet. Children who use the Roman alphabet need to understand that English letters not only have different names but also different sounds, and that capital and small letters for each letter have the same sound – the only difference is the size. Children who write in non-Roman letters need more informal experiences of seeing written text before they are ready to find out how to decode such written text.

It is interesting to note that stories that involve some special character like an animal, a make-believe creature or even a robot seem to be most meaningful to children. Boys are often attracted to stories about special fantasy superheroes. Children seem to build up some personal relationship with these characters, which allows for interaction. Stories that have no identifiable character do not seem to excite young children in the same way. Thus, when choosing stories for beginners, teachers would be well advised to look for picture books that have a character to which both boys and girls can relate. Many of the character-based picture books have support materials that come with the books and help children to understand the stories more easily.

7.4.1 Pre-presentation

Before reading a picture book decide which key words or key phrases in the text (eg animal names – *an elephant* – or phrases like *clap your hands*) to introduce beforehand through realia, an activity game or creative work. It is better not to introduce all the text as this may spoil the thrill of the story for some children.

Practise reading the text aloud to yourself slowly beforehand, without altering the intonation pattern. Work out where you will pause to add suspense and which words you will stress, taking care not to distort the reading. Decide what body language you will use to dramatise the story to make understanding easier. It is important to feel confident that you know the story well so that you will not be fazed by unexpected interruptions! It is also important to plan these details carefully, as children will expect the same dramatisation each time you re-read the story.

7.4.2 Presentation

To get children used to picture book activities, it is better to have a regular Book Time in the teaching programme. Many teachers find sharing picture books is best in Phase Three of a lesson (see Figure 4). In this way children can anticipate the activity and prepare themselves to listen. Children who do not have similar book experiences in SL classrooms need time to learn how to get meaning and information from books (text and pictures), as well as how to look at and listen to the adult reader. Concentration may be short to begin with as children are used to the fast-changing pictures from TV and DVDs. With exposure, children gradually learn to expand their concentration span. It is accepted that most girls find it easier than boys to sit still and listen.

Select a comfortable and different place like a corner mat in the classroom to read books. The adult should sit at a higher level than the children. Make sure children are able to be close enough to observe the adult's mouth movements, as they pick up information about pronunciation by watching and imitating the adult. Check that children who have problems with seeing and hearing – this includes temporary difficulties due to colds and teething – are also close to the reader.

Reading picture books is about constructing some personal meaning from the text and pictures. Begin the story by looking together at the cover, endpapers (if they are decorated), as well as the title page, as these are part of the total design of the picture book. The first time you introduce a picture book you may feel that it is better to talk about it in English then SL (if you can), and then finish by reading the text in English.

Make story reading fun and interesting and enjoy it yourself too; in this way your own passion will come across. Each time you re-read a story, speed up your reading a little, but keep it fresh. With each re-reading, children deepen their understanding of the story and gain more from it. As you re-read, point to each word. As children pick up more of the text by heart they will soon be ready to add the last word or words to phrases if you indicate by hesitating and signalling by your face gesture that you expect them to join in. They are used to doing this in SL, so it only involves a skill transfer for them.

Translation of some words and phrases may be necessary in the first reading. Where possible, code-switch in your translation to include the key words and key phrases –which you included in your pre-presentation

— in English. Use a whisper for the translation so children get used to the idea that the translation is not permanent and will not be there when you re-read. If young children know that you will translate each time you read, the less engaged children may not bother to listen to the English as they see no point in making the effort!

After the first reading, or as soon as possible, only read the text in English. Children have an amazing and often underestimated ability to cope and they will try to work out what they do not understand using gist understanding skills. Young children do this continually in their home language, as they do not always understand all that adults say to them in L1 or SL.

Be sure to pause before you turn a page and add your own commentary like *And then what happens?* or *Look at the…*, pointing to the new picture. Children need time to scan the pictures if they are to decode meaning from them.

At this beginning stage it is better not to ask too many questions as these can come between the child and the story and may intrude and irritate, as children may be still in the story world.

As children begin to join in they may make mistakes in pronunciation. Make no comment, as criticism can demotivate. Praise them for joining in and repeat the word back to them in the phrase in which it is used. *Bad. Yes, the wolf's bad.* They will notice the difference and self-correct either straight away or later as they are used to refining their pronunciation to match adult's speech in L1 and can transfer the skill.

A story is successful when children gradually begin to complete the end of sentences or phrases themselves, filling up the pauses you leave as you read aloud. This leads on to them picking up all the language of the story. If the story is right for their developmental level, you will find that some soon know it off by heart — something that doesn't happen so easily with language in a textbook unless it is a song or rhyme.

Presentation is most effective in sequential steps over a period of time:

- **pre-presentation** to introduce new vocabulary before a child sees the book
- **presentation** of part or all the book
- **re-presentation** many times until the text is well known
- **follow-up** activities where suitable, remembering that a picture book is not a teaching tool.

Use the voice in presentation to aid learning and increase fun. Here are some suggestions:

- stress exciting or vital language
- alter the tone of voice to insert excitement and suspense
- pause to give a child the opportunity to complete sentences or say refrains himself
- use *teacherese* language techniques to help children use and develop English naturally (see 1.2.3).

7.4.3 Re-presentation

Read to children as often as they request it and as often as you can. If you encourage and praise them, they soon join in finishing off words or phrases. If a short text is well presented and is at the right level for a child's English, a child generally picks up a lot of it after five or six readings on different days. The value of repeated reading of the same books, even if they are not necessarily the children's top favourites, is vital as without repetition deep learning cannot take place. Also it is through absorbing text in these natural experiences that children begin to teach themselves to read. If at all possible, it is a good idea to use English native speakers as teachers' aids for additional role-model speakers to share the picture books and play games with the children.

7.4.4 Translation

Use of translation depends on:

- whether the teacher is monolingual English or bilingual
- whether the children are monolingual or plurilingual
- whether one or two children are native English speakers
- the aims of the teacher (maximum English input or English embedded in holistic classroom work).

When to use translation depends on each situation and on the teacher's own judgement. The following are merely suggestions:

- to introduce a new activity or picture book (but make only one translation of the text)
- to answer a child's question in SL in order to develop thought and cognitive knowledge (either reflect back in simple English what the child asked or discuss outside the English lesson. In the next and following lessons be sure to revisit the same discussion, scaffolding the language where possible; see 1.2.3).

Use a whisper for translation in the English lesson to show that translation is not a regular part of an English lesson. If children have not understood after one translation, do not translate it a second time. Ask a child who has understood to explain. If the language content is at the right level, children usually feel proud that they can give accurate translations.

7.5 Decoding pictures (visual literacy)

Obtaining information and meaning from pictures is an important and fast-developing method of communication in this global, technological world. Not only do adults need to be text literate – capable of decoding the different print forms of letters and reading them to get meaning, they also need to be capable of getting information from pictures, maps and symbols. The better adults and children are at decoding visually, the more successful they are likely to be at gathering information.

Have you ever introduced a new picture book to a young child and watched how, in silence, he concentrates as he scrutinises the picture, his eyes gliding from top to bottom, side to side? Suddenly, when he has made sense of it and absorbed all he wants, he looks up at you to show he is ready for you to turn the page. If you do not rush him, he will focus on the picture far longer than an adult would. Unlike most adults, he hasn't yet developed scanning skills by which his eyes scan a picture to pick up relevant detail, disregarding what is irrelevant. Scanning skills in 'reading' pictures, as in reading text, develop through experience and at a child's own speed.

What does a child bring to a picture?

- his own visual ability – how he sees colours
- his own meanings – based on previous experiences with illustrations, photographs, media
- his own creativity – based on previous experiences
- his own cultural influences – books, toys and daily life in his society.

7.5.1 Ways of decoding a double-page spread

A *spread* means text on left, picture on right or pictures and text on both pages. Anyone who is used to reading picture books with a young child will have noticed that when you or the child turns a page to a new spread, whether or not he can read, he nearly always looks at the picture first, following more or less the same routine of skim, scan and review.

Skim

The child gets a general impression from looking at the picture first and then, if they can read, the text. (The young learner who cannot yet read is used to getting information from pictures. Compare this with the adult who generally reads the text first and then secondly, glances at the picture, possibly regarding it as decorative, but not vital for information.)

Scan

The child looks at the picture, scrutinising detail. The child moves from place to place in the picture and moves on only when he has obtained sufficient information to make meaning. The young child is an astute observer as he learns much through imitation (copying) and decoding facial gestures.

Review

The child, satisfied that he has gleaned sufficient information, returns to review the whole picture, incorporating the connections made between the details and his own experiences. The child then, if he can read, appears to pass through the same routine in looking at the text, possibly reading sentence by sentence or reading blocks of text. Where different styles of type are used, little is known about how he decodes. Does he read the speech bubbles first? Does a general pattern emerge?

Browse

The child needs opportunities to return again and again to the visual experience in order to make new connections and obtain deeper meaning. Pictures (and text) provide multi-layered experiences, which alter and become more profound each time the child returns to the picture book, as each time the child is older, more mature and more experienced. He possibly has added confidence too, as his newly acquired daily life experiences make additional connections to the decoding experience, so deepening meaning. *What we see is not simply given but is the product of past experience and future expectations* (Gombrich 1982).

Apart from learning English through picture books, children's observation skills develop, and they become more confident about how to look at and then decode new and different styles of illustration and photographs. These experiences help them develop valuable lifelong skills for use in both English and SL in today's media-led society where, each year, visual literacy is becoming more important and influential.

In the same way as a child's drawing usually carries more detail than his verbal explanation, so picture books with simple texts often carry more sophisticated narrative in the details of the illustration or photographs, than in the accompanying text.

Teachers sometimes worry that some illustrations are too sophisticated for their children, who may have had a diet of only cartoons or very soft, fairy-tale-like illustrations or even only screen experience. Again, it is only too easy to underestimate the child. On-screen graphic illustrations appear 'real' and more frightening and threatening than those in picture books. It is up to teachers to act as mediators, helping children to manage the emotional experience of a picture book and enjoy the richness in:

- the styles of illustration
- the types of illustration media, including collage, embroidery, oil, watercolours, crayon or photography (these can be discussed and even experimented with as art forms in the classroom; many picture books include details about the artist and their other works)
- colour (many children have never played with paints, seeing how the addition of a new colour can change the original colour; some only know one shade of purple – the one in their box of 24 crayons).

What does a child get visually from a picture book?

- a visual experience beyond their own environment – an airport, a jungle
- details that expand understanding of an unknown society/culture
- consecutive illustrations with a beginning and an end
- chances to stretch the imagination
- opportunities to 'meet' different peoples and creatures – Eskimos/Gruffalo

- exposure to other people's feelings and finding out how to cope with own feelings
- stimulation, motivation, fun, relaxation, all of which contribute to the 'feel-good' factor
- ideas about the physical properties of a book – the endpapers, the title page etc.

7.6 Decoding alphabet letters

Without knowing the names of the 26 alphabet letters in English, it is difficult to talk about words and their letter content. The 26 letters make 44 sounds (see 4.5). Many parents may be confused by the letter sounds and, as a result, when reading with their children, often confuse them. Most adults know the names of the letters in English, and many can even sing the *Alphabet song* and *Doe, a deer, a female deer* from *The Sound of Music*. This means they can be encouraged to provide some back-up at home by using the letter names.

If children already write in Roman letters, it is better to use the same letter shapes they already use. If children's SL is in a different script, but they are taught Roman letters as a different way of writing their language (in Japanese Romaji), it is also better to use the same Roman style letters that are taught and are used in the school. Once children can recognise some of the letters, it is possible to refer to words by saying *Find the word that begins with the letter d* and wait for the children to point to it. *Yes that's right. Listen, this word says dog,* stressing the letter *d*. Children find this simple activity fun and it is valuable preparation for later reading.

Oral language needs to be established before children begin reading in English, otherwise they tend to use SL decoding methods of sounds, which results in them reading English with a foreign accent.

French boy aged 9 years, pushed by his parents to read before he had much oral ability and knew about the sounds of English, read a simple English text with a French accent. As he progressed he never lost his French accent as he had got used to decoding English using French sounds.

That young children cannot read English does not mean that they are not ready to enjoy picture books, as they hear the text read by an adult. This gives them another and different exposure to simple English in spoken form that, once picked up, can be directly transferred to other situations.

A boy aged 6 years, when asked by his mother in LI to help her, replied in LI with a recycled English phrase from a version of the *Little Red Hen* story *'I'm sorry, I'm busy.'*

If some children are interested in the letters of the alphabet, introduce alphabet starting games and sing the *Alphabet song* (see 4.5.2).

Children who can already read in SL are often keen to read in English once they know the letters of the alphabet. At this point they may try to read text they have already memorised by recognising the first letters of whole words as these give a clue to their sound. This type of reciting–reading also occurs in 'reading' rhymes – reciting together with an adult who points to each word as she reads aloud (see Chapter 6).

To be able to do this *pretend reading*, which is a recognised and important step in the journey that is learning to read in English, children need to be given times when they can browse through the picture book. Children who do not try to decode by themselves through working out the sound of the first letter or letters have not yet reached a stage of *reading readiness*. Teachers should not try to teach them, but continue reading new and familiar books to them until they are more mature and a structured learning-to-read programme can be introduced.

7.7 Post-presentation

Some classrooms make their own small art gallery of four or five picture books, opening each book at a special picture. Children enjoy looking at picture books over and over again and, if given an opportunity, they like to discuss the pictures amongst themselves or even copy a picture from a book. For this reason plain paper, pencils and crayons should always be made available.

In the same way as you may talk in more detail about a story in SL which was introduced in the English lesson, talk about the pictures. Ask the children which is their favourite picture and tell them yours, explaining why. Enthusiasm is infectious and contributes to influencing lifelong attitudes to enjoying art. In fact children, when they are grown-up, often remember their teacher's favourite picture when they see it in a bookshop or library. Lifelong attitudes are laid down by the age of 8 years and these types of experiences with picture books contribute to developing character, imagination and creativity. Each child imagines stories and sees pictures through his own eyes, involving his own emotions and feelings. *Tread softly because you tread on my dreams* (W. B. Yeats 1865–1939).

7.8 Follow-up

Follow-up activities should be fun, with hidden learning and can include:

- drama – puppets, plays, group rhyme recitals
- making books – copying pictures, illustrating own version of the story eg changing the ending
- reading aloud together, with the child finishing off words and lines
- book browsing in a Book Corner (see 7.9).

Books that children know well can be put in the English Corner or the Book Corner for everyone to pore over and enjoy. Children need time to browse and discuss books amongst themselves. At this stage, discussion is in SL, as few children have sufficient English to communicate ideas and feelings in depth.

Children benefit from being able to borrow books they can 'pretend read' to take home. Family involvement, interest and admiration of reading skills is motivating! Some teachers make CDs to go with the storybooks that have no CD or DVD.

Children also benefit from further opportunities to discuss the story in SL. If you are not a monolingual teacher it is important to encourage any discussion as, apart from developing thought and language, it helps you to know how the children think. Their opinions may be quite different from what adults imagine. In SL discussions the adult should code-switch to include the English story language.

Listen to children's ideas and suggestions as these provide clues to their interests. Child-led activities usually need hidden guidance from an adult, as without this the activities may not develop to provide further learning opportunities. This guidance usually entails scaffolding the experience to the next conceptual and linguistic level.

Be prepared to provide opportunities to draw, paint, act, dance and sing or for children to make their own books. These activities help to consolidate the learning experience at the child's level. Be sure that children do not feel that, after a lovely story they 'have to do work', which is sometimes their comment about worksheets etc.

It is important to feel the children's mood, as some books may not need any immediate follow-up, whilst others may need only a quick one.

Include a 'Favourite Book Day' in the programme. Let a child know in advance that on 'Favourite Picture Book Day', the adult will re-read a storybook selected by them. Ask them to make their request beforehand so that you can prepare. Gradually develop this into a day when a group of children take over the organisation and share the reading of their favourite picture book aloud, either as individuals, in a group or with the teacher.

Adults are the child's initial mediators of picture books in English, but with re-presentation the adult's role diminishes as the child takes on a personal relationship with the book. The depth to which this multifaceted relationship develops depends greatly on the quality of the adult mediator's presentation and is also affected by the amount of post-presentation contact with the book, including browsing, that the child has. Book browsing or child-led activity with picture books should be the ultimate goal of a picture book experience, as it will consolidate and deepen the experience and at the same time influence the child's holistic development, including linguistic ability in SL as well as in English. Like all children, those learning English need to have opportunities to book browse and 'play' with books.

> *If a story is to become their own and deeper learning is to take place, children need to get beyond listening to stories at the speed of the adult to controlling their own speed of reading, turning each page when they are ready. Children need their own space with a picture book if they are to enjoy their own 'dream time'.*

(Dunn 2001)

7.8.1 Asking questions about the story

Listening to a story is a very personal experience. The relationship between the words and pictures is different for each child. It is most important not to break the magic the story creates for each child by questioning too much and too soon. Reading a picture book is not an exercise in comprehension! Adults are often keen to get an immediate reaction and many children are not ready to answer straight away. Given time, children often tell a caring adult what they feel about a story, even relating it to their own experiences. Teachers can learn a lot about how individual children think and feel through creating shared opportunities, like tidying-up together, when a child is able to talk to the teacher about how he felt about a story. Picture books are a special holistic maturing experience and should primarily be seen as offering enjoyment rather than as teaching tools.

In the early years questions serve three general functions:

- language development in SL
- language development in English
- thought (concept) development.

If the main aim is to teach English, it seems better that the questions are aimed generally at developing English by keeping them simple, using question words *What? Where?* and using the reply to start scaffolding familiar and story language. Of course these questions help the child think, but helping language acquisition is their main aim. For example, before you turn a page you can ask the children to predict what is coming *What's next?* with a pause that is sufficient for them to reflect and then reply. Young children are not bored if you ask some of the same questions each time you read the story, directing your question at different children each time and possibly altering the scaffold to include different story language.

If, in their excitement, children answer in SL or their home language, recast the reply in simple English for them. Don't ask them to repeat it in English, just say it naturally once or twice in English. When you re-read the story in the next lesson, the same child may answer in English: children are quick to pick up language.

Other questions may help children focus attention on the story or encourage a closer look at the picture.

> *Look at the ... What's he doing?*
> *Where is the ...? I can't see the ...*
> *What does he look like? Is he sad?*

Questions that need a *yes* or *no* answer confirm children's understanding of the story, but give no opportunity to build on a scaffold.

More complicated questions that develop reflection and extend and sustain children's thinking are best asked in SL lessons at this stage of learning English. Later, as children have more developed spoken, reading and writing skills, they will be better equipped to answer these questions in English.

One of the best ways to find out how children feel about a story, is to ask them to make their own illustration for one episode in the story or to draw a different ending to the story. Young native speakers put more details into their pictures than they can write; children learning English generally do the same. Look at their pictures and comment, but do not be tempted to question them too much about the content. Young children will tell you as much as they can or want to about their picture. If they tell you in SL or their home language, rephrase some of it in English. Later, use the same English phrases to tell the rest of the class about the picture in Phase Three of the lesson, when each child shows his picture. By doing this, the child who drew the picture has had the opportunity to hear the same language at least twice. Mount the pictures onto background paper, then write some or all of the spoken text under the picture and display it on the classroom wall. If you are not allowed to display material in the classroom, stick it into a book, which children can 'read' in the English Book Corner. This leads on to making class picture stories and eventually children writing their own picture book stories (fold A4 paper and cut to make a six-page booklet). Remember that, to begin with, the pictures will tell more of the story that the text. However, as children's fluency increases so does the size of the book and the length of the text.

> *However it works, drawing is thinking aloud, a powerful route into knowledge.*
>
> (Sedgwick and Sedgwick in Arizpe and Styles 2003)

7.9 English Book Corners

Once children are familiar with a book and have memorised most of the text, place the picture book in the English Book Corner, as it is now time for children to have opportunities to book browse. Children need to have a place where they can easily find picture books in English and sit down quietly to browse. Creating an English Corner in which there is a Book Corner or even an English bookshelf is important. Displaying the picture books, front forwards, is much more stimulating than stacking them with only their spines showing. Ideally the English Corner should have somewhere comfortable to sit and read and possibly a table where children can draw.

> *To learn to read a book, as distinct from recognising the words on a page, a young reader has to become both the teller (picking up the author's view and voice) and the told (the recipient of the story, the interpreter). This symbolic interaction is learned early. It is rarely, if ever, taught, except so far as an adult stands in for the author by giving the text a 'voice' when reading to the child.*

(Meek 1988)

Suggested titles

The forms in which children's picture books are being published are changing as publishers try to increase sales. Some classic books are being reprinted as novelty books, creating opportunities for more interaction. Other character books like *Spot* are being sold with an accompanying character soft toy dog. Increasingly, editions of picture books have CDs or DVDs included. Before buying it is advisable to research what is available.

Many of the books included below lead on naturally to activities or projects like planting seeds or collecting postcards of famous buildings. Some of them have been selected as they fit in with suggested projects (see Chapter 8). The first story books listed in Step 1 in each section are

257

Figure 18 An English Book Corner: sample layout

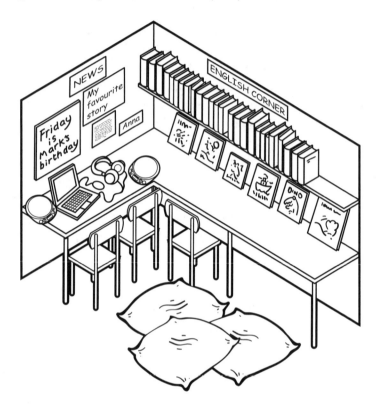

the easiest for beginners to understand and enjoy. Once children recognise that English picture books provide easy-to-understand interest and fun, they are ready for slightly more challenging text. It is important that children remain positive that they will be able to understand the English text they hear. Even if they only lose confidence on one occasion, it takes time to regain the 'feel-good' factor about 'reading' picture books.

Depending on the frequency of lessons, it is ideal to introduce a minimum of five or six books per term. Where parents ask for suggestions for birthday presents, try to suggest buying a familiar picture book used in class, so that children own their own copy.

Some of the books listed may be out of print, but quality used copies may be available. For additional descriptions of more suitable books for young beginners refer to the *Archive* section of *Realbook News* at www. teachingenglish.org.uk/teaching-kids/real-books.

Young Learners – 6–8+ years
Step 1 (in order of ease of understanding)

Good Night Gorilla Peggy Rathmann, Puffin Books
The story is told in the pictures, the text consists of three speech bubbles: *Goodnight, Goodnight zoo, Goodnight dear.*

Freight Train Donald Crews, Phoenix Yard Books
With minimum language A train with a black engine, and purple, blue, green, yellow, orange trucks and a red guard's van at the back moves across the track through tunnels, going by cities. crossing bridges, going, going until gone to where? The graphic illustrations excite the reader showing how the train gathers speed.

Run, mouse, run! Petr Horáček, Walker Books
In ten phrases a mouse runs away from a cat and *just in time* runs quickly *into his hole*. The shaped pages and hole add fun to the book, which is a springboard for creative ideas like making your own mouse or making your own picture story book of a mouse.

Beep Beep Petr Horáček, Walker Books
A family car ride as *We're all going to visit Granny*. Plenty of car noises to join in with as they drive *through the town, across zebra crossing* to *Stop! At the traffic light*. This fits well with project work (see Chapter 8).

Next Please Ernst Jandl and Norman Junge, Red Fox Books
Short, repetitive phrases about a common experience – a doctor's waiting room. Ideal for dramatising, with a chorus narration. *Five waiting./Door opens. One comes out./Next please. One goes in./Four waiting./Door opens. One comes out./Next please. One goes in./Three waiting …* until *One waiting all alone. None waiting* and then finally the readers sees the doctor …

From Head to Toe Eric Carle, Puffin Books

Twelve animals ask children to copy their actions. *I am a giraffe and I can bend my neck. Can you do it?* The child replies, *I can do it.*

Ready or not Mr Croc? Jo Lodge, Hodder Children's Books

Mr Croc are you ready or not? This colourful novelty book shows Mr Croc at home putting on his clothes to go out. When he is finally ready he says *I'm coming to get you.*

Rosie's Walk Pat Hutchins, Red Fox Picture Books

A dual narrative book – the pictures tell how a fox chases Rosie, a hen, through a farm, whilst the text narrates Rosie's pre-dinner peaceful walk in one long sentence. *Rosie, the hen, went for a walk … and got back in time for dinner*, with no mention of the fox! The rest of the sentence tells how Rosie went *across the yard, around the pond, over, past, through, under*, which can all be understood by simple actions.

Something To Do David Lucas. Gullane Books

The story of a little bear who believes There is nothing to do. Told simply through outline illustrations, minimal colour and a few phrases a little bear is taken on an adventure that stimulates imagination and creativity.

'Pardon?' said the Giraffe Colin West, Walker Books

The frog wants to know *What is it like up there?*, where the Giraffe, with its long neck is, but the Giraffe is so far away, he can't hear. So the frog jumps onto the back of a larger animal. Other animals ask the same question and follow the frog's example, until the Giraffe sneezes.

Step 2 (alphabetical order)

10 Minutes till Bedtime Peggy Rathmann, Puffin Books

All Aboard! Corinne Albaut and Grégorie Mabire, Zero to Ten Books

A bit lost Chris Haughton, Walker Books

Buzz, Buzz, Buzz, went Bumble-Bee Colin West, Walker Books

Chocolate Mousse for Greedy Goose Julia Donaldson and Nick Sharratt, Macmillan

Come for a Ride in a Ghost Train Colin and Jacqui Hawkins, Walker Books

Conjuror Cow Julia Donaldson and Nick Sharratt, Puffin Books

Dogs Emily Gravett, Panmacmillan

Fox's Socks Julia Donaldson and Axel Scheffler, Macmillan

Hop on Pop Dr Seuss, HarperCollins

How Kind! Mary Murphy, Walker Books

Inside, Outside, Upside Down Stan and Jan Berenstain, HarperCollins

I want my hat back Jan Klassen, Walker Books

Love Monster Rachel Bright, Harper Collins.

Mr. Cool Hildegard Müller, Franklin Watts

'Not Me,' said the Monkey Colin West, Walker Books

One Fat Cat Vivian French and Liz Million, Walker Books

Rainy Day Caroline Jayne Church, Campbell Books

Shark in the Park! Nick Sharratt, Corgi Children's

Something Beginning with BLUE Nick Sharratt and Sally Symes, Walker Books

Stomp, Dinosaur, Stomp! Margaret Mayo and Alex Aycliffe, Orchard Books

Susan Laughs Jeanne Willis and Tony Ross, Red Fox Books

There are cats in this book Viviane Schwarz, Walker Books

You Choose Nick Sharratt and Pippa Goodhart, Random House

Rhyme/Song books

A Dark, Dark Tale Ruth Brown, Red Fox Books

Cats Sleep Anywhere Eleanor Farjeon and Anne Mortimer, Frances Lincoln Children's Books

In a Dark, Dark Wood Jessica Souhami, Frances Lincoln Children's Books

There was an Old Lady who Swallowed a Fly Pam Adams, Child's Play International

This is the House that Jack Built Pam Adams, Child's Play International

We're Going on a Bear Hunt Michael Rosen and Helen Oxenbury, Walker Books

Information Books

All Kinds of People Emma Damon, Tango Books (novelty book)

Banana Monster Peter Bentley. Qed Publishing.

Busy Airport Rebecca Finn, Campbell Books

Can You See It? Square! Sally Smallwood, Zero to Ten Books

Ella's Bath Peter Bentley Qed Publishing

First Shapes in Buildings Penny Ann Lane, Frances Lincoln Children's Books

First the Egg Laura V. Seeger, Frances Lincoln Children's Books

I Like Bugs Lorena Siminovich, Templar Publishing

Let's Go Driving! Gus Clarke, Walker Books

Skeleton Hiccups Margery Cuyler and S. D. Schindler, Simon & Schuster Children's Books

Ten Seeds Ruth Brown, Anderson Books

Very Young learners – 3–5+ years
Step 1 (in order of ease of understanding)

Happy Dog, Sad Dog Sam Lloyd, Little Tiger Press
A fun story in which comic illustrations focus on contrasting two dogs on seven spreads *big dog – little dog; clean dog – dirty dog; happy dog – sad dog* and so on until the last spread where there is *no dog.*

Teddy Bear, Teddy Bear! Annie Kubler, Child's Play International
A traditional action rhyme that can be said or sung. The teddy bear

touches *his nose*, then *toes*, and turns around and finally *turns off the light* and says *Goodnight*.

Monkey and Me Emily Gravett, Macmillan
Monkey and me, we went to see a lot of animals and got *home for tea*. Detailed drawings narrate an amusing adventure told in very few repeated words and phrases.

'Have You Seen the Crocodile?' Colin West, Walker Books
Jungle animals in turn ask *Have you seen the crocodile?* Finally the crocodile says *I've seen the crocodile* and *snap, snap, snap*.

Choo, Choo Petr Horáček, Walker Books
Children can join in the train noises as they follow the train on its journey through the woods, over the bridge, into a tunnel and beyond. The cutout pages give the feel of trees and mountains and even of being inside a tunnel.

Whose Tail? Sam Lloyd, Little Tiger Press
This story is about animals pulling tails. *The cheeky monkey pulled the tail of the stripy zebra, the grizzly bear pulled the tail of the very tall giraffe* and so on until *the sleepy lion woke up and ROARED*: a fun book to dramatise.

Brown Bear, Brown Bear, What Do You See? Eric Carle, Puffin Books
Eleven animal pictures accompanied by repetitive text *Brown Bear, brown bear, what do you see? I see a [animal name] looking at me.*

Dear Zoo Rod Campbell, Campbell Books
The zoo sent animals as presents, but they were all wrong. *They sent me a (guess). He was too grumpy! I sent him back.* On each page the same phrases repeat until finally a perfect present was sent. Lift the flap to find out what it was.

Step 2 (alphabetical order)

A Dragon on the Doorstep Stella Blackstone and Debbie Harter, Barefoot Books

Arabella Miller's Tiny Caterpillar Clare Jarrett, Walker Books

Bear on a Bike Stella Blackstone and Debbie Harter, Barefoot Books

I'm a Car Woody, Bloomsbury Books

Maisy Likes Driving Lucy Cousins, Walker Books

Maisy's Train Lucy Cousins, Walker Books

Mimi's Book of Opposites Emma Chichester Clark, Anderson Books

Ready, Steady, Go! Shigeo Watanabe and Yasuo Ohtomo, Red Fox Books

Shh! (Don't Tell Mister Wolf) Colin McNaughton, HarperCollins

The Selfish Crocodile Faustin Charles and Michael Terry, Bloomsbury Books

Tiger Nick Butterworth, HarperCollins

What Do I Look Like? Nick Sharratt, Walker Books

What Shall We Do With the Boo Hoo Baby? Cressida Cowell and Ingrid Godon, Macmillan

Where is Maisy's Panda? Lucy Cousins, Walker Books

Where's My Teddy? Jez Alborough, Walker Books

Whose Baby Am I? John Butler, Puffin Books

Whose Tail is That? Christine Nicholls and Danny Snell, Happy Cat Books

Rhyme/Song

Head, Shoulders, Knees and Toes... Annie Kubler, Child's Play International

If You're Happy and You Know It... Annie Kubler, Child's Play International

Publishers often change, and are sometimes different, depending on the country. The books mentioned above are available at time of publishing on *Amazon Children's Books* or *Book Depository* as new or used books.

8

Oral projects – holistic activities

8.1 Oral projects

Children learn holistically, using their senses where necessary, discovering new ideas and approaches, whilst confirming what they have recently learned. Projects are holistic activities that are cross-curricular. The following are suggestions for oral projects that help to consolidate learning English and provide opportunities to use English in meaningful and motivating ways. In project work the process is generally more important than the final product, although the final product needs to be shown off, as the interest and praise offered by other children, as well as by adults and parents, helps to further motivate learning.

Projects arise out of mini-activities; they are rarely initiated by the children, but by the teacher who 'sets the scene' for project work as they know what is logistically possible at this stage of learning English. However, the teacher should leave space for the children to initiate and develop their ideas within 'the scene'.

The content level of a project can be adapted for VYLs or YLs but the management for either group is more or less the same. Written words and phrases are introduced where they would occur in real life situations eg *Birthdays in March, This week's news* above photos or *Our jungle* above a picture. The teacher reads these natural examples to the children, pointing to each word as she reads. Chatting is important and it needs, within reason, to be encouraged if it is in English, as it is through dialogues, however short and simple, that language is heard, acquired and used. Teachers should give a running commentary on what children are doing as well as giving them space to chatter amongst themselves and with the teacher.

For projects to work smoothly, it is important to keep parents in the loop of information. This can be done by short notes written in simple English for each child to take home and read aloud: *Toy Pet Show tomorrow. Please bring your Toy Pet to school.* Messages to parents can be confirmed by email. This can lead on to a photo show of any real pets and to making mini-picture stories about pets.

8.1.1 Management

Children may want to take part in groups or work by themselves, as young children are not always ready to share or compromise on creative ideas. For this reason, it is advisable, where possible, to make provision for group work and also for children to work individually. Gradually most children will grow to feel they want to take part in a group; this is more likely to happen where children have opportunities to see and discuss amongst themselves the photo (or video) documentation of the development of a project. Visible documentation tends to stimulate learning and socialising. Young children should have visual proof of the advantages of co-operating.

Although working on projects stretches children conceptually, this is not the main aim. Teachers will find it easy to manage an all-English activity – a mini-total-immersion experience in English – if the project is managed around concepts already learned in SL and known to the children, although not used in the same creative, holistic ways. The initial management of this experience depends a lot on the teacher's input of English, which includes a sustaining and managing running commentary and quick dialogues with each child. Most young children are sufficiently mature to understand and pick up some of the English that is spoken to a group or to other children and not directly to them, as long as they feel secure in the all-English environment of the classroom.

New technology makes information and visual material (photos, pictures and maps) more available for this type of work.

8.1.2 Repetition

Repetition in learning is important as it gives children a second chance to achieve. It is a natural way of absorbing prefabricated language, so that children can begin to use it themselves. Children learn by doing and most learners welcome another try to improve their skills. Visual documentation provides natural opportunities for children to talk about their contribution to the project – a natural form of repetition that helps to consolidate learning.

Suggestions are given in the following section for similar types of projects which give children opportunities to try again to achieve their potential once they understand the organisation of the project and can concentrate on the content material – content that will be different from a previous project. Some children want to recreate an experience or make a picture or story picture book at school or at home. Make sure that materials are available for them and encourage their initiative.

8.1.3 Translation

Taking part in a group project leads to discussion and children often revert to SL or code-switching in their enthusiasm to participate. It is important to prepare content and management language, working out the logical progression before introducing a new project. It is also best to make sure that children are familiar with most of the content language before they embark on the project. In this way children will be able to understand what the teacher says and so be more prepared to speak in English. When children use SL, the teacher should reflect back what they have said in English (*teacherese*), so that they hear the English version, including any new vocabulary.

If any discussion topics arise, it is best to save them for an SL speaking time or, in the case of a monolingual teacher, explain the children's interest and questions to the SL class teacher and ask her to follow up. Learning is not compartmentalised for children; what is learned in English is not only for the English lesson. Children have a remarkable ability to transfer learning and also creativity and imagination across languages and, at some later stage, what has been learned in one language will be used or referred to in another language environment.

8.1.4 Follow-up

The process of making a project is more important than the finished product for the child's holistic development and enjoyment. Oral commentary is valuable and also gives opportunities to reuse language in a meaningful way. *Aisha painted the bird in the sky. The bird's a beautiful blue. I like Abdul's car. There are no bicycles. I can ride a bicycle.*

Children get satisfaction from their achievement and this should not be underestimated. There should be a session when the class and teacher together discuss the results and make positive suggestions about where improvements or additions could have been made, building on young children's desire to self-correct and their enthusiastic inner drive to improve their own performance.

It is a good idea to send a photo of a group work activity by email to parents, asking them to download it for their child to show the family. Alternatively, send each child home with a photo to show their parents. Parents' interest and praise always stimulates, even if their English is limited or non-existent. Some young children create a small-scale version of the latest school project at home; this may be equal to browsing (see 7.8) and consolidating learning in their own time.

8.2 Suggested projects

1) The road

Materials

- paper for picture (two lengths stuck together)
- paste
- scissors
- crayons/felt-tip pens.

Pre-project

- Children know names of *a car, a bus, a taxi, a bicycle, a scooter, an airplane, a helicopter, a tractor, a train* (from playing *What's this?* memory game; see Chapter 5)
- Children ask parents to help them cut out pictures of the above list from magazines or download from the Internet

- Picture books – introduce books on road transport in Phase Three of a lesson.

Project

- Teacher makes long paper drawing of a road, with line down the middle. Larger classes need two pictures. With children who are 6–8 years old, include a crossroads and see if the children suggest a crossing and also traffic lights and even a river.
- In Circle Time (Phase One of a lesson), the teacher introduces the outline of the road and shows a picture of a car and asks children where to stick it. *Where do I put my car? There/Here. Yes. Pass me the paste, please. Thanks. Look,* (pasting) *there's my car on the road.*
- Whilst children stick on cars, creating the road, the teacher keeps up a commentary and takes some pictures as documentation for visible learning.
- Recap on the picture.
- Suggest next time children can bring more transport objects.
- Finish by reading a picture book with a transport theme.

Follow-up

- Display a picture made of photos of children doing their 'The road' project and talk about it.
- Add any new transport words.
- Talk about ON the road and IN the sky (*In the sky* can be the next project). If you have added a river, talk about *A boat on the river* and *A fish in the river.*

Figure 19 *A Road* project

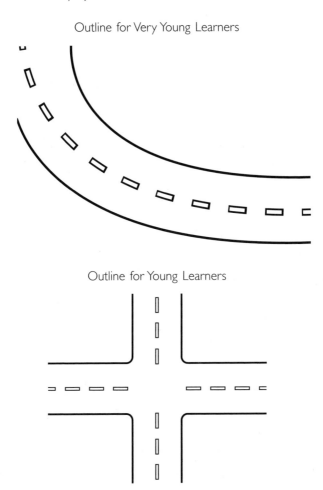

Outline for Very Young Learners

Outline for Young Learners

Leaving room for children to add any extra things

Related projects using the same type of organisation

In the jungle

- Discuss a jungle with the whole class and make sure children know the names of jungle animals. Reinforce the idea with a picture book and introduce the rhyme *I am walking through the jungle* (see 6.2.7).
- Teacher makes an outline picture of trees in a jungle and asks the children to complete the picture. Explain that for the next lesson children can ask parents to help them cut out a picture of a jungle animal.
- Children in turn then stick on their animal in the jungle. *Look, you have got a snake. Where are you going to put it? There. In the tree, Leo's got a monkey. What's this? It's an elephant. An elephant. Look, your butterfly is on a leaf, a big leaf.*
- Introduce picture books about jungles.
- **Rhyme game** *Walking through the jungle/What can I see?/I can see a tiger/ Looking at me. ROAR.* Pass on to the next child, who says the rhyme and selects his animal. Teacher recaps, saying *(child's name) can see an elephant. And (child's name) can see a tiger. Who's next?*
- **Follow-up** Make the jungle picture with the photos the children have brought from home.

In the forest (a small group, pair or individual project)

- In Circle Time discuss a forest and look at picture books that depict a forest. Then suggest children draw a forest and add a small house in the forest and a small road going to the house. Children can add some forest animals (different from the jungle animals). *Who lives in the house?* (children may suggest ideas such as *The Three Bears, Hansel and Gretel*); the teacher suggests: *A little boy? A little girl? Their mother? Their father? Have they got a dog? How do they go to school? Draw the mother and the father. Then draw the little boy and the little girl. Now draw a road from the house into the forest.*

- **End of lesson** Show and talk about the pictures and let children make suggestions for additions they can make in the following lesson. By now the group, pairs or individual children will have imagined their own story. If there is time the teacher can write some simple phrases under the pictures about the stories.

2) Soft Toy Show

- In Circle Time explain to very young children and send a simple note home to parents that next English Time children can bring in their cuddly toy to put in the show. During the explanation the teacher can show her own soft toy with a label round its neck, *Teacher*, to confirm children's understanding and as a bit of fun.

- For the next session the classroom is arranged so that there is a flat area where the soft toys can be placed for the show and for everyone to see. Overhead, the teacher puts the label *Toy Show* and adds some additional labels like *Boys' toys*, *Girls' toys*. Some schools ask parents to put a label with the child's name on the soft toy for the duration of the toy's school visit.

- Teacher welcomes each toy, *Hello. What's your toy's name?* and child replies. Then the teacher tells everyone *(Name of child.) Look. Her toy is a dog. The dog's name is …*

- Children introduce their pet *My toy is a dog. His/her name is …*

- Then children and teacher count *How many dogs? One dog, two dogs … How many cats?* etc.

- Teacher writes simple invitations to other teachers, which the children decorate. *Come to the Toy Show.* Other classes can be given *Tickets* made by the children to visit the Toy Show.

- **Game** Each child holding their toy: *Touch your pet's nose. Touch your pet's ears* etc. Take photos for visible documentation of children with their toys.

- Children take soft toys home at the end of the lesson. Teacher says *Thank you for coming, goodbye* to each toy. Children make a pretend voice for their pet, who says *Thank you. Goodbye.*

3) A Mountain

- In Circle Time with young children introduce mountains by looking at picture books and also travel brochures. Some young children may know the names of mountains and also which mountain is the highest in the world and in their country. Talk about *going up a mountain* and *going down a mountain. Up to the top, down to the bottom.*
- In Phase Two explain that the class are going to make a mountain by folding paper. If possible take some coloured origami square paper with a white back, or white A4 paper, and cut it into a square.
    - Fold the square into a triangle.
    - Fold it again to make a smaller triangle.
    - Open it up to the first triangle and on one side of the main fold tear the paper and fold it over to make the snow at the top of the mountain.
    - Fold the paper back into the cone shape.
    - Leave the snow white and colour the mountain (if using plain paper) and add trees and a path up the mountain.

Rhyme

Up the mountain, up, up we go *(Climbing up the mountain with their fingers then climbing down)*

Up to the top without a stop.
Down, down we go, on the path down.
At the bottom, we're in the town.

- **Follow-up** Add more photos of mountains and the rhyme card to the English Corner. Talk about volcanoes.
- Make a mountain range picture by each child folding another mountain with snow on the top and pasting it onto a big piece of paper. Add paths and flags. Add a town at the bottom of the mountains.

Figure 20 *A Mountain* project

1. Fold the square into a triangle.

2. Fold the triangle again to make a smaller triangle.

3. Open it up to the first triangle. On <u>one side</u> of the main fold, tear the paper.

4. Open the paper to the original square. Fold the torn portion over on the main fold. (This is the 'snow' for the mountain.)

Fold into the larger triangle again, keeping the 'snow' visible on top.

5. Fold the larger triangle back into the smaller triangle shape. Now you have a mountain with snow on top!

6. Make several mountains and decorate them.

4) Family photo or picture book *My Family Book*

- Children make a family book. Drawings can replace photos if they are difficult to obtain.

- Take two pieces of A4 paper and fold, then cut in half. Fold again to make into a hand-sized book for each child.

- Although this is a visual/oral book, the teacher can write a name or short phrases under the photos or drawings as she talks to each child about their picture. The following are merely suggestions and need to be adjusted to modern family circumstances. The book is made over several lessons. For the first lesson ask for photos or drawings for pages one to three, the second lesson pages four and five and so on.

Page 1 *This is me… I am (name)*, plus photo or drawing.

Pages 2 and 3 *This is my brother. His name is … This my sister … These are my sisters.* (If a child has no brother or sister use these pages for additional photos of the child. *This is me as a baby.*)

Page 4 *This my mother. Her name is …*

Page 5 *This is my father. His name is …*

Pages 6 and 7 (double spread) *This is my home.*

Pages 8 and 9 *These are my grandmothers.*

Pages 10 and 11 *These are my grandfathers.*

Pages 12 to 16 are left open for cats, dogs or special people. *This is my teacher. Her name is …* etc.

5) Birthdays

- All young children look forward to their birthdays and it is fun to be able to celebrate them in the English lesson with a party snack and even playing a birthday party game together in Phase Three of the lesson, followed by the 'birthday boy' or 'birthday girl' choosing their favourite picture book to be read at the end of Phase Three to calm the excitement before *'It's time to go home.'*

- Of course any birthday in the class will involve singing the birthday song: *Happy Birthday to you/Happy Birthday to you/Happy birthday dear (name)/*

Happy Birthday to you. The tune can be heard on YouTube for those who do not know it. Try to follow this with the reply sung to the same tune. Most children may need a little help, some others like to practise it beforehand at home:

I say thank you to you/I say thank you to you/I say thank you to each one/ I say thank you to you.

- YLs can draw birthday cards. Show how to make simple pop-up novelty cards. Examples can be found on the Internet.

- If you have an English-speaking toy or puppet, use it as a role model, making sure you celebrate his or her birthday early in the first term so that children are familiar with birthday language and how birthdays will be celebrated in your classroom.

- **Birthday game *Musical statues*** Children dance round the room to the music. When the music stops, they have to freeze. The last child to stand completely still (freeze) is out and comes to help the teacher to judge by sitting down next to her. With bigger classes this can be played in pairs.

6) My favourite food

Lesson 1

- In Phase One of the lesson talk about favourite (fa/vou/rite) food.
- *My favourite food is chocolate cake. I like chocolate cake.* (Show a picture).
- Ask children *What's your favourite food?* Ask children in turn to answer the question.
- In Phase Two of the lesson (see Figure 4) children draw their favourite food and as the teacher cuts the drawings out she talks to them about their favourite food. *Yes I like it too. It's scrummy. It's yummy.*
- Teacher draws a shop window with two shelves and tells the children they can put (stick) their food on the shelf in the window.
- In Phase Three of the lesson ask the children to point to their favourite food in the food shop window and tell everyone *My favourite food is … I like …*, adding *I like it too. It's scrummy. I don't like orange cake.*

Lesson 2

- In Phase Three look at the food shop window and discuss again.
- **Game** In turn, each child tells the class what they want to buy *Can I have this one, please?* and the teacher writes the child's name by the food. Usually everything will be bought!

    Look at the scrummy things in the shop.

    I like this one. Can I have this, please? (pointing to some food)

This can be followed by making similar projects like a toy shop window and a clothes shop window.

> *Adults who know their children well do not need to have somewhat superficial exchanges in order to find a more meaningful starting point for a conversation.*

> Oxfordshire Adult–Child Interaction Project

9

Culture

9.1 Culture – an introduction

For many families and school children, the teacher is their first experience and role model of an English-speaking adult. Of course, many may have seen English-speaking adults and children on screen and heard them speak English, but this is different from actually socialising with an English speaker. Young children are open-minded and since they trust the teacher, they believe anything the English role model says.

In multicultural classrooms VYLs and YLs hardly notice the differences between children of different cultures and races. Their aim is to socialise and they are programmed to find the similarities and common interests amongst other children as they play games together. Empathising comes naturally to balanced young children; they are to be seen crowding round when one of their group cries in the playground, curious to find out what is wrong and at the same time feeling sorry for their classmate. The idea that their friends are racially different is often put into the heads of young children by their parents and other adults.

From infancy a child learns much from imitation, from observing, modelling their behaviour on others and using this information to decode relationships, recognising where to empathise, motivate and encourage. *Social intelligence is the interpersonal part of intelligence. The brain is wired to acquire social intelligence from birth on. The first time a mother and baby meet eyes, that baby has started to lay down a blueprint of how you interact* (Goleman 2007).

9.1.1 What is culture?

Culture is man-made. It has to be learned. Language and culture are interrelated as, in picking up English in activities that involve 'doing', as long as the activity is based in English culture, a young child will also be picking up the accompanying culture.

Effective communication cannot take place without understanding meaning; and meaning is influenced by the culture behind the spoken words, and facial and body language. For example:

- Words can differ in meaning from one language to another – the word 'bath' spoken in English by a Japanese living in Japan may have quite a different concept (style and use) from the bath in a Western-style hotel outside Japan.
- Words can be used differently – 'thank you' in English is used differently in Gujurati, where it is used only occasionally and then as an expression of deep gratitude.
- The use of body language, for example, hands and fingers, can differ, and what is acceptable in one country can be unacceptable in another.
- The use of facial language can differ. In some cultures it is considered rude to 'look someone in the eye' when you speak to them, whilst in others it is impolite not to look at someone when you say 'thank you'.

Culture is about how groups of people understand and interpret the world and solve problems. Culture is many layered, but only the outer layer is explicit.

The outer layer of culture

The outer layer consists of things that can be seen, felt, heard or tasted, such as historical monuments, mosques, churches, art, music, scenery, food, homes and climate etc. Most adults have visual images of these sort of things stored in their minds as representing the culture of a certain country. In fact these images are symbols of deeper, invisible, inner layers of culture.

The middle layer of culture

The middle layer consists of norms and values. The norms represent the principles of right or wrong, which are controlled by laws and social conventions. Values are a group's concepts of good and bad, which reveal the group's aspirations and hopes. In many cultures the middle layer is influenced and even tied to their system of education and religion. This may still be the case even where the practices of religion have been abandoned, as religion is still part of that culture's history.

The inner core of culture

The inner core is implicit. It is about how the group survives the elements of nature and their effect on the environment. It is concerned with coping strategies – whether these be in earthquake zones, in countries with severe winters and little daylight like in Northern Europe, or where life is governed by lack of water as it is in deserts.

Culture consists of the basic assumptions about life: the unquestioned routine solutions for surviving daily life problems that are accepted, taken for granted and generally not discussed. To begin to understand the basic differences between cultures and what influences the families of the children, it is essential to refer back to this inner core of human existence.

9.1.2 Stereotypes

Stereotypes are cultural symbols and, often, broad generalisations. They are useful in that they provide an essential simplified form or symbol that can be immediately understood or related to and learned. Stereotypes are like stepping stones, as they can provide ways into a culture. With greater experience they may be found not to be truly representative of the culture, and can then be discarded.

Whether it is good to use stereotypes or not is open to debate. However, within reason, and if used sensitively, they have their place and value, providing they are up-to-date and not an over-exaggeration. Sometimes British traditions are better preserved outside the United Kingdom. It is important not to introduce out-of-date examples that record what surprises rather than what is familiar. Today it is rare to meet English men who wear bowler hats, but Scots still wear kilts!

9.1.3 Child culture

An identifiable child culture exists in every society as well as in every home. The way the child is expected to behave and is disciplined within the family and society differs from country to country, although the way children are dressed has become international (except at festivals).

The place given to the child within the family and society also differs from culture to culture as do the expectations of what children can or should do at certain ages. In some societies children up to the age of 6 years are more protected than in others, like the UK, where compulsory education begins at 5 years old, but many children go to school before. In some societies boys and girls are not treated equally and behavioural expectations can be different, too.

Expectations for the eldest child in a family can also vary from society to society. Being the firstborn and thus the only child for some time means the eldest will have had more parent interaction and more one-to-one language experience than the second or other children in the family, who will always have had to share their parents' affection and time. This can be reflected in their behaviour, their L1 ability and their skills in acquiring English.

To expect young beginners, whose home life is very different from that in a Western home, to respond to material and activities in the classroom like an American, Australian or British child of the same age is not realistic. The type of teaching and the relations with the teacher in local schools will influence a child's behaviour and expectations in the English class. If the child is otherwise taught by the very formal methods of a distant, authoritarian teacher, he will probably have difficulty responding initially to an active, informal style of teaching.

Parents might also react to different teaching methods, feeling that this is not the way young children are taught in their country and that their child is not receiving sufficient instruction. Where this type of situation exists, new style programmes in the English class have to be built up gradually and parents need to be given explanations, translated into their local language, about how English is absorbed through structured playful activities, rhymes and sharing picture books. Without this, parents, especially those with high aspirations for their children, may find it difficult to be positive and to support their young children's efforts to learn English.

Taking part in dialogues related to meaningful activities also results in the teacher–child relationship being less formal, and more relaxed, friendly and fun. To understand each child's behaviour in the classroom and to be able to plan the right type of activities from which the child can benefit, teachers need to find out as much as is possible about a child's background. Knowing about the cultural and home situation as well as the type of home support likely to be given can help teachers, who are faced by the challenges of managing the varying concentration spans and differing maturational stages amongst boys and girls in the same class.

This has implications for selecting picture books as maturity levels and picture book and screen experiences differ from country to country. Types of illustration also differ from society to society, too, and many young children brought up on Disney-like illustrations may initially find decoding some other styles of illustration and the accompanying content difficult, as most illustrations are culturally based. *Seeing is conditioned by the conventions of his culture, an artist's seeing is conditioned by the traditions from which he emerges* (Gombrich 1982).

Sometimes it is difficult to find out what cultural input there is 'at home' and more especially what happens in binational (dual heritage) families where, usually, the mother's culture is dominant, as she is likely to spend more one-to-one time with her child and be responsible for his life-routines and discipline.

When selecting materials and mediating them it is important that the English teacher is positive, but also sensitive to children's own culture. Young children trust their teacher and their first impressions as mediated by her can influence later learning. This is particularly the case in selecting picture books, rhymes and jokes: teachers need to respect the local society's culture, parents' beliefs and their way of bringing up children. Some picture book illustrations that make adults laugh in Northern Europe may offend readers from other cultures.

It is also important to bear in mind the latest cultural neuroscience research on:

- how culture shapes the brain
- the fundamental cultural differences between races.

> *It is as if the West conceives numbers just as words, but the East imbues them with symbolic, spatial freight. One would think that neural processes involving basic mathematical computations are universal, but they seem to be culture-specific.*
>
> (Ambady in Begley 2010)

Cultural neuroscience research may alter thinking in the future as a result of findings that show what were considered to be universal notions are more culture-specific than was thought. After all it is only recently, due to neuroscientists' research using new scanning technology, that experienced teachers have been able to confirm what they felt about the learning differences between young developing boys and girls.

9.1.4 Body language

Body language and facial gestures differ from culture to culture. Young children may not comment on this, but as they become more fluent they often include the right type of body language to go with English.

> A Japanese girl aged 7 looked an English-speaking woman straight in the eyes when speaking to her in English, but hung her eyes down when speaking to a Japanese as she knew it was not polite in Japanese society to make eye contact.

In some societies laughter is used differently; it can represent amusement in some but in others embarrassment. If teachers are to connect with the children they teach, it is important they find out about the children's culture and also a little about their L1 and accompanying body language. *Knowledge of children's first language should alert teachers to features of English language that are contrary to children's expectations* (Tough in Brumfit et al. 1991).

9.2 Absorbing culture

Interest and curiosity about a foreign culture can serve to motivate English learning. In discovering English culture, children learn how to identify aspects of their own culture and understand it better. Children have the analytical ability to work out for themselves the systems for analysing and matching how to behave in different cultures.

The young child learns culture and language simultaneously, consciously or unconsciously, whilst doing things or listening to others narrate their stories or experiences. If these are culturally laden, the child will absorb some of the culture without realising it. Some young children have already been to many countries and towns on their TV and computer screens and may tell you what they saw in New York or about the Egyptian pyramids. Some of them, or members of their extended family, may have taken an airplane to other countries. Most of today's children have already had many different second-hand global experiences.

> *An enormous amount of learning from infancy and childhood goes through modelling – through observing how others act – and bringing that into the brain as part of a repertoire for behaviour and then using it in the right situation.*
>
> (Goleman 2007)

Where a child is exposed to two cultures in the home from an early age, he appears to be able to distinguish which things belong to which culture. He has also worked out which language the adults in the family use and rarely makes a mistake in addressing them with any language other than their own. Young children are shrewd observers and good imitators and from a young age develop skills with which to decode situations.

9.3 Culture shock

'Culture shock' describes the impact of moving from a familiar culture to one which is unfamiliar.

(UKCISA 2008)

Culture shock is an experience that adults feel if, when they travel abroad, they encounter a new environment with different peoples and different habits. Culture shock in adults is an accepted state and, in time and with understanding, most adults living in a different culture adjust to their new surroundings.

Few people realise that young children can also suffer from a form of culture shock in an English classroom or when seeing something on screen that takes them far beyond their familiar 'comfort zone' and ability to make meaning. Children do not need to change country to experience culture shock. Children may not be capable of expressing their feelings of shock as these are new sensations to them, and adults may fail to 'tune into' their feelings and recognise them. Adults think children are resilient, but sometimes some shocked children turn off their efforts to engage or decode the situation and retreat, often temporarily, into their personal 'comfort zone'. There is little research into culture shock in children who are already bilingual and who know and live their life adapting to two or even three different cultures.

Culture shock can also happen through reading picture books where the illustrations are far removed from the children's ability to interpret them without detailed mediation by the teacher. Teachers often think children have understood the whole story, but most may only have understood a little and are carried along by the teacher's love and enthusiasm for the picture book. Young children may have never seen a typical English countryside with the village church or may be surprised by images of the African bush. Ghosts and witches may play a different and important role in certain cultures, and stories about them need to be introduced carefully if children are not to be scared. A badly mediated cultural experience at a young age can leave lasting anxieties; many adults

287

can tell you of a childhood shock they never managed to absorb. Teachers, like parents, need to be sensitive, seeing the new culture 'through the children's eyes', and:

- prepare children before introducing new cultural material, linking it from what they know to the unknown
- mediate a new cultural experience slowly, as some families are more conservative and resistant to change and girls may be less prepared to take risks; carefully explain and talk about similarities and differences
- discuss again in LI/SL or let children retell the experience/story in their own words
- respond to any comments or reactions made by children
- help children who have not been able to engage in the picture book
- keep parents informed, as children need parents' support and understanding.

9.4 Cultural activities

9.4.1 Planning cultural encounters

It is through adults that young children learn about English and the culture that goes with English-speaking societies. Teaching children in very different cultures like China, Malaysia or Africa can be a great challenge for teachers. Young children's first impressions of a very different culture can easily influence lifelong attitudes, since they have little experience of life and are still open-minded.

> Girl aged 7 years, taught by an American exchange teacher of Dutch origin, who had come to a UK primary school as an exchange teacher in order to explore her Dutch roots during the school holidays. The teacher visited Holland many times and passed her enthusiasm for Dutch culture to her class. When grown up, several of these UK children visited Holland and made efforts to make Dutch friends.

9.4.2 Selecting activities

In selecting activities to introduce culture to young children include activities that:

- encourage curiosity and also keep interest alive – young children enjoy exploring and finding out something new; facts about the biggest and the smallest eg animals, buildings, etc, are fascinating for them
- help children to understand that there are several ways of doing the same thing, like making bread
- develop understanding that there are similarities (matching), and later acceptance that there are differences, between cultures
- develop empathy and respect for other peoples, especially other young children
- demonstrate that the meaning of the same word may differ between cultures
- demonstrate the differences in customs between cultures
- develop awareness of their own culture.

Some children may break into SL during a discussion to ask about a cultural observation; reply in SL before switching back to English. Questions leading to discussions might occur at other times too, when children have had time to reflect. *Why was that ... ?* Keep parents informed about the cultural content of a lesson so that they can follow up at home. These discussions are opening *a window on the world* and are part of holistic learning.

9.4.3 Suggested activities

All activities are, to some degree, culturally based. Since language and culture are integrated, children taking part in activities pick up the culture at the same time as they pick up language. A child looking at an English picture book hears the written language and uses the pictures to help work out the full meaning of what is being read. Without realising it the child is absorbing the English text and another culture.

Suggested activities can include:

- inviting native speakers to visit the classroom and play games with groups of children on a regular basis
- inviting other nationals who speak world Englishes to the classroom to introduce their countries
- talking about festivals in other cultures
- playing football and using football language
- talking about airplanes and where they go
- using superlatives: the highest mountain in the world etc.
- talking about and looking at shapes of world buildings – Eiffel Tower, Big Ben, the Pantheon, the Gherkin
- reading picture books (see Chapter 7)
- playing a game from another culture
- singing a song from another culture
- looking at world art masterpieces
- food (talking about different foods and collecting pictures).

English Corners or English Tables (see 7.9)

An English Corner, or a simple English Table, helps to set the scene for English lessons. It is the focus for anything related to English as it provides:

- storage space for games
- a mini-library space for displaying picture books
- space for displaying new discoveries about English culture like pictures, flags etc.
- a place where children can sit and browse (browsing is a type of self-initiated and self-directed play, important for consolidating learning).

Culture forms the root of most of our actions, although generally we are not aware of its role. It is often not until adults come in contact with a different culture that they begin to examine their own culture and think beyond the visible outer layer. If children are to grow up into sensitive, open-minded adolescents and adults, who respect other peoples and are willing to find out more about other cultures, it is important to lay foundations in the attitude-forming years of early childhood. As mediators, teachers have opportunities to introduce young children to other children in the world who speak English.

Without some inclusion of cultural information about English-speaking countries, YLs may begin to adopt other people's preconceived ideas and prejudices. *A second language programme which teaches cultural information along with language can produce a more tolerant, less prejudiced child* (Donoghue and Kunkle 1979). We are now living in a global village and as mediators, teachers and parents, we have opportunities to introduce young children to other children and societies in the world who also speak English.

> *A different language is a different vision of life.*
>
> Federico Fellini (1920–1993)

Final thoughts

Education is not about the filling of a vessel, but the kindling of a flame.

(Socrates 469–399 BCE)

Most very young children and young children have an inner drive to learn language and communicate, but depend on a teacher and on family support. To 'bathe' them in play-like English language experiences is important but equally important is 'tuning in' to their holistic development levels and their emotional needs. Learning language is not a new experience; they have already learned one or more languages in the warmth of home and need to find some of this special emotional relationship with a teacher to 'feel good' and be motivated to succeed in English.

Each detailed chapter in this book aims to help teachers understand more about the young children they teach and kindle this passion, which will later form the basis of lifelong positive attitudes to English.

Opal Dunn
2012

References

Arizpe, E., and Styles, M. (2003) *Children Reading Pictures: Interpreting Visual Texts*. London: RoutledgeFalmer.

Barnes, Jonathan (2005) 'Is This Intelligence?', *Nursery World* (April).

Begley, Sharon (2010) 'West Brain, East Brain. What a Difference Culture Makes', *Newsweek* (March 1 2010).

Bettelheim, Bruno (1991) *The Uses of Enchantment*. (4th ed). London: Penguin.

Bromley, H. (2012) 'Positive Relationships: Working with parents' *Nursery World* (January 22 2012).

Brumfit, C., Moon, J., and Tongue, R. (1991) *Teaching English to Children*. London: Collins.

Bryant, P., Bradley, L. et al. (1989). 'Nursery Rhymes, Phonological Skills and Reading', *Journal of Child Language*, (16).

Corder, S. Pit (1977) *Error Analysis, Interlanguage and Second Language Learning. Language Teaching and Linguistics: Surveys.* Cambridge: Cambridge University Press.

Department for Education and Skills (2007) 'Letters and Sounds: Notes of Guidance for Practitioners and Teachers', *Primary National Strategy*. Norwich: Crown.

Deustcher, G. (2011) *Through the Language Glass – Why the world looks different in other languages*. London: Arrow/Random House.

Donaldson, M. (1978) *Children's Minds*. London: Fontana.

Donoghue, M. R., and Kunkle, J. F. (1979) *Second Language in Primary Education*. London: Newbury House.

Dunn, Opal (1994) *Help Your Child with a Foreign Language*. USA: Berlitz Kids.

Dunn, Opal (2000) *Acker Backa Boo! Games to Say and Play from Around the World*. London: Frances Lincoln.

Dunn, Opal (2001) Feature article, www.realbooks.co.uk (10): (November 2001).

Dunn, Opal (2000) Feature article, www.realbooks.co.uk (8): (November 2000).

Dunn, Opal (consultant) (2008) *Learnenglish Family Booklets*. London: British Council.

Dunn, Opal (forthcoming) *Introducing English to Young Children: Reading and Writing*. Glasgow: North Star ELT.

Dunn, O., and Winter, S. (2006) *Acker Backa Boo! Games to Say and Play from Around the World*. London: Frances Lincoln Children's Books.

Dweck, Dr Carol S. (2007) 'The Secret to Raising Smart Kids' www.scientificamerican.com (December 2007).

Farren, Anne, and Smith, Richard (2004) *Bringing it Home*. London: CILT Publications.

Field, John. (2004) 'Blame the Left Hemisphere', *EL Gazette* (295).

Gardner, Howard (1983) *Frames of Mind: The Theory of Multiple Intelligences*. London: Heinemann.

Garvie, C. (1979) *Play*. London: Fontana.

Goleman, Daniel (2007) *Social Intelligence*. London: Arrow Books.

Gombrich, E. H. (1982) *The Image and the Eye*. Oxford: Phaidon Press.

Grenier, J. (2011) 'To the Point' *Nursery World* (December 2 2011).

Hawkes, N. (1981) *Communication in the Classroom*, ed K. Johnson and K. Morrow, London: Longman.

HMSO (1967) *The Plowden Report: Children and their Primary Schools*. London: Crown.

I can (children's communication charity) Newsletter (2010): www.ican.org.uk

Karpf, Anne (2006) *The Human Voice*. London: Bloomsbury.

Krashen, S. D. (1981) *Second Language Acquisition and Second Language Learning*. Oxford: Pergamon Institute of English.

Krashen, S. D. (2004) *The Power of Reading*. Oxford: Heinemann.

Lindon, Jennie (2005) *Understanding Child Development*. London: Hodder Arnold.

Lynn, Richard (2010) Femail Magazine. Daily Mail (September 16 2010).

Meek, Margaret (1982) *Learning to Read*. London: Bodley Head.

Meek, Margaret (1988) *How Texts Teach What Readers Learn*. London: Thimble Press.

Montessori, Maria (1967) *The Absorbent Mind*. USA: Delta Publishing.

Morris, Desmond (2010) 'You Can't Overturn Millions of Years of Evolution', *Daily Mail* (September 16 2010).

Newberger, Eli (1999) *The Men They Will Become – The Nature and Nurture of Male Character*. London: Bloomsbury.

OECD Report (2011) BBC News (November 2011).

Oxfordshire Adult–Child Interaction Project (2012) Time to Talk Part I: Learning and Developing Practitioners *Nursery World* (Jan 12 2012).

Pluckrose, H. (1979) *Children in their Primary Schools*. London: Penguin.

Slobin, D.I. (1973) in Tough. J. *Young Children Learning Languages* in Brumfit, C., Moon, J. and Tongue, R. (1991) *Teaching English to Children*, London:Collins

Stewart, Nancy (2011) *How children learn – The Characteristics of Effective Early Learning*. London: Early Education Publishers.

Swain, M. (1981) 'Time and Timing in Bilingual Education', *Language Learning*, vol 31:1 (June): pp.1–15.

Taeschner, Traute (2005) *Learning a Foreign Language at Nursery School*. CILT Publications.

Tough, J. *Young Children Learning Languages* in Brumfit, C., Moon, J., and Tongue, R. (1991) *Teaching English to Children*, London: Collins

Tucker, Nicholas (1977) *What is a Child?* London: Fontana.

UK Council for International Student Affairs (UKCISA) (2008) 'International Students and Culture Shock'. London: http://www.ukcisa.org.uk/student/info_sheets/culture_shock.php (October 16 2010)

de Villiers, P. A., and de Villiers, J. G. (1979) *Early Language*. London: Fontana.

Vygotsky, L. S. (1978) *Mind in Society*. Cambridge, MA: Harvard Press.

Waterland, Liz (1985) *Read with Me*. London: Thimble Press.

Wells, G. (1981) *Language through Action – The Study of Language Development*. Cambridge: Cambridge University Press.

Whitehead, Marian R. (2002) *Developing Language and Literacy with Young Children*. London: Paul Chapman Publishing.

Zimmer, Ben (2010) 'Language – Chunking', *International Herald Tribune* (September 20 2010).

Appendix

Letters and Sounds: Principles and Practice of High Quality Phonics
Notes of guidance for Practitioners and Teachers

Tables 1 to 4: The representation of phonemes

Table 1: Phonemes to graphemes (consonants)

Phoneme	Correspondences found in many different words		High-frequency words containing rare or unique correspondences (graphemes are underlined)
	Grapheme(s)	Sample words	
/b/	b, bb	bat, rabbit	
/k/	c, k, ck	cat, kit, duck	s<u>ch</u>ool, mos<u>qu</u>ito
/d/	d, dd, -ed	dog, muddy, pulled	
/f/	f, ff, ph	fan, puff, photo	rou<u>gh</u>
/g/	g, gg	go, bigger	
/h/	h	hen	<u>wh</u>o
/j/	j, g, dg	jet, giant, badge	
/l/	l, ll	leg, bell	
/m/	m, mm	map, hammer	la<u>mb</u>, autu<u>mn</u>
/n/	n, nn	net, funny	<u>gn</u>at, <u>kn</u>ock
/p/	p, pp	pen, happy	
/r/	r, rr	rat, carrot	<u>wr</u>ite, <u>rh</u>yme
/s/	s, ss, c	sun, miss, cell	<u>sc</u>ent, li<u>s</u>ten
/t/	t, tt, -ed	tap, butter, jumped	<u>Th</u>omas, dou<u>bt</u>
/v/	v	van	o<u>f</u>
/w/	w	wig	pen<u>gu</u>in, *one*
/y/	y	yes	on<u>i</u>on
/z/	z, zz s, se, ze	zip, buzz, is, please, breeze	sci<u>ss</u>ors, <u>x</u>ylophone
/sh/	sh, s, ss, t (before -ion and -ial)	shop, sure, mission, mention, partial	spe<u>c</u>ial, <u>ch</u>ef, o<u>ce</u>an
/ch/	ch, tch	chip, catch	
/th/	th	thin	
/th/	th	then	brea<u>the</u>
/ng/	ng, n (before k)	ring, pink	to<u>ngue</u>
/zh/	s (before -ion and -ure)	vision, measure	u<u>s</u>ual, bei<u>ge</u>

In the last column words printed in italic are from the list of 100 words occurring most frequently in children's books.

Table 2: Phonemes to graphemes (vowels)

	Correspondences found in many different words		High-frequency words containing rare or unique correspondences (graphemes are underlined)
Phoneme	Grapheme(s)	Sample words	
/a/	a	ant	
/e/	e, ea	egg, head	s<u>ai</u>d, s<u>ay</u>s, fri<u>e</u>nd, l<u>eo</u>pard, <u>a</u>ny
/i/	i, y	in, gym	w<u>o</u>men, b<u>u</u>sy, b<u>ui</u>ld, pr<u>e</u>tty, engin<u>e</u>
/o/	o, a	on, was	
/u/	u, o, o-e	up, son, come	y<u>ou</u>ng, d<u>oe</u>s, bl<u>oo</u>d
/ai/	ai, ay, a-e	rain, day, make	*th<u>ey</u>*, v<u>ei</u>l, w<u>eigh</u>, str<u>aigh</u>t
/ee/	ee, ea, e, ie	feet, sea, he, chief	th<u>e</u>se[1], *p<u>eo</u>ple*
/igh/	igh, ie, y, i-e, i	night, tie, my, like, find	h<u>eigh</u>t, <u>eye</u>, *<u>I</u>*, goodb<u>ye</u>, t<u>y</u>p<u>e</u>
/oa/	oa, ow, o, oe, o-e	boat, grow, toe, go, home	<u>oh</u>, th<u>ough</u>, f<u>ol</u>k
/oo/	oo, ew, ue, u-e	boot, grew, blue, rule	*t<u>o</u>*, s<u>ou</u>p, thr<u>ough</u>, tw<u>o</u>, l<u>o</u>se
/oo/	oo, u	look, put	c<u>ou</u>ld
/ar/	ar, a	farm, father	c<u>al</u>m, *<u>are</u>*, <u>au</u>nt, h<u>ear</u>t
/or/	or, aw, au, ore, al	for, saw, Paul, more, talk	c<u>augh</u>t, th<u>ough</u>t, f<u>our</u>, d<u>oor</u>, br<u>oa</u>d
/ur/	ur, er, ir, or (after 'w')	hurt, her, girl, work	l<u>ear</u>n, j<u>our</u>ney, *w<u>ere</u>*
/ow/	ow, ou	cow, out	dr<u>ough</u>t
/oi/	oi, oy	coin, boy	
/air/	air, are, ear	fair, care, bear	*th<u>ere</u>*
/ear/	ear, eer, ere	dear, deer, here	p<u>ier</u>
/ure/[2]			s<u>u</u>re, p<u>oor</u>, t<u>our</u>
/ə/	many different graphemes	corn<u>er</u>, pill<u>ar</u>, mot<u>or</u>, fam<u>ou</u>s, fav<u>our</u>, murm<u>ur</u>, <u>a</u>bout, cott<u>on</u>, mount<u>ai</u>n, poss<u>i</u>ble, happ<u>en</u>, cent<u>re</u>, thor<u>ough</u>, pict<u>ure</u>, cupb<u>oar</u>d... and others	

In the last column words printed in italic are from the list of 100 words occurring most frequently in children's books.

[1] The 'e-e' spelling is rare in words of one syllable but is quite common in longer words, (e.g. *grapheme, phoneme, complete, recede, concrete, centipede*).

[2] The pronunciation of the vowel sound in *sure, poor* and *tour* as a diphthong (a short /oo/ sound followed by a schwa) occurs in relatively few words and does not occur in everyone's speech.

Table 3: Graphemes to phonemes (consonants)

Grapheme	Phoneme(s)	Sample words	Correspondences found in some high-frequency words but not in many/any other words
	Correspondences found in many different words		
b, bb	/b/	bat, rabbit	lamb, debt
c	/k/, /s/	cat, cell	special
cc	/k/, /ks/	account, success	
ch	/ch/	chip	school, chef
ck	/k/	duck	
d, dd	/d/	dog, muddy	
dg	/j/	badge	
f, ff	/f/	fan, puff	of
g	/g/, /j/	go, gem	
gg	/g/, /j/	bigger, suggest	
gh	/g/, /-/	ghost, high	rough
gn	/n/	gnat, sign	
gu	/g/		guard
h	/h/	hen	honest
j	/j/	jet	
k	/k/	kit	
kn	/n/	knot	
l	/l/	leg	half
ll	/l/	bell	
le	/l/ or /əl/	paddle	
m, mm	/m/	map, hammer	
mb	/m/		lamb
mn	/m/		autumn
n	/n/, /ng/	net, pink	
nn	/n/	funny	
ng	/ng/, /ng+g/, /n+j/	ring, finger, danger	
p, pp	/p/	pen, happy	
ph	/f/	photo	
qu	/kw/	quiz	mosquito
r, rr	/r/	rat, carrot	
rh	/r/		rhyme
s	/s/, /z/	sun, is	sure, measure

Table 3: continued

ss	/s/, /sh/	miss, mission	
sc	/s/	scent	
se	/s/, /z/	mouse, please	
sh	/sh/	shop	
t, tt	/t/	tap, butter	listen
tch	/ch/	catch	
th	/th/, /th/ thin, then	Thomas	
v	/v/	van	
w	/w/	wig	answer
wh	/w/ or /hw/	when	who
wr	/r/	write	
x	/ks/ /gz/	box, exam	xylophone
y	/y/, /i/ (/ee/), /igh/	yes, gym, very, fly	
ye, y-e			goodbye, type
z, zz	/z/	zip, buzz	

In the last column words printed in italic are from the list of 100 words occurring most frequently in children's books.

Table 4: Graphemes to phonemes (vowels)

	Correspondences found in many different words		Correspondences found in some high-frequency words but not in many/any other words
Grapheme	Phoneme(s)	Sample words	
a	/a/, /o/, /ar/	ant, was, father	water, any
a-e	/ai/	make	
ai	/ai/	rain	*said*
air	/air/	hair	
al, all	/al/, /orl/, /or/	Val, shall, always, all, talk	half
ar	/ar/	farm	war
are	/air/	care	*are*
au	/or/	Paul	aunt
augh			caught, laugh
aw	/or/	saw	
ay	/ai/	say	says
e	/e/, /ee/	egg, he	
ea	/ee/, /e/	bead, head	great
ear	/ear/	hear	learn, heart

Table 4: continued

ed	/d/, /t/, / ed/	turned, jumped, landed	
ee	/ee/	bee	
e-e	/ee/	these	
eer	/ear/	deer	
ei	/ee/	receive	veil, leisure
eigh	/ai/	eight	height
er	/ur/	her	
ere	/ear/	here	*were, there*
eu	/yoo/	Euston	
ew	/yoo/, /oo/	few, flew	sew
ey	/i/ (/ee/)	donkey	*they*
i	/i/, /igh/	in, mind	
ie	/igh/, /ee/, /i/	tie, chief, babies	friend
i-e	/igh/, /i/, /ee/	like, engine, machine	
igh	/igh/	night	
ir	/ur/	girl	
o	/o/, /oa/, /u/	on, go, won	*do*, wolf
oa	/oa/	boat	broad
oe	/oa/	toe	shoe
o-e	/oa/, /u/	home, come	
oi	/oi/	coin	
oo	/oo/, /oo/	boot, look	blood
or	/or/, /ur/	for	work
ou	/ow/, /oo/	out, you	*could*, young, shoulder
our	/owə/, /or/	our, your	journey, tour (see table 2, footnote 2)
ow	/ow/, /oa/	cow, slow	
oy	/oi/	boy	
u	/u/, /oo/	up, put	
ue	/oo/, /yoo/	clue, cue	
u-e	/oo/, /yoo/	rude, cute	
ui			build, fruit
ur	/ur/	fur	
uy			buy

In the last column words printed in italic are from the list of 100 words occurring most frequently in children's books.

To avoid lengthening this table considerably, graphemes for the schwa are not included, but see table 2.

Source: *Letters and Sounds: Principles and Practice of High Quality Phonics, Notes of Guidance for Practitioners and Teachers* (DfES Publications 2007, pages 23–26)

Index